WHY THE WEALTHY GIVE

WHY THE WEALTHY GIVE

THE CULTURE OF
ELITE PHILANTHROPY

FRANCIE OSTROWER

PRINCETON UNIVERSITY PRESS

PRINCETON, NEW JERSEY

Library of Congress Cataloging-in-Publication Data

Ostrower, Francie.
Why the wealthy give : the culture of elite philanthrophy /
Francie Ostrower.
p.   cm.
Includes bibliographical references (p.   ) and index.
ISBN 0-691-04434-1
ISBN 0-691-01588-0 (pbk.)
1. Philanthropists—New York City (N.Y.)   2. Charities—
New York City (N.Y.)   3. Voluntarism—New York City (N.Y.)
4. Elite (Social sciences)—New York City (N.Y.)   I. Title
HV99.N59085   1995   361.7'4—dc20   95-2854

To my father, with thanks

CONTENTS

TABLES

ACKNOWLEDGMENTS

I FIRST started the research for this book as a doctoral student, and I remain deeply indebted to Juan J. Linz and Paul J. DiMaggio for all the assistance they so generously provided as I formulated, carried out, and first synthesized my study. I have benefited greatly as well from Paul DiMaggio's ongoing suggestions as I revised and reworked the study into this book. I wish to extend my sincerest thanks to Joseph Galaskiewicz and Jerome Himmelstein, who read the book in its entirety, and whose comments proved most valuable in making the final revisions. I am grateful for comments on individual chapters by Peter V. Marsden and Andrew Walder and for the assistance on statistical matters provided by Tony Tam on numerous occasions. My thanks as well to Mary Murrell, my editor, for all her assistance. For their support and encouragement throughout, I thank Nancy Nasr and Roland Ostrower.

I greatly appreciate all the help I received from the Yale University Program on Non-Profit Organizations. I am thankful as well to John G. Simon and Bradford Gray for their encouragement, support, and assistance over the course of the study, and for many informative and enjoyable conversations about philanthropy and nonprofit organizations.

For providing financial assistance that was invaluable in carrying out this study, I am grateful to the Yale University Program on Non-Profit Organizations, the New York Community Trust (for a grant to the Program on Non-Profit Organizations in support of my work), the Center for the Study of Philanthropy of the City University of New York (for a Center for the Study of Philanthropy Research Award), and to Yale University (for a John F. Enders Research Assistance Grant). I am thankful as well to Yale University for the fellowship that enabled me to attend graduate school. A semester's junior faculty Presidential leave of absence from Harvard University was invaluable in bringing the project to completion, and is gratefully acknowledged.

I also wish to express my gratitude for the assistance received at Yale University from the staffs of the Computer Center, the Social Science Library, the Social Science Data Archive, and the Social Sciences Statistical Laboratory, who were extremely helpful in obtaining and using relevant materials.

My deeply felt thanks go to the ninety-nine donors who so generously took time from very busy schedules to speak with me about their philanthropic attitudes and practices. Their thoughtful comments and willingness to speak in such depth made the hours spent gathering the data for this study very interesting and enjoyable ones. I am also very grateful to the nonprofit institutions that generously provided me with information for this study. My sincere thanks as well to the various fundraisers, nonprofit executives, and other individuals knowledgeable about the nonprofit world who spoke with me during the course of this research.

In closing, I would also like to express my general thanks to all, too numerous to name, who have shared their comments and questions, at talks or in conversations, over the years.

WHY THE WEALTHY GIVE

INTRODUCTION

S IGNS OF the philanthropic involvements of the wealthy are not hard to find. Buildings, programs, and even entire institutions are named for wealthy benefactors. The playbills of many performing arts organizations offer long lists of their donors. In museums, placards next to works of art identify the men and women by whom they were donated. Hospital wings and endowed university chairs carry the names of large contributors. The sources of elite philanthropy, however, are less visible than its results. The purpose of this book is to explore those sources and to examine the place of philanthropy within elite groups. The result is an account of an institution that, I found, plays a central and defining role in upper-class culture. It is also an account of how this institution has been adapted, and has thus endured, in the face of changing circumstances.

This book is based on a series of personal interviews that I conducted with ninety-nine wealthy donors who live and/or work in the New York City area. Eighty-eight of these men and women were selected through a formal sampling procedure described later in this chapter. Eleven additional individuals were interviewed as part of a pretest. These donors are at the center of this book, but I will also consider organizational data that I compiled on boards of directors and donations to major New York City nonprofit organizations. Taken together, these materials provide an understanding of the character, sources, and consequences of elite philanthropy among a set of affluent donors in a major American city.

The following pages of this Introduction present the definitions, background, methodology, and context for the particular themes and arguments of the book. These themes are first introduced individually in their particular context. At the end of the Introduction, the multiple themes are drawn together and presented in an overview and outline of the book as a whole. Although the formal analysis is reserved for remaining chapters, this Introduction will also present preliminary material from the interviews. The purpose in doing so is to convey to the reader both a sense of the normative character of philanthropy among these donors as well as how they were drawn into the philanthropic world. This general and substantive background sets the stage for the more specific and specialized discussions to come.

THE SCOPE OF PHILANTHROPY

"Philanthropy" is often used interchangeably with "charity," but the two differ in important ways. Charity is specifically directed toward the poor, and often focuses on the relief of severe and immediate needs. Philanthropy is a broader concept, which includes charity but also encompasses the wider range of private giving for public purposes.[1] Thus, contributions to universities, museums, hospitals, churches, temples, mosques, environmental causes, social service institutions, parks, and research institutes all fall under the category of philanthropy, whether or not they are directed to poor recipients.[2] In short, as one woman I interviewed put it, philanthropy covers "the whole range of what's acutely necessary to what is desirable."

This understanding of philanthropy was commonly expressed by donors, including those who did make large "charitable" gifts. For instance, one such man said,

> This is not a hard-and-fast antiseptic view, but basically we pay heavy taxes, and I have, and I feel that should do most of the work that I can do towards relieving poverty problems, although I respond to those as well. . . . But basically, where the individual can make the biggest impact is in the quality of life—things that are hard for the government to do or justify, but that would have a big impact on everybody's feeling of well-being.

In a comment that expresses a similar view and also highlights the organizational nature of contemporary philanthropy, another donor observed,

> A lot of people don't understand what philanthropy is. I do not give money to buy clothes and food for individuals. My tax money goes for that. I think that's a government responsibility. And I think there is a responsibility. You can't leave people starving. . . . That is not to me philanthropy. Philanthropy, to me, is the support of institutions, rather than life-or-death issues—the richness of one's life. Supporting one's church, to me, is philanthropy.

Particularly among those critical of elite philanthropy, there has been a tendency to analyze philanthropy as if it were, in principle, charity. One consequence is that "noncharitable" donations are treated as deviations from, and abuses of, the intended purposes of philanthropy. Explanations accordingly take on an exposé flavor, in which philanthropy and donors' motives are revealed as other than what they claim to be.[3] Although one might believe things should be otherwise, for the purposes of analysis, we must begin from the fact that, legally and historically, the broader range of giving has been an explicit part of philanthropy.[4] Moreover, donors themselves are in fact quite forthright concerning their belief that such giving is as legitimate as charitable giving. Indeed, historically some millionaires, such as Carnegie, have even rejected the view that the role of philanthropy is to provide support for the destitute.[5]

Noncharitable giving is by no means confined to the wealthy. In reality, relatively few of all the donations made in the United States go to poor recipients.[6] To the extent that elite philanthropy is distinctive, the difference does not lie in this aspect of it. The fact that charity is comparatively atypical, moreover, makes it all the more imperative not to transfer assumptions and definitions about it to the study of the wider phenomenon of philanthropy. What is vital is explaining and understanding the variations in people's philanthropy, which is one major purpose of this book.

To this point, I have focused on gifts of money, but volunteer activities, too, are a part of philanthropy. For the majority of the donors in this study, giving and volunteering are intimately connected. As one woman said, "It isn't just money. Philanthropy is time and mental work, and it's all tied in together." Similarly, one man described the importance of philanthropy to him personally as "the fulfillment I get out of being able to support my convictions through the use of my resources in association with, in most cases, my personal efforts."

Volunteer activities, particularly board membership, turned out to be of an importance for giving among the wealthy that even exceeded my initial expectations. Among the elite, contributions of money are part of an overall involvement with nonprofit organizations. To understand why the wealthy give, we must accordingly understand the nature and significance of their connections to nonprofit institutions more generally.

This discussion of the scope of philanthropy clearly parallels legal and tax-related definitions. There are those who advocate defining philanthropy instead in terms of the "social signals" it responds to, rather than in reference to formal institutional characteristics such as tax status.[7] Such approaches are useful for drawing attention to other properties of philanthropy. I believe, however, that legal definitions and formal institutional characteristics are central to the nature of contemporary elite philanthropy, including how donors themselves conceive of and define their philanthropic activities. It is a belief that received confirmation numerous times over the course of this study.

THE SIGNIFICANCE OF ELITE PHILANTHROPY

The most readily apparent reason for wanting to understand why the wealthy give lies in the role elites have played in philanthropy. Giving and voluntarism are distinctive and important aspects of American society. Elites, in turn, have traditionally played a major role in founding, sustaining, and overseeing nonprofit organizations.[8] The efforts expended by nonprofit organizations to raise money from wealthy donors, even as they have diversified their funding sources, testifies to their continued importance. So, too, does the ongoing prominence of members of the elite on the boards of major nonprofit organizations. The study of elite giving and volunteering, in short, is one integral part of the general study of philanthropy and nonprofit organizations.

Less apparent, perhaps, but equally important for the purposes of this book, is that studying philanthropy also contributes to our understanding of elites. Philanthropy is an integral and defining element of elite culture. I believe that it also provides a case study in the nature and functioning of upper-class culture in American society. Robert Bellah and his associates observe that American culture has been dominated by the middle class and that a genuine upper-class culture has failed to develop.[9] The United States does indeed lack the aristocratic traditions and sharply defined class distinctions of societies such as England. The case of philanthropy, however, shows that American elites do fashion a separate cultural world for themselves by drawing on and reformulating elements and values from the broader society.

When they participate in philanthropy, elites share in a set of activities and values that are widespread in American society. Elites take philanthropy, however, and adapt it into an entire way of life that serves as a vehicle for the cultural and social life of their class, overlaying it with additional values and norms. In the process, philanthropy becomes a mark of class status that contributes to defining and maintaining the cultural and organizational boundaries of elite life. As donors themselves put it, philanthropy becomes a "way of being part of Society" and "one of the avenues by which Society makes its connections." In this respect, philanthropy is also one of the activities that contributes to facilitating cohesion among elite groups.[10]

At the same time, the values, interests, commonalities, and divisions that characterize elite groups come to shape attitudes and behavior in the philanthropic arena. One of the major themes of this book is that philanthropy grows out of the donor's sense of identity. Class affiliation is one basis of identity available to members of the elite, but there are others as well, rooted, for instance, in ethnicity, religion, and gender. I argue that the relative strength and availability of different sources of identity provides one key to understanding variations in giving among donors. Because of the connection between giving and identity, moreover, the study of philanthropy provides an opportunity to examine the relative strength of class and alternate sources of identity within the elite. This is yet another example of how research in this area furthers our general understanding of elites.

The connection between diverse sources of identity and diverse types of giving, moreover, is one example of my more general emphasis on philanthropy and elites as heterogeneous phenomena. From the outside, the privileged men and women in this book appear to be quite similar. Yet from an intra-elite perspective, they are far from a homogeneous or tightly knit group. I contend that distinctions and hierarchies that differentiate members of the elite carry over into a set of distinctions and hierarchies within philanthropy itself. Variations in philanthropic giving, too, grow out of differences rooted in the social organization of the elite groups to which donors themselves belong.

PHILANTHROPIC DIVERSITY

As we have seen, the term *philanthropy* covers a broad range of giving. Up to a point, it is nonetheless useful and legitimate to regard philanthropy as a unified cultural construct. There are a set of political, social, and cultural attitudes underlying philanthropy that cut across the diversity of giving and volunteering. In considering how philanthropy is actually conducted, however, I argue there is a need to disaggregate the concept of "philanthropy." I do so by distinguishing giving according to different areas of activity, such as culture, social services, education, and health. Although there are overlaps, important variations exist in the factors that influence giving to different areas of activity. The same holds true for board membership, showing that the factors that facilitate achieving positions of organizational prominence in elite philanthropy also vary in different areas of activity. Furthermore, there are also differences in the way in which donors themselves think about and account for their giving to different areas. This holds true even when we look at giving to organizations that are seemingly quite similar, such as prestigious cultural and educational institutions. In short, I propose that before we can determine why the wealthy give, we must amend the question to ask—give to what?

In placing this emphasis on area of activity, this study clearly diverges from the perspective, offered elsewhere, that looking at the cause or purpose of philanthropic gifts fails to help us "comprehend the mode of participation of givers."[11] By contrast, I maintain that the purpose of the gift, or the nature of the activity engaged in by the recipient organization, is a central element in how donors think about and carry out their philanthropy. Accordingly, attending to the area of activity of the gift is important both to understanding the meaningfulness of philanthropic participation to donors and to explaining the form that their participation assumes.

THE ORGANIZATIONAL AND INSTITUTIONAL NATURE OF ELITE PHILANTHROPY

Philanthropy is a social institution that takes on meaning in the context of a cultural emphasis on individualism and private initiative and a mistrust of governmental power and large-scale bureaucracy.[12] These underlying values provide a framework in terms of which philanthropy as a social institution makes sense. The existence of such a framework is important, for it is not obvious or necessary that philanthropy would be valued by elites, or anyone else. It may be noted, for instance, that the introduction of tax incentives for giving in other countries has not automatically resulted in fostering comparable levels of philanthropy.[13]

For these reasons, I believe it is critical to distinguish the particular phenomenon of philanthropy, and its specific institutional manifestations, from the more general issue of altruism or helping behavior. Generosity can take many different forms, and what we must understand are the particular social institutions that exist and are encouraged for channeling generosity in various specific societies, and how these are maintained.[14] The fact that elites widely praise philanthropy as a beneficial *social* institution is also indicative of the fact that it is deeply connected to certain conceptions of how society should be organized.

The distinction between philanthropy and helping behavior more generally is also important because philanthropy is as much about the idea that individuals should "do their share" to support the organizations from which they benefit as it is about giving to others. Although instances of giving to support causes used by wealthy donors have been criticized as abusive of philanthropy,[15] such giving is in fact typical, and not only among elites.[16] The recognition that this is true is important not only for understanding philanthropy but also for accurately assessing its capabilities and limitations.

Of course, donors can give to organizations that they use, while also wanting to help others. This occurs, for example, when donors who feel they have benefited from an organization give so that the institution can continue to provide services to others. At the same time, as donors themselves were aware, philanthropy can occur in the absence of either generosity or a desire to help. As they further recognized, less than noble motives, such as a donor's desire for prestige, have also contributed to the strength of elite philanthropy. Indeed, affluent individuals who are deeply committed to particular causes are often masters at appealing to such motives in order to elicit donations from their less magnanimous peers.[17]

Philanthropy may also be differentiated from helping behavior more generally in terms of the type of recipient being helped. Contemporary elite philanthropy is organizational in nature, with most donations going to nonprofit institutions rather than directly to individuals.[18] This was certainly true of contributions made by donors in the present study. Some even explicitly emphasized the organizational nature of recipients in their definition of philanthropy. As we saw earlier, one man described philanthropy as the "support of institutions." Another defined it as gifts of money to "voluntary organizations." The distinction between support for organizations and direct support for individuals was one of the bases on which some donors differentiated philanthropy from welfare. In evaluating the role, benefits, and limitations of philanthropy, donors consistently referred to organizations. Indeed, their comments indicate that they simply take the organizational nature of elite philanthropy for granted.

The organizational character of elite philanthropy has a profound effect on how and why individuals give. Involvements and identifications with organizations become a central focus of donor loyalties and concern, which in turn foster and perpetuate their donations. I further believe that the nature of philanthropy among the elite today is the product of the dynamics of both class and organizational factors, as elaborated below.

ELITE PHILANTHROPY: TENSIONS, CONTINUITY, AND CHANGE

The entire world of elite philanthropy is built around a series of organizations. The character of elite philanthropy is shaped not only by the values and priorities of the elite, but also by the needs and evolution of the nonprofit organizations they support. The two, moreover, do not always coincide. As Paul DiMaggio and Michael Useem point out in the case of cultural institutions, elite concerns with status exclusivity can come into conflict with organizational requirements for funds. Traditional upper-class board members, for instance, have resisted including trustees capable of contributing large sums but who are perceived as "outsiders." Historically, elites have also endeavored to monopolize organizational services, resisting their extension even to the upper middle class.[19] On the other hand, if elites are totally unwilling to adapt, the organizations that they value will die. The response of elites in the face of precisely such tensions is one of the major themes of this book. As we shall see, one reason the organizational nature of contemporary philanthropy is so important is that financial needs of recipient organizations do indeed influence the thinking and behavior of the elites who serve as their donors and trustees.

The tensions we have been discussing always exist, but they can become more marked at certain times. Changes within both the elite and the nonprofit world made them quite pronounced during the late 1980s, the time of this research. This was a decade that witnessed a dramatic increase in wealth accumulation and in the number of new millionaires.[20] These developments were very much in evidence in New York, a national financial center and home to Wall Street. In short, there was an enormous pool of "newcomers" with ample funds to contribute, yet who were viewed as "outsiders" by many considering themselves to be part of the "old guard." At the same time, the financial needs of New York's nonprofit organizations have only increased. Even many of the oldest and most prestigious nonprofit institutions have evolved into enormous operations whose financial needs cannot be met by any small group of donors. In the wake of such developments as New York City's financial crisis during the 1970s, moreover, organizations became increasingly geared toward expanding their pool of private donors and finding new ways to generate funds. One sign of these changes is that many boards of major New York nonprofit institutions expanded in size during the 1970s and 1980s.[21] Although boards may also expand to diversify in other respects, one purpose of a large board is that it serves as an important fundraising tool, permitting organizations to incorporate greater numbers of wealthy donors. The creation of other mechanisms to incorporate large donors,[22] and the implementation of more formalized fundraising efforts also testify to this trend.[23]

A major argument of this book is that elite philanthropy has indeed evolved and changed, but within the context of a larger continuity. Elite philanthropy has remained exclusive with respect to those outside of the elite. At the same time, however, status barriers to achieving prominence within elite philanthropy, particularly valued seats on the most prestigious boards, have weakened. Thus, within the elite, philanthropy has become more open. As a consequence, there has been a shift both in the importance of the various criteria for attaining prominence in elite philanthropy, as well as in the people who achieve prominence. The result, however, is that the institution of elite philanthropy itself (and the nonprofit organizations valued by elites) has endured and been strengthened. A fundamental insight of elite theory has been that elites and their institutions must change in order to survive.[24] I propose that precisely such a process occurred in New York City's philanthropy. For this reason, moreover, philanthropy provides a case study in the evolution of status processes within the elite.

A further and related theme of this book is that the way in which philanthropy is conducted permits it to continue in its role as a mark of class status, even under changing organizational circumstances. From the standpoint of the elite, many valued nonprofit institutions have evolved from formerly more exclusive and clublike ways of operation. For instance, in an effort to generate earned sources of income, some have entered into marketing and retail activities. These activities give the organization a commercial, businesslike flavor that is at odds with those more exclusive earlier ways of operating. A good example may be found in Smith's comparison of the Metropolitan Opera's vigorous marketing efforts during the early 1980s with the situation thirty years earlier—when even finding out about the performance schedule and ticket availability was a challenge for all but the regular subscribers.[25] Current attendance figures for some of these organizations are similarly at odds with more exclusive ways of operating. The Metropolitan Museum, for example, reported fully 4.5 million visitors during the 1991–1992 year.[26] The two organizations that I have just cited are particularly appropriate examples, because they command enormous prestige in the eyes of the elite. They therefore illustrate well how organizations have maintained such prominence even as they have moved in directions that seemingly run counter to elite emphases on exclusivity. This book offers a discussion of how this situation is being accomplished.

I argue that the organization of elite philanthropy has allowed the re-creation of a relatively homogeneous elite environment, even under such shifting circumstances. Within the sphere of philanthropy, elites carve out a distinctive niche for themselves and maintain a separate set of relationships with prestigious recipient organizations. This permits them, in turn, to retain a special sense of identification between these institutions and their class, even as the organizations themselves have changed.

THE SOCIAL ELITE: A PRELIMINARY NOTE

Much of this book is concerned with philanthropic patterns among various subgroups of donors. Some of the distinctions made, such as those between women and men, and Jews, Catholics, and Protestants, are relatively straightforward. One distinction, however, does require some preliminary explanation. It concerns the subgroup of these elite men and women who belong to the social elite or social upper class.[27]

The social elite is an elite of status. It is characterized by solidarity within the group, social exclusivity, and a distinctive cultural identity.[28] Families in this group interact in a variety of exclusive organizational settings, such as clubs and prep schools. Through intermarriage, the group is perpetuated over time. In the United States, the social elite has consisted primarily of white Anglo-Saxon Protestants. Accordingly, it is the group sometimes called the "Protestant Establishment."[29] It is also this group that people often have in mind when referring to "blue-bloods." We can thus see how people can be wealthy or members of the elite, without necessarily being members of this particular group within the elite.

The social elite may be thought of as an elite within the larger elite. It has been characterized as a core or dominant group within the elite, whose behavior, values, and culture are admired by, and serve as a reference point for, other members of the elite.[30] On the other hand, it has also been argued that today the social elite represents a class in decline, increasingly replaced by a more atomized collection of corporate managers.[31] Historically, such elites have often managed to exert an influence in the cultural sphere after their authority in other arenas, such as politics, has been eclipsed.[32] A central focus of this book will be on continuity in the face of change in contemporary elite philanthropy. A key part of this analysis will be to examine the place of the social elite in philanthropy today, including its relative dominance and relationship to other groups. I conclude that while the social elite's position in philanthropy has declined in one sense, its values have been institutionalized more broadly among elite donors.

In order to distinguish the donors in this sample according to whether or not they belong to the social elite, I employ a standard indicator from elite research, developed by G. William Domhoff, building on the earlier work of Digby Baltzell. A donor is classified as a member of the social elite if he or she is listed in the *Social Register* (a national society bluebook), or is a member of an elite club, or is a graduate of an elite prep school.[33]

THE NORMATIVE BASIS OF ELITE PHILANTHROPY

The men and women who are the focus of this book live in a milieu in which giving is a norm, and characterize philanthropy as an obligation that is part of their privileged position. They want to give, and believe they have a right to give, and to give as they choose. In some cases, they even have etiquettes concerning how to give. These donors defend, moreover, an ideological position according to which it is legitimate (and desirable) to maintain, through philanthropy, a set of institutions whose mission is "public" but that remain under private, rather than governmental control.[34] Although there are differences in the kinds of giving found among subgroups of these donors, members of all these subgroups share a fundamental orientation toward, and emphasis on, philanthropy.

The vast majority of donors agreed that "for wealthier members of our society, philanthropy is not only a matter of personal choice, but is an obligation."[35] Specific interpretations of "obligation" may vary among individuals and particular charitable traditions. One donor emphasized that "obligation" be viewed positively, saying, "There's a certain responsibility that goes with success, let's put it that way." A Jewish donor explained that "the Hebrew term for charity is a word called *tzedaka*—and that means justice, not charity. So it's considered as an obligation."

Some donors talked of "giving back." Thus one man explained, "The principal reason that I give money is, having started with very little, and having been the recipient of aid and scholarships, and having a sense of how people that are disadvantaged can be helped by philanthropy . . . I've always felt it was the right thing to give back something of the largesse that you make in this country."

Some tied their giving to personal lifestyle, explaining that they did not choose, or even felt uncomfortable with, higher levels of spending on luxuries. As one donor said, "What I should tell you is that I'm driving [an old, less expensive model car], not a BMW. This is a decision we've made about the way we want to live. We're not ascetics. We live very well and eat at good restaurants. We're just not into things like fur coats. It's just not us." In one unusual case, a donor who truly did appear to live in middle-class surroundings explained, "We have more money than we can sensibly use. Neither one of us is interested in large Cadillacs and diamond rings. We weren't brought up that way. They're simply unimportant to us."[36]

Others pointed to guilt as a motivating factor. One man readily acknowledged that he enjoys the material advantages of wealth, but feels he must put some money aside, explaining, "I think I'd feel very guilty if I didn't give any money away." Such comments suggest the role of philanthropy in legitimating wealth. Philanthropy has also been postulated as a method of legitimating the upper class to the rest of society.[37] I found, however, that wealthy donors are generally more focused on their peers, rather than those outside their class, as the audience for their philanthropy. At the same time, philanthropy may well help to legitimate their own position to donors themselves, allowing them to feel more comfortable with their wealth. As Weber observed, the well-off are not content to merely enjoy their good fortune; they want to feel that it is deserved: "Good fortune thus wants to be 'legitimate' fortune."[38]

While characterizing philanthropy as an obligation, donors readily acknowledged that it is also enjoyable. It is something they want to do. One donor, for instance, noted that even if you receive no explicit reward for making donations, "there's a return in my own head that I've been a person who is generous, and have helped some person or some cause. So I think all philanthropy does have a payback, if not in kind then in sort." Yet another explained, "It's something I feel everyone has to do. It's just simply a sense of obligation, which is then tied into a sense of pleasure, by choosing a philanthropy in which one can get emotionally and intellectually involved." As this comment highlights, donations of money are bound up with donors' broader interests and priorities. One reason that philanthropy is a source of satisfaction to donors is precisely because of the connection they feel to specific organizations and causes. Indeed, some were frustrated when they felt forced to make gifts in response to external pressures (such as business considerations), without having a personal interest in the recipient.

The picture of philanthropy conveyed by these affluent men and women did encompass an interesting blend of both constraint and voluntarism. Donors feel it is important to support causes of their own choosing, but readily acknowledge that a considerable amount of giving is done in response to requests from friends and associates. Their readiness to characterize philanthropy as an obligation was of particular interest, because many also strongly defended the idea that people are free to use their wealth as they choose. In fact, this very freedom is one of the rationales they offer in support of philanthropy. Some comments expressed the tension between these views. For instance, one man said that, "I dislike as a [New England] Yankee, people telling me what my obligations are, but I do feel if you are fortunate enough to have something, that you should share it." Donors generally regarded the actual selection of particular causes as a matter of personal choice. Yet a number felt people have an obligation to support causes in their local community and, in practice, felt personally obligated to support certain organizations.[39]

Furthermore, many were highly critical of affluent people who they feel do not make adequate contributions, and said they thought less of people they know who fall into that category.[40] Some expressed bewilderment over the failure of some wealthy individuals to give, and speculated that something must have "gone wrong" for this to happen. Thus one person accounted for an acquaintance's lack of generosity as "perfectly understandable if you know him. He's just a warped person, unhappy, insecure, damaged by his past."[41]

Individuals from wealthy backgrounds expressed the view that training in philanthropy is part of a proper upbringing. When one such man sees people who contribute little,

> it gives me a real clue about them as people, especially if they have the same background as I do. In other words, if they've been brought up with money and choose not to give when their parents were givers . . . I wonder about them. And I wonder what went wrong. . . . You see, I was brought up with that idea of stewardship and obligation. And I'm sure that's very capitalist and very old world. But nevertheless, that's a large component in a lot of our lives. And I simply do not understand people who don't give to anything. You know, they will give money to the small animal league because they have a poodle. Forget nuclear disarmament!

Disapproval of nondonors was by no means confined to those who grew up wealthy.[42] One woman who was not from a wealthy family finds it "revolting" when affluent people do not give. Another, who described his family and childhood as "very poor," commented,

> There are many very, very wealthy people who give hardly anything, and who give only under extreme pressure when they can get some powerful advantage . . . in our New York society. And I think they're looked upon with disdain, disfavor, and are highly criticized. . . . There's such an enormous amount of need. . . . It doesn't matter where you give—as long as you give to something.[43]

A number of factors lend strength to attitudes concerning nondonors, in addition to any feelings concerning the obligations of those with so much money to contribute. The majority of these donors also raise money for causes they support, and attitudes toward those unwilling to contribute can reflect their role as fundraisers. In speaking of such people, one woman who raises money said, "It annoys me when I see them going off on expensive trips, and yet if they're asked to subscribe to some contribution . . . they'll say they can't afford it, or they'll make a very modest contribution." Another donor said she does not think less of people who do not give much, but then qualified her response by adding that she does "resent" their attitude when trying to raise money.

An additional factor that may contribute to donors' views is that they interpret philanthropy as involving support for organizations in the community. One donor expressed this view as follows: "Every city has certain institutions which make it the city that it is. . . . They give it the color, substance of a civilized aggregation of people. There are a number of such [places] in New York, and I think that people in New York owe it to the city to preserve those institutions."

Accordingly, wealthy people who do not contribute risk being perceived as not "doing their share," while benefiting from organizations supported by other people. One man observed that people who live in his suburb and work in New York (as he does) tend to donate to New York projects, but should do "a helluva lot more" for their own town. Another donor emphasized that people should give to several institutions in a community, and referred to those who do not as "free riders."[44] Thus, when wealthy people do not give, they are failing to conform to expectations of their peers and to support institutions that other members of the elite believe it is important to maintain.

It should be emphasized that few background characteristics distinguished donors who regard philanthropy as an obligation from those who regard it as a matter of individual choice. These differing views are unrelated to variations in donor occupation, age, religious affiliation, religiosity, gender, ethnic background, educational attainment, asset level, income, or to whether donors inherited or made their wealth. The ideology of "noblesse oblige" associated with the social elite might suggest a greater willingness among its members to characterize philanthropy as an obligation, but this was not the case. Similarly, according to another view, held by some donors, growing up in a philanthropic family inculcates a sense of obligation. While this may be one way it can develop, it is clearly not the exclusive one. Donors raised in families with a philanthropic background were no more likely than others to regard giving as an obligation.

The sole factor that had a clear association with donors' willingness to characterize philanthropy as an obligation was membership in a religious congregation. Those who belonged to a church or temple were more likely than nonmembers to view philanthropy as an obligation.[45] This may stem from the fact that religious teachings present giving as an obligation. Accordingly, people who are involved enough with organized religion to join a congregation might be more likely to support that view.[46] Additional findings suggest a further explanation. Higher percentages of donors who identified themselves as either Republican or Democrat viewed giving as obligatory, than did Independents who split their vote. Taken together, the findings concerning congregation membership and party affiliation suggest that donors who view philanthropy as obligatory may generally be more likely to identify with and become involved in organized social groups.[47] While noting the interest of these differences, however, we must also keep in mind that the majority of donors from all subgroups viewed philanthropy as an obligation.

Paths to Philanthropic Involvement

Although individual experiences vary, there are certain typical routes through which wealthy donors become involved in philanthropy. As we shall see, the very pervasiveness of philanthropy in donors' social milieu contributes to drawing individuals into giving and volunteering. It is not surprising, therefore, that one donor said he had not planned to spend this part of his life involved in philanthropic activities, but "just slipped into it."

Some people are introduced to philanthropy by their family. Inheritors told of how exposure to giving began for them as children. The example of one donor, whose parents expected her to set aside a portion of her allowance each week for charitable purposes, illustrates this process. Another woman's family taught her that "no matter what, no matter how busy your life is, this is something you must be involved in. And it isn't something that simply involves giving money . . . it's something that involves time." Some described various ways that they encourage their own children to be philanthropic, and "teach" them how to give. One donor, for instance, said that she and her husband view this as part of preparing their children for the fortune they will inherit. Typical mechanisms for encouraging children's philanthropy included involving them in a family foundation and providing them with a set sum each year to give away. Sometimes, parents leave funds in a foundation after their death, which ensures that children will engage in philanthropy. Sometimes, where relationships have developed between particular nonprofits and particular families, donors may also become involved with those specific institutions.[48]

Another route into philanthropic activity is through marriage to someone who is involved. One woman thus described how after her marriage to a wealthy man, numerous organizations began to approach her for donations. Initially, she was very uncomfortable and at a loss about how to handle such requests. She discussed this with her husband, who told her, "It's your duty as a woman with money to hear everyone, and then you can decide whether you want to support them." Over time, she said, she learned from her husband's family, and has become quite active as a donor and volunteer.

Exposure to philanthropy may also occur through business associates. Some donors described people who served as their "philanthropic mentors." One man was cautioned at a young age by a senior person in his field whom he greatly admired that, as he accumulated wealth, he should remember that someday he would "have to give it back to society." Another man became involved after going to work for a firm where he "was surrounded . . . with a tradition of giving." As his interest developed in this setting, his associates arranged for him to go on the board of a nonprofit organization.

Religion provides yet another setting in which exposure to giving may occur. One donor remarked that "like everybody who has gone to Sunday school or church" he was "indoctrinated early in putting something into the plate every Sunday." This brings up the more general fact that philanthropic involvement may begin because someone is a member of, or uses the services of, a nonprofit organization. Throughout their lives, members of elite groups are likely to be involved with organizations that ask for donations. Indeed, the donor cited above, whose exposure began in church, added that he attended a private prep school, college, and professional school. When you graduate, he said "you're badgered incessantly by the alumni fund," so that "my obligation to be philanthropic was not something that I was allowed to forget." These comments further testify to the importance of the organizational character of contemporary philanthropy.

There are certain characteristic times in the lives of the wealthy when they are predisposed toward greater philanthropic involvement. For men, retirement from business is such a time. Having generally led active professional lives, philanthropy provides an arena into which energy and expertise can be directed after retirement. One business executive, who became involved and started devoting time to nonprofit boards after retiring, said, "I'm retired and I have nothing other than these activities to take up [my time]. They take it up and it's very interesting." Similarly, another donor became involved with a particular cause "when I stepped back from the day-to-day operations" (of his business).[49]

Wealthy women, who are frequently not employed, may seek greater involvement as their children age. One woman said earning money was not important or necessary for her, but that she did need to do something where she could make an impact. Therefore, when her children began school and she had free time during the day, she turned to volunteering on a full-time basis, becoming deeply involved with one particular organization for many years.[50] The relationship between philanthropic involvement and stages in the life cycle reinforces the point that philanthropy is an activity that many donors find fulfilling and enjoyable, allowing them to pursue their own interests and goals, while feeling that they are helping others as well. Indeed, the woman just described explained that "doing good" did not even initially enter into her volunteer activities.

Personal tragedy, such as an illness or death of a family member, also proved to be a catalyst for philanthropic involvement. For some, an initial involvement that occurred for this reason later led to a greater commitment. One man told me that prior to a relative's accident, he had never been a major contributor and was "oblivious to charitable causes." Another did make donations before a close relative developed a serious illness, but said it had "been unemotional, with no distinct feeling of accomplishment or pleasure. I've given because I should give and was supposed to give. Now I *want* to give, and there's a helluva difference." First motivated by a desire to find a cure, he emphasized that "that feeling will carry over" to supporting other causes, because the type of experience his family has undergone "unblocks your thinking."

The examples concerning family illness highlight the individual and even emotional aspects of philanthropy. Indeed, as we shall see, philanthropy as a social institution derives strength from the fact that it becomes a channel through which individuals can express various personal experiences, attachments, and relationships with other people.

THE STUDY: SELECTING THE SAMPLE

A methodological goal of this research was to develop and explore a new way of identifying and selecting wealthy donors. Developing procedures of this type is important because no single, comprehensive list of donors from which to sample is available. Although more detailed information is presented later,[51] it is important to explain at this point the basic way in which donors were selected. Accordingly, the two-stage sampling approach that I employed is described below, following a discussion of the study's geographical focus.

A geographical focus was desirable for a number of reasons. First, contributions are typically raised and expended in the same community.[52] Furthermore, people from the same area live in proximity to the same nonprofit institutions and therefore share a common set of philanthropic choices. Donors from separate areas might contribute differently simply because different kinds of nonprofits were located, or had greater stature, in their respective communities. Since I wished to examine the impact of differences among donors themselves (such as gender and ethnicity), it was important to minimize that possibility through a geographical focus. For similar reasons, it was also desirable to interview a group of individuals who share a common elite context.[53] For example, particular lines of differentiation (such as religion, or the distinction between old versus new wealth) might be more important in some cities than others. The geographical focus, accordingly, was well suited to my interest in analyzing the influence of subgroup affiliations on philanthropic patterns. A further benefit of a geographical focus is that it facilitates our understanding of how individual donors function within the context of the organized philanthropic worlds of their community.[54]

A major advantage of New York City as a research site is that it offers a large and diverse group of wealthy, influential individuals and non-profit organizations. This is reflected, for instance, in the fact that fully ninety of the four hundred wealthiest Americans listed by *Forbes* at the time of the study lived in New York City. This was a higher number than lived in any other metropolitan area.[55] The New York City metropolitan area is also by far the largest center of households listed in the *Social Register*.[56]

Since there was no master list of New York donors in existence, some procedure had to be devised for sampling donors. Since the study was to examine the influences on, and characteristics of, elite philanthropy, it was important to identify a sample that would be representative of some clearly defined larger pool. It was also important that the sampling method make as few prejudgments as possible about the characteristics and behavior of wealthy donors, given that these were the very topics to be investigated. Accordingly, I designed the two-stage sampling procedure mentioned earlier. First, I compiled a list of the largest New York City nonprofit organizations in seven areas of activity: animals and environmental causes, hospitals, other health and rehabilitation, education, culture, social services, and youth development organizations not classifiable elsewhere. All are private institutions that offer services that are "public," in that they are not confined to immediate members. All fall under Section 501(c)3 of the Internal Revenue code and are eligible to receive tax deductible contributions.[57]

Once the organizational sample was established, I collected lists of donors of $1,000 or more from forty-eight institutions.[58] The result was a database of 12,289 gifts made by 9,973 people. One of the major benefits of sampling donors through organizations was that it produced this large database, which provides an additional source of data to be used in this book. Next, I drew a random, stratified (by size of contribution) sample of donors from the database, with the top strata consisting of those who had made at least one gift of $100,000 or more. The primary reason for stratifying the sample was to ensure an adequate number of very large donors, a group critical for a study of philanthropic attitudes and practices. Although $1,000 would not generally be considered a "large" gift by the kinds of individuals included in this study, I decided to include a set of people whose gifts were in the low thousands because it seemed likely that someone making a single gift of that amount might be contributing larger sums elsewhere, doing their major giving through a foundation, or might be younger in age.[59] Pretests confirmed the reasonableness of these expectations.

The level of giving among the donors in the final sample (ascertained during the interviews) confirmed that this procedure had successfully identified affluent and large donors. During the interviews, donors were asked about the total amount of money they had contributed during the past year. Fully one-fourth had contributed $500,000 or more, close to half had contributed $100,000 or more, over three-quarters had contributed $20,000 or more, and the remainder contributed between $5,000 and $20,000.[60] As one might expect, these affluent donors were commonly occupationally based in business or related realms (such as law) or, in the case of women, married to individuals with such a connection.[61]

It should be emphasized that the point of the sampling strategy was to identify large numbers of bigger donors from a variety of institutions. It was not the study's intention to focus on donors who concentrated their philanthropy on the particular institutions in the organizational sample. Rather, during the interviews, donors were asked detailed questions about their donations, including where they had made their largest gifts. These gifts, discussed throughout this book, must be distinguished from the donations used as part of the sampling process. One man, for example, was identified for the sample because he made a gift of between $1,000 and $10,000 to one of the large New York nonprofits used to sample. During the interviews, however, I discovered that the three largest gifts he made during the past year, each for more than $20,000, had gone to other organizations. Of course, many had made a largest gift to one of the organizations in the sample as well.

To further understand the rationale for the sampling approach employed, it is useful to compare it with other possible approaches. Alternatives included identifying people through newspapers and other media sources, or based on reputation or referrals.[62] These approaches, though useful in other contexts, were not suited to the present study. First, it would be difficult to know which group or groups the donors selected in such a manner would be a part of, and how their proportions in the sample would relate to their actual presence in philanthropy. These considerations were particularly true in New York, a very large city where one could not hope to identify all wealthy donors. Moreover, these approaches could be prone to selecting donors who are highly visible, who know more people, or who have a greater reputation for philanthropy.

The donor lists, by contrast, had the advantage of providing comparatively objective information about the donative behavior (actual contributions) of a very large number of people. This is particularly important because judgments about other people's philanthropy may be "contaminated" by evaluations of their overall generosity or character. During the course of this research, for instance, a newscast appeared in which one "expert" on the rich explained that a failure to give had led to one particular New Yorker's unpopularity. Yet this very individual had recently made a gift of several million dollars. Apparently, it was this person's lack of popularity that resulted in a reputation as a nongiver, rather than the reverse.[63]

With respect to the types of people in the sample, it is important to keep in mind that all are donors. Consideration was given to the alternative of trying to sample wealthy individuals per se. This was rejected, however, because no suitably inclusive list of wealthy New Yorkers existed from which to draw a sample. Using a smaller, partial listing (such as New Yorkers on the *Forbes* magazine list of wealthiest Americans) would not have provided a representative sample of the wealthy, and would have been biased in ways that were not desirable for the present study. Since the various partial sources are based on disparate criteria, moreover, combining multiple lists would not have resulted in greater representativeness or inclusiveness (as was true of the donor lists) but in a hodgepodge of all varieties of individuals. I should emphasize that it is certainly legitimate and important to conduct studies of philanthropy among various individual subgroups of the wealthy.[64] This would not have been appropriate for the present study, however, which sought to examine which groups are active in philanthropy in the first place, and how the interactions between the groups affect philanthropy. Furthermore, particular characterizations of elite philanthropy have been criticized on the grounds that they overstate (or understate) the importance of particular elite groups in philanthropy[65]—a risk that is minimized by starting with involvement in philanthropy itself. Moreover, it should be emphasized that by working through donor lists, I was indeed able to capture important segments of the wealthy. This is illustrated by the fact that fully 82 percent of New Yorkers from the *Forbes* list of wealthiest Americans appeared in the sampling base of my study. That the percentage was so high also testifies to the fact that the organizations used in my sampling procedure do indeed attract donations from a large portion of New York's wealthy.

In the absence of the ideal sampling situation, the ultimate decision reflects a process of weighing the limitations and advantages of the alternatives in terms of the study's particular questions. I believe that the method used here offers considerable advantages, but it certainly has its limitations as well. One obvious boundary imposed by the sample is that the study can deal only with donors, not with the wealthy who do not give. Thus, even when referring to individuals in the study as "the wealthy," I mean wealthy donors. Most affluent individuals, it should be noted, do make contributions. Internal Revenue Service figures reveal that around the time of the study, fully 94 percent of those with an Adjusted Gross Income of $100,000 or more had made contributions during the previous year.[66] The extensive representation of members of the *Forbes* list in my sampling base further testifies to the commonality of giving among the wealthy.[67] To study nondonors would thus probably require a highly specialized and targeted sampling procedure to ensure adequate cases for analysis. Understanding what differentiates these individuals from their peers, and why they do not give, are interesting areas for future research, but represent issues that are beyond the boundaries of this study.

Even within the world of donors, the sample overlooks certain groups. By selecting donors who contributed to the largest and wealthiest nonprofits, this study may well overlook donors with more exclusively "offbeat" philanthropic patterns who do not contribute to such mainstream institutions. By selecting donors who contribute to New York City institutions, it necessarily overlooks those who direct all their donations elsewhere. Furthermore, members of some groups who are a statistical minority are not represented in the sample. To include individuals from such groups, it may be necessary to use a more purposive sampling procedure, which takes characteristics of donors into account. Alternately, one might identify organizations likely to receive larger gifts from members of those groups and sample their donors. Finally, as useful as they are as a source of data, the donor lists have limitations as well. They vary in the contribution categories used to group donors, forcing the researcher to adopt categories that might not otherwise be best, in order to make the lists compatible. Ideally, for instance, I would probably have set the baseline somewhat higher than $1,000, but this would have rendered some of the lists unusable.

In sum, the procedure employed has several benefits in relation to the goals of this particular research. It also offers an approach that is conducive to comparative and cumulative research on philanthropy. Since the base from which donors are sampled is clearly defined, it would be possible to redo the study in a few years to examine whether change has occurred, or to adopt a comparable procedure in another city, thereby permitting a comparison among cities. Given the absence of any comprehensive listing of wealthy donors or individuals, the development of procedures that permit comparison of findings from different studies is a vital task. Absent the possibility of constructing a truly representative sample, moreover, it is equally important that systematic alternatives be devised whose biases are knowable. Ultimately, a complete knowledge of elite philanthropy requires multiple studies in which a variety of samples are examined. In short, then, no implication is made that this sampling procedure is perfect, or that it represents the sole legitimate technique. It was, however, well suited to this study's goals. Moreover, by following through a new technique to the point where its advantages and limitations can be assessed, the study contributes to making additional options available to researchers interested in elite philanthropy.

THE DONORS

Having compiled a sample, I was ready to begin the interviewing process. Donors proved surprisingly willing to take time from their very busy schedules to grant an interview. Eighty-eight donors agreed to be interviewed, representing a response rate of 80 percent. Respondents spoke freely and at length, with interviews lasting an average of one hour and forty minutes (the median was one hour and thirty minutes), and ranging from thirty minutes (due to the respondent's illness) to four hours. As noted, eleven additional donors were previously interviewed as part of a pretest, and provide further qualitative materials for this book. With rare exception, interviews were conducted at the donor's home or office.

Why did these donors agree to participate in the study? There were a variety of reasons, but I believe that their widespread willingness to speak with me was an initial indicator of the fact that philanthropy is something they are convinced is important, take seriously, and find of interest. That many large donors are also fundraisers, and as such have a natural interest in the factors that influence giving and volunteering, was likely a further help to me. Some donors indicated that they wanted to communicate a particular piece of information they felt was critical for the study. Many expressed an interest in learning of my results, and they sent enthusiastic thank-you letters back after these were received.

Furthermore, in asking to speak to people about their philanthropy, I was asking them to speak about an activity that they perceive as good. This may also have contributed to their willingness to be interviewed. On the other hand, the topic also suggested that the interview might include rather personal questions. Some people, for instance, asked whether I would be inquiring about specific sums of money. In such cases, I frankly told them that this was the case. At the same time, I added that there were many other kinds of questions as well, and that I'd be grateful for whatever topics they felt they could discuss. My assurance that the interview would be confidential surely contributed to people's willingness to speak and share certain personal information with me.

Interestingly, some donors (who were clearly eligible) occasionally questioned their eligibility for the study, warning that they were not "philanthropists" or not really wealthy. Such a claim was made even by someone who readily acknowledged that he had many millions of dollars. This response also provides an initial sense of an important and recurrent theme of this book—that the reference point for these donors are other members of the elite. As Domhoff observes, "Even people with millions of dollars are likely to deny they are rich if they are asked directly. This reaction is in part genuine, for they always know someone else who has much more money and makes them feel poor by comparison."[68] A further explanation for this phenomenon is provided by Simmel. He observes that since each class has "typical needs," and "the impossibility of satisfying them means poverty," the poor (those unable to satisfy status-related ends) exist in all classes.[69]

OUTLINE AND OVERVIEW

This book offers several interlocking arguments and themes whose purpose is to provide a larger picture of contemporary elite philanthropy. The themes, moreover, cut across individual chapters. Although one chapter deals specifically with religion and another with gender, for example, both are related to the book's larger arguments concerning identity and philanthropy. For these reasons, although the arguments have been presented individually, it is useful to review them together here, so as to provide an overview.

Starting by distinguishing giving and volunteering from the more general phenomenon of altruism or helping behavior, this book focuses on the meaning and sources of philanthropy as a social institution among the elite. Elites take philanthropy, a more widespread social practice, and adapt it into an entire way of life that serves as a vehicle for the social and cultural life of their class, overlaying it with additional values and norms. In the process, philanthropy comes to function as a mark of class status that is connected to elite identity. The specifically class-based adaptation of philanthropy, in turn, influences the types of causes and organizations that elites choose to support, and the types of volunteer work that they undertake. To understand why the wealthy give, and why they give as they do, in short, we must understand the class context in which their philanthropy is shaped.

At the same time, the book contends that both elites and philanthropy must be seen as heterogeneous phenomena, showing how and why various types of causes are supported by various types of donors. In doing so, I argue that internal distinctions and hierarchies within the elite are carried over into a set of distinctions and hierarchies within philanthropy itself. As we shall see, a dominant and widespread class-based pattern of giving coexists with divergent patterns rooted in alternative sources of donor identity, such as religion, ethnicity, and gender. I also argue that the relative strength and availability of divergent identities provides a key to understanding which donors are more or less likely to deviate from the prestige hierarchy of their class when choosing the causes they are willing to support.

Drawing on data on changing board composition, historical information gathered during the interviews, and findings from earlier studies, this book offers a further and related argument, concerning continuity and change. Specifically, I argue that in the face of considerable change within nonprofit organizations, the elite, and the urban environment, elite philanthropy in New York City has survived by adapting and rejuvenating itself through the assimilation of new people. Within the elite, barriers to achieving positions of prominence in philanthropy (seats on prestigious boards) have weakened. Consequently, certain formerly excluded members of the wealthy now enjoy greater access. At the same time, there has been a fundamental continuity of values among the participants, so that the role and character of philanthropy within the elite endures. The position of the social elite, has, in one sense shifted within elite philanthropy as it has been increasingly forced to share coveted positions in philanthropic institutions with those outside its ranks. Its values, however, have been institutionalized and accepted among donors more broadly. Moreover, elite philanthropy has remained exclusive with respect to those outside the elite; it has remained *elite* philanthropy. Even as valued organizations themselves become more open, elites have re-created a relatively homogeneous environment within elite philanthropy under shifting circumstances. Thus, the book concludes that change has occurred within a larger continuity and consensus concerning philanthropic values.

In this respect, the book highlights the fact that philanthropy is intimately connected to, but does not merely reflect, larger elite culture and organization. There is, for example, greater fluidity in intra-elite boundaries within the philanthropic world than within the elite as a whole. Thus, while philanthropy must be studied in relation to the broader functioning of the elite, the two must never be equated. The distinction, I contend, points to a set of tensions that characterize philanthropy's ability to serve as a mark of class status. By identifying these tensions, in turn, the study sheds light not only on philanthropy's relation to elite status processes, but also on the ongoing potential for status competition, shifts, and evolution within the world of elite philanthropy. In exploring these themes, I hope to contribute to the study of elite philanthropy by simultaneously emphasizing homogeneity and heterogeneity, continuity and change, as well as to the broader study of elites, particularly with respect to elite culture, identity, and cohesion.

Chapter 1 presents the basic characteristics and meaning of giving and volunteering within the elite context, including their relationship to status processes, boundaries, and networks within the elite. The significance and determinants of board membership are discussed, and initial evidence is presented concerning shifting status boundaries within elite philanthropy. Chapter 2 examines the influence of religious and ethnic identity on philanthropy, with a particular focus on Jewish donors. The relative importance of class and ethnic identity are compared, and the evolution of barriers faced by Jewish donors is explored, including the consequences for giving to religiously linked institutions. The book's arguments concerning various sources of identity and willingness to deviate from the philanthropic prestige hierarchies of the class are introduced. Chapter 3 expands upon the discussion of identity and variations in philanthropic patterns, through an analysis of the influence of gender. Philanthropy is also examined as a household activity, with consideration to the distinctive nature of couples as donors, and the comparative impact of marriage on the philanthropy of men and women. Chapter 4 completes the book's discussion of the relationship between philanthropic and elite hierarchies and its analysis of philanthropic prestige by focusing on giving to education and culture and patterns of philanthropy within the social elite. Conclusions are presented concerning the wider institutionalization of the social elite's values and continuity in elite philanthropy. The final two chapters focus on the broader cultural attitudes and ideological assumptions that underlie the practice of elite philanthropy. Chapter 5 examines giving by bequest, to consider the place of philanthropy within donors' plans for the overall disposition of their fortunes. In doing so, I show how philanthropy is influenced by donors' assessments of other available options for the use of wealth, namely leaving wealth to children or to government through taxation. Chapter 6 explores donors' views concerning the respective roles, advantages, and limitations of government and philanthropy. The political, cultural, and social attitudes that provide the rationale for elite philanthropy are examined. The relationship between elite attitudes toward philanthropy and those of members of other classes is also considered. The Conclusion reviews the main findings and offers some more general implications and observations concerning elite philanthropy today.

Chapter One

PHILANTHROPY AND STATUS BOUNDARIES
AMONG THE ELITE

THE INTRODUCTION to this book focused on a series of developments that formed the context for philanthropy in the 1980s, raising a series of questions about continuity and change in this elite activity. This chapter begins to address those questions. The significance of the emergence of new wealth for philanthropy and established philanthropic elites, the meaning and persistence of exclusivity in elite philanthropy under changed organizational circumstances, and challenges to existing status boundaries in elite philanthropy—these are the topics of this chapter.

To address these subjects requires going beyond the earlier discussion of the normative character of philanthropy, to examine the relationship between philanthropy, individual prestige, and status within the elite. It also requires analyzing the close links between organizational involvements and philanthropy. The two topics are connected, for status processes related to philanthropy are influenced by the very interconnection of elites and formal organizations. This is because contemporary philanthropy exemplifies the more general phenomenon whereby the bases of elite status have become increasingly associational and organizational in character.[1]

Taken together, the analyses presented in this chapter illustrate that philanthropy and elites must be viewed from a dual perspective. Philanthropy, on the one hand, occurs within a broad boundary that encompasses a group of wealthy individuals who share certain widespread commonalities. Indeed, one thesis offered in this chapter is that philanthropy itself contributes to defining the cultural identity and organizational boundaries of the elite. Equally important, however, is to look at the hierarchies, competition, variations, and even tensions that occur within the general boundaries of elite philanthropy. This is a theme to which we shall return throughout this book, beginning, in this chapter with an analysis of the multiple determinants of prominence within contemporary elite philanthropy. This also includes a consideration of how philanthropy becomes a scene of status competition within the elite. Taken together, these analyses will show how philanthropy adapts, is revitalized, and shifts under changing circumstances, while retaining a central role within the elite.

DONATIONS, ORGANIZATIONAL INVOLVEMENT, AND SOCIAL TIES

Elite philanthropy involves far more than monetary contributions. Among those interviewed, giving does not occur in isolation but is part of an overall involvement with nonprofit organizations. Fully 75 percent of these donors served on at least one nonprofit board, and over 60 percent sat on multiple boards (see Table 1.1). Furthermore, 78 percent raised funds for various organizations, and others had done so in the past. These figures are particularly striking because sample selection for this study was done solely on the basis of monetary contributions, with no regard to volunteer activities. Accordingly, they show that where we find the affluent giving money, we can also expect to find them involved with nonprofit organizations in other ways.

Looking at the connection between specific donations and organizational involvement reinforces this point. During the interview, donors were asked to identify the three largest gifts they had made during the previous twelve months and to explain their reasons for making these donations.[2] Their responses indicate that with striking frequency, these gifts went to organizations with which the donor had some other (i.e., nondonative) relationship, such as serving on the board or using the organization's services (see Table 1.2).[3] This was true, for instance, of 66 percent of all gifts to culture, and 56.3 percent of gifts to education.

It is interesting to note that the donor often had a direct, personal involvement in the organizational structure of the recipient. To take an example, 43.4 percent of largest gifts to culture were made to organizations where the donor was a board member. In the case of gifts to churches and temples, donors were generally members of the congregation. In short, donors often not only had a relationship to the organization but were themselves a part of the organization, as members or leaders.

TABLE 1.1
Number of Board Memberships Held by Donors

No. of Board Memberships	% of Donors
0	25.0
1	13.6
2	18.2
3	14.8
4	11.4
5 or more	17.0

$N = 88.$

TABLE 1.2
Relationships Cited in Connection with Donors' Largest Gifts (Percentages by Area)

			Health		Social Services					
	Culture	Educ.	Hosps.	Other[a]	Jewish Affil. Fund	Other[b]	Youth (n.e.c.)[c]	Church/ Temple	Anim./ Env.	Rights/ Advocacy/Policy
NO. OF GIFTS	53	87	22	15	16	11	5	13	9	9
DONOR'S RELATION W/ORGANIZATION										
Board member (other volunteer)	66.0	56.3	72.7	46.7	0.0	63.6	60.0	76.9	66.6	55.5
Uses services/attends programs	43.4	23.0	22.7	33.3	—	36.4	60.0	15.4	33.3	44.4
Professional relationship	18.9	—	50.0	13.3	—	9.1	—	—	33.3	—
Attended school	3.8	1.1	—	—	—	18.2	—	—	—	11.1
Member church/temple	—	42.5	—	—	—	—	—	76.9	—	—
Good experience	—	—	—	—	—	—	40.0	—	—	—
DONOR'S RELATION W/OTHER PERSON										
Spouse, family involvement/interest	30.2	42.5	40.9	53.3	31.3	36.4	20.0	38.5	22.2	22.2
Friend's involvement/interest	18.9	8.1	9.1	6.7	25.0	27.3	20.0	15.4	22.2	—
Contact w/employee of org.	9.4	4.6	13.6	6.7	6.3	9.1	20.0	7.7	—	22.2
Business associate's involve./int.	—	—	4.6	6.7	—	—	—	—	—	—
Honor memory	1.9	8.0	—	6.7	—	—	—	7.7	—	—
Illness of family member	—	1.1	9.1	—	—	—	—	—	—	—
Spouse/child attended school	—	24.1	4.6	33.3	—	—	—	7.7	—	—
Other	—	1.1	—	—	—	—	—	—	—	—
TOTAL: W/ORG. OR W/OTHER PERSON	90.6	90.8	90.9	93.3	31.3	81.8	80.0	92.3	88.9	77.8

Note: The top row shows the percentage of all times that the donor's relationship with an organization was cited by the donor as a factor in a largest gift. Below, the various organizational relationships and the frequency of their mention are itemized. A similar procedure is followed for the donor's relationship with another person. The bottom row gives the total percentage of times that a relationship of either type was mentioned as a reason for a largest gift. Since multiple relationships could be cited for a single gift, totals do not necessarily equal the sum of the individual percentages.

[a] Includes health and rehabilitation organizations other than hospitals, such as those concerned with a particular disease and/or a particular type of physical disability.

[b] Includes social service organizations other than the Jewish-affiliated fund, such as agencies providing services to families, runaway youth, and the elderly.

[c] The abbreviation "n.e.c." indicates that this category includes youth organizations not elsewhere classifiable. Organizations in other areas of activity can also provide services for the young.

In many cases donors' largest gifts were connected to a relationship with another person, who in turn often had some involvement with the organization. This was true of 30.2 percent of largest gifts made to culture, 40.9 percent made to hospitals, and 53.3 percent made to other health organizations. For instance, one donor had made a largest gift to an organization concerned with a particular disease. He explained that although he had always "given a little bit" to causes in this general field, he began to "dedicate" and "focus" larger gifts to this particular organization after friends of his became involved there.[4]

In short, the vast majority of largest gifts were made to nonprofits with which donors had some involvement, and/or grew out of donors' relationships with other people, who in turn usually had some involvement with the organization. This was true of over 90 percent of all gifts made to the areas of health, education, culture, and to churches or temples. In fact, these figures may even understate the frequency with which donors' gifts were associated with such ties, because they are drawn from answers to open-ended questions. Thus, some donors may have given to organizations that they or a friend are involved with, but not mentioned this as a reason for their contribution.[5] The fact that donors so often cited organizational and social ties is significant, for it reveals that they themselves regard such involvements as an important consideration when making gifts.

These patterns are by no means limited to largest gifts. Other gifts made by donors, as well as charity benefits, also exhibit a pattern of giving accompanied by social ties and organizational involvement. The benefit that donors had attended most recently was virtually always linked to the donor's involvement with an organization (37.5 percent of benefits) and/or the donor's relationships with other people (60 percent of benefits).[6] Similarly, donors frequently reported that they make their "smaller" gifts[7] at the request of friends.[8] Indeed, the world of elite philanthropy is characterized by a system of exchange in which individuals support one another's causes. One donor described the "tit-for-tat" that goes on, where "you give to me, I give to you," a category of giving she and her husband typically do by taking tickets to benefits. Another donor explained that when you're chairman of an organization, it "costs you money" for that organization, and also "costs you money for all the people you ask [to give], because they then come back to you and say, 'Give me money for my pet charity.' And if you get money from them you have to support their charity. It's a circle."

With respect to their larger contributions, donors often spoke of the importance of having an involvement with recipient organizations. One, who feels it is important to give time along with money, said, "Anything that I'm giving at a level that's material to me, would inevitably be associated with personal involvement of me or a member of my family." Another donor explained how she first started giving to an organization as follows: "Actually I was invited to join the board. Which, I consider that some sort of involvement like that is essential to significant giving."

Many respondents emphasized that organizational involvement, in the form of board membership, entails an obligation to make contributions. One donor explained that "you don't dare go onto a board without being prepared to give." Another said, "I look at my other board members and [whether] they contributed. There's pressure to give because you're on the board. . . . And you try to put the bite on them. But . . . I'd call it community. It's your circle of friends." As these quotes suggest, the question of why the wealthy give is closely connected to the question of why they serve on nonprofit boards, to which we return later in this chapter.[9]

Involvement also promotes familiarity with an organization, which in turn fosters donations. One donor who is quite interested in health said that "most of the money has gone to [Hospital X], mostly because we use that hospital and got to know the doctors there. . . . So you get connected with things that you get caught up in, and respond to their needs as you get to know them."

As this example suggests, involvement with an organization can develop through use of the organization's services, by the donor or a family member. One man made two of his largest gifts to schools he attended, although culture is his area of interest. He explained that he feels he has "been successful and that I ought to share some of that success, for which they are in no small way responsible, and pay them back so that other people can take advantage of what they offer."

It is important to note that among elites, involvement with organizations is often tied to family identity and to the social networks in which the donor participates. In accounting for gifts to her school, one donor noted that she had met her husband in college, where she had also developed lifelong friendships. Thus, her evaluation of the high quality of the school, social life, and family ties all contribute to her ongoing involvement. As we shall see, close associations between families and particular schools may lead individual donors to contribute even where their own sense of involvement is weak.[10]

Fostering a sense of involvement is a strategy that is quite consciously incorporated into fundraising among elites. One respondent who does fundraising stressed that when requesting money, "You have to have a fundamental belief in [the cause] and . . . why they owe something. The nature of it should appeal to them, or reflect some part of their life." A donor who spends considerable time raising money for a school emphasized the importance of "cultivating" prospects, such as doing things that "involve them in the [organization]. And once they get involved . . . they become interested donors." Another donor feels that his fundraising efforts have been helped by working on the principle that "if you're involved in something, if you have a title in something, you're more apt to give."

Apparently, fundraisers employed by nonprofit organizations agree. An executive in the development office of one organization I spoke with during the course of the study emphasized that "people don't just give one million dollars because someone comes to see them." He explained that it is "crucial" to get donors (or potential donors) involved, and "most important" to maintain relationships over the long run.[11] His comments are particularly relevant because he works for just the kind of prestigious nonprofit to which these donors so often made their largest contributions.

As we have seen, contributions of money are accompanied by social relationships and organizational involvements. It is important to note that social relationships with other members of the elite and organizational involvements, in turn, overlap and reinforce one another. A characteristic route by which donors join nonprofit boards, for instance, is through their social relationships. A typical example was one respondent who joined a board because he knew the organization's president. He explained that without the connection he would not have become involved, yet as a trustee he made one of his largest gifts to this organization. This story illustrates well how donations of money, social ties, and organizational involvements feed into one another.

This does not mean that donors become involved solely "because" of a connection. People have reasons for perpetuating these involvements, and donors believe that the organizations they support are worthy, of interest, and of importance. Social relationships, however, often interact with donors' general predispositions and interests, bringing together particular individuals with particular nonprofit institutions. A typical example was one donor who reported that a few years ago, he "was looking for something basically to do, because I'd sold my business and retired." When an associate of his son's asked him to join a nonprofit board, he did, and became a major donor to, and fundraiser for, the organization.

The characteristics of giving that have been discussed are indicative of the closure that characterizes elite philanthropy. Donors were often quick to note that there are many worthy causes, more than they could possibly support. It would seem that of the numerous causes that exist, elites more frequently direct their largest gifts toward organizations with which they or someone they know (who is likely to be a fellow member of the elite) have had personal experience. Indeed, the fact that many organizations with which donors come into contact in the course of their lives (such as a school) are seen as needing funds may even deter donors from searching more broadly for less familiar institutions to support with their largest gifts. As one donor said, he and his wife occasionally see advertisements for nonprofits that seem worthy and "we might give a minor amount through mailings, but either they don't get to us or we don't get to them."

THE LONG-TERM NATURE OF ORGANIZATIONAL INVOLVEMENTS

The relationships that develop between donors and the recipients of their largest gifts are ongoing and longlasting. On average, the donors in this study were 62.7 years old and had been contributing to recipients for 18.5 years. Simmel's analysis of the genesis of obligation from acts of assistance provides a useful context for understanding these enduring involvements. He observes that "when an act of assistance has been performed . . . although it be spontaneous and individual and not demanded by any obligation, there is a duty to continue it, a duty which is not only a claim on the part of the one who receives the assistance, but also a sentiment on the part of the one who gives."[12]

Indeed, some expressed firm beliefs concerning the responsibility of donors to provide regular support. For example, one woman said that she has about one "switchable" organization a year, but otherwise "I think they expect your gift. They expect your money and . . . they have to have this core of support, and to switch that around all the time I think is not fair to them." When asked whether she feels pressure to support any particular organizations, another donor responded that she feels pressure "to keep up what I've been doing."[13] One donor was taught to maintain donations as part of the philanthropic training she received from her parents. She was also taught that if she must stop donations, she should do so gradually, and give an explanation to the organization. Donors may even take measures to continue gifts beyond their lifetime. One man, for instance, is building up a fund because "a top priority" of his is to ensure a comparable level of support for a favored charity after his death.

In some cases, a surviving spouse or other relative even carries on the donor's relationship after his or her death by continuing to make contributions. One widower continues to support his wife's church, although he belongs to a different religion. Another donor said that although he has "no interest in any toe dancer," he gives annually to an arts organization because his mother had supported the cause while she was alive.

A crucial point to highlight from these examples is that involvement with particular organizations becomes part of donors' own identity in the eyes of those they know. This is illustrated by the practice of honoring a friend by giving to his or her favorite charity. A woman who has volunteered at the same organization for over forty years spoke about this custom as follows: "Well, I recently had a big birthday. And most of the people who are close to me made gifts to [the Hospital] instead of sending me a gift. . . . It becomes a way of getting people to be aware of a charity. It also becomes a way of giving . . . not only as a memorial thing, but as a very happy way of honoring." Another donor's family had a tradition of contributing to a particular health organization on special family occasions, such as births, deaths, anniversaries, and birthdays. The organization was founded by the family and their friends, and they have been contributors for more than fifty years. Given the high degree of personal identification that develops between donors and "their" organizations, it is easier to understand why respondents feel they must take acquaintances' requests for contributions to their favored causes so seriously.

The ongoing nature of organizational commitments made by donors further exemplifies the closure that characterizes elite philanthropy. It illustrates that giving perpetuates itself, for donations lead to a greater sense of involvement, identification, and obligation toward organizations, which in turn promotes additional giving. Rather than exhaustively reviewing and evaluating solicitations in order to fund the "best," donors already have commitments, which limit their very ability to consider new proposals. When asked how she decides which organizations to support, one donor said, "It's usually somebody asks us, or organizations that we're involved with." Since she and her husband "are really closely involved with the growth of lots of organizations," they have little left to give elsewhere. Another respondent feels priorities must be set for "major gifts," because there "just isn't enough money." He gives smaller amounts at the request of friends, but guards the bulk of his funds for these priorities. Asked whether he is therefore not looking for new things to fund, he said, "Nobody is. Absolutely nobody is. Because the money needs of this community are enormous."

The identification that develops between individuals and institutions may have various meanings. In terms of the present discussion, one important implication is that individuals derive prestige from their identification with organizations and the elite networks with which they are associated.

PHILANTHROPY, PRESTIGE, AND STATUS AMONG THE ELITE

A theme that emerged throughout the interviews is that philanthropy clearly remains a sign of prestige among the elite. We have seen that donors view giving as an obligation of the privileged. Philanthropy, however, is not merely something that members of the elite do, nor is it isolated from other aspects of upper-class life. Rather, philanthropy is itself a mark of privilege and high social status. It is a part of elite standing, which is perceived as one of the very defining characteristics of being upper class. Thus, one donor wryly described nonprofit board membership as a virtually mandatory "accoutrement." Said he, "I am a trustee of a hospital. You have to be a trustee of a hospital if you're wealthy. It's required. . . . But I know nothing about hospitals." Another donor observed,

> Part of the activity of a certain class of people is to be philanthropic. . . . I don't know if people do it more out of obligation or that's their way of being part of society. Everybody wants to belong. In our culture, in our way of doing things, that is the role of the wealthy. . . . And poor people go to the local church or temple, right? Make suppers, cake sales.

Her comparison with the local church is appropriate, for it highlights donors' involvement with recipient organizations. Nonprofit organizations are focal points around which upper-class life revolves. Through their philanthropy, wealthy donors come together with one another and sustain a series of organizations that contribute to the social and cultural coherence of upper-class life.

The association between philanthropy and privilege means that philanthropic involvements are viewed as symbolic of the donor's personal success and affluence. Speaking of why he agreed to head the alumni fundraising drive among his classmates, one person confessed, "Honestly, I was well motivated by about 80 to 90 percent, but certainly there was a factor in there that it improved my visibility. . . . Just among my classmates, because everybody knows that someone who takes on the chairmanship of a class reunion is prepared to give, and has the time and interest to give, and as you say, that's a luxury in society."

While some expressed regret that prestige and even snobbery are influential, donors also emphasized their usefulness in raising money. Said one, "If an organization is going to exist, I suppose it has to have a certain amount of snobbery." Another observed that "social snobbery is a device of fundraising."[14]

At one level, the sheer display of wealth through giving indicates one's success. The connection between prestige and philanthropy, however, involves far more than giving money, and extends to identification and involvement with prominent nonprofits and the elite networks with which they are associated. One man, for instance, acknowledged that "there are some aspects of philanthropic work which are connected with social snobbery. I recognize it myself." Thus, he was "thrilled" when asked to join the board of one prestigious arts organization. Said he, "Naturally I want to be known as an expert on [the organization]. That may be a form of social snobbery, but I'm delighted that this is happening!"

The connection between status and philanthropy may be related to the perspective that philanthropy represents a form of exchange that brings returns to the donor.[15] Observing that modern philanthropy typically goes to organizations, Blau suggests that returns to the donor come from fellow members of the elite, who reward him or her for conformity to the norms of the group.[16] Donors themselves freely discussed how they "use" the desire for prestige as a tool in fundraising from their peers. Discussions with these donors reveal that the prestige of association with nonprofit organizations, particularly board membership, is itself a powerful reward.[17] Speaking of the connection between status and philanthropy, one respondent confessed, "Sometimes I've taken advantage of that in raising money from other people. A couple of weeks ago there was a potential member of the board, and to tell you the truth, we were desperate for money and I took advantage of the fact that he wanted to be on the board, wanted to make an impression on everyone. And I nudged him verbally . . . so that he gave."

Being identified with prestigious nonprofits serves as a symbol of "having arrived" socially. One respondent observed that "someone or his wife gets very concerned about their status in society" and will try to get involved with organizations so that "they can take their—as the British would say—'rightful place in Society.'"

Prestigious nonprofits and charity benefits become the target of "social climbing" and networking. As one donor put it, philanthropy "is one of the avenues by which Society makes its connections." Charity benefits, for instance, provide exclusive settings for elite interaction. Donors viewed benefits as a prominent component of New York social life, which 89 percent said they attend.[18] As one respondent explained, he enjoys himself at benefits because "there are a lot of people like me there." Another brought up benefits during a discussion of social snobbery and philanthropy, saying, "I will admit I'm partially guilty. . . . I very much like the black tie . . . dance at [Organization X]. . . . It's an opportunity to meet some people and do some things, which in my mind is more networking than anything else." One donor volunteered that he knew someone who attended benefits for "purely social reasoning—she wanted to meet people and marry a wealthy husband." More generally, he observed that "in some of these organizations there is complete social snobbery. Pick an organization and it has benefits, and people go. And those who can't afford to go, can't go. Also, its a way of meeting people. It is an important part of social life."

As these quotes suggest, charity benefits further illustrate the closure characterizing elite philanthropy. Here, we often find elites giving at the request of other elites to attend functions with other members of the elite, often in support of organizations that are used by and have prestige in the eyes of the elite.

The connections between giving, elite interaction, and prestige are also found surrounding nonprofit boards. Several donors reported that it is because of the elite interaction associated with philanthropy that people want to become trustees of prestigious organizations. One donor described how someone had asked a family member what it would cost to get on a board he serves on: "What's the tab? That's pretty straightforward." Explaining why the person wanted to join, she said, "Social profile. A new forum of making social connections. Actually, the person in this case was someone from out of town who wants to spend more time in New York." Her anecdote highlights the fact that nonprofits and elites are connected with one another in the minds of the wealthy, with organizational involvement being seen as a way to establish relationships with members of the elite. Another donor, who believes that philanthropy is a prerequisite for membership in certain social circles said,

> I'll give you an example. . . . If you move to [X] and you want to be accepted by the OK people, you break your back to get on the board of the museum. . . . The entrées leading off that board are not to be believed. . . . You cannot imagine the vying that goes on to get onto that board. It really is crazy. . . . There's only one rival . . . and that has come up because the museum couldn't take these people on. So the offcasts—this sounds awful to say this, but it's true, and I have seen people try to rise to the top in the museum and they haven't made it, so they pull out . . . and go to [the other organization].

He added that membership on that museum board did indeed offer valuable social and business connections. Another donor explained that "one gets into philanthropic efforts or involvements the way some people get involved in club activities, because you like and enjoy the caliber of the people you're doing this with."

Implicit in the discussion to this point is that a good deal of elite philanthropy takes place within the same generally well-to-do ambiance that characterizes the work and social environment of these donors. Indeed, privileged access to prestigious settings represents another return to donors for philanthropic contributions, as seen, for instance, in charity benefits and private performances.[19] The lavish backdrop against which philanthropy occurs, in turn, contributes to retaining the identification between philanthropy and prestige. Many donors, who are also fundraisers for causes, stressed the importance of this. Discussing whether too much money is generally spent enhancing the setting of charity benefits,[20] a donor who organizes such benefits emphasized the importance of surroundings as follows: "I think it's money well spent. When a charity becomes attractive to people, they're going to raise more money. . . . One time we used to say, 'People are paying a hundred dollars for dinner.' Now they're paying a thousand dollars for dinner! You have to give them flowers. You have to give them a decent meal."[21] Another donor made a similar observation with respect to boards. Said she,

> Organizations today have to do a lot for board members. . . . You have to have an interesting board of directors, have it in a pretty place . . . have decent food . . . because they're used to it. They really like things the way they're used to. So to say, if you've given us ten million dollars, but you're going to have a two-cent paper napkin to have your sandwich on—no plates! They'll be happier if things are done in a style that they're comfortable with.

Similar considerations come into play in the fundraising process as well, with respect to the stature of the person requesting donations. Among the wealthy, a characteristic of fundraising is that it involves elites personally asking one another for contributions. This might be a friend or someone who is in a comparable social or business position. Donors often reported cases of nonprofits sending such an individual to request contributions. When asked if (and by whom) he had been asked to make one of his larger gifts, one man said,

> [Nonprofit X] was very active on that. Which I think is in a certain sense, reason to do it—if somebody else is interested enough to come over to your office. The guy who came over the first time was the president of [Corporation X] across the street here, and if he thought it was worth his time—maybe it was just ego massaging—but he thought it was a worthy venture. I thought it was much better than a form letter.

Considerations of organizational prestige are influential in channeling largest gifts as well. As some of the above quotes indicate, nonprofits do not enjoy equal stature among the elite. Rather, philanthropy is structured by a prestige hierarchy. One factor influencing an institution's position in that hierarchy is the area of activity in which it is engaged, as illustrated by the distribution of largest gifts made by donors.[22] With striking frequency, these gifts went to precisely the kinds of educational and cultural organizations that are used by, and have prestige among, the elite.[23] Education received largest gifts from the greatest number of donors, followed by culture (see Table 1.3). Indeed, these two areas alone received fully 58.6 percent of all (244) largest gifts made, with the remainder divided among six areas. The particular or-

TABLE 1.3
Distribution of Donors by Area of Giving (Largest Gifts)

Area	% of Donors Giving
Education	69.4
Colleges/Universities, related[a]	61.2
Schools, related[b]	14.3
Culture	42.9
Health	30.6
Hospitals	22.4
Other	15.5
Social Services	29.4
Jewish Affil. Fund	20.0
Other	11.9
Churches/Temples	15.5
Animals/Environment	10.7
Rights/Advocacy/Policy	10.7
Youth (n.e.c.)	6.0

Note: Based on the three largest gifts made by donors during the past twelve months. The base number of donors is 85 except for the areas of schools (precollege), culture, other health, other social services, churches/temples, animals/environment, rights/advocacy/policy, and youth, where it is 84 because for two donors there are data on some, but not all largest gifts. These cases are treated as missing for all areas except those where they are known to have contributed.

[a] Most donors in this category (94.2 percent) gave to a university or college. Also included are "related" gifts, such as to a college scholarship fund or a research institute. One donor gave gifts of both kinds.

[b] Most donors in this category (92.3 percent) made gifts to a precollege level school, or, in one case, to an organization that supports schools. Also included are "related" gifts to organizations providing educational services at this level. One donor gave gifts of both kinds.

ganizations within these areas, in turn, were among the most prestigious in their fields. For instance, most gifts in education went to universities and colleges. Of these 63 gifts, in turn, fully 42.9 percent went to Ivy League schools, with many others going to competitive smaller colleges.[24] In both education and culture, moreover, we find a concentration of giving whereby certain organizations received gifts from multiple donors. In the case of education, this reflected gifts made to particular Ivy League schools; in the case of culture, these were arts institutions described by various donors as among the most prestigious, prominent, and "chic" nonprofits in New York.

The frequency with which culture and education were selected was not confined to largest gifts, but was also found in an examination of donors' recent smaller gifts ($1,000 or less). These two areas were again the primary recipients, receiving 50.6 percent of all such gifts. Their prominence in philanthropy is further indicated when we turn from the interview data to look at the median numbers of gifts of $1,000 or more received by a set of New York City's largest nonprofit organizations (using data from the donor lists collected as part of the sampling procedure). Organizations in culture and education received the highest number of such donations by far. The median was 461 gifts in education and 362 in culture, and then dropped to 210 for hospitals, the area with the next highest median.[25]

An analysis of variation in giving to education further demonstrates that prestige is one factor channeling gifts to certain organizations. Among college graduates, donors who attended more prestigious schools were also more likely to have made one of their largest gifts to their alma mater.[26] This finding also reveals the importance of prestige hierarchies within, as well as between, areas. It indicates as well that even when a donor has familiarity with an organization, its prestige will still be a factor in eliciting largest contributions.

Taken together, the results we have been considering reveal that it is not only giving money or organizational involvement that makes philanthropy prestigious. It is also a question of where that money or involvement is directed. Particular organizations, like philanthropy itself, carry symbolic status values, which influence the distribution of donors' gifts.

Donors themselves expressed an awareness that a status hierarchy exists among nonprofits, and that culture and education are privileged in this regard. When deciding about whether to attend various benefits, one donor is influenced by the involvement of friends, whether the events sound like fun, "or if they're very prestigious, let's be honest." Another donor said, "There are certain institutions, that if you're a volunteer for them, then you're a big deal. If you are on the board of something else, nobody's heard of it. People don't tend to come to meetings." She added that while volunteers are hard to get elsewhere, "they line up by droves" to volunteer for a prestigious arts organization with which she is familiar.

Another respondent, who raises money for a health and rehabilitation organization, noted that this same cultural organization has a waiting list for people wanting to buy benefit tickets, despite their extremely high price. Said she, "I can't stand it. I would love to say, 'Let me have the waiting list. I'll take the waiting list!'" Similarly, executives at service organizations I spoke with during the study referred to the relative lack of prestige enjoyed by their organizations, noting that they do not have the "glitz" that cultural causes enjoy in the eyes of donors.

It is important to emphasize that this discussion has been considering donors as a whole. When donors are broken down into subgroups, very different patterns of *concentration* of giving to culture and education emerge. It would therefore be incorrect to draw conclusions about the relative position of culture, education, and other areas at this point. Nonetheless, culture and education may legitimately be singled out as privileged because they are common choices of so many different sub-groups of donors (Jews and non-Jews, women and men, those with inherited wealth and those with self-made wealth).[27] This, in turn, shows their privileged association with elite status per se. This association, I maintain, derives from the connection between such institutions and the social elite. This view is confirmed not only by the long historical association between social upper classes and such institutions,[28] but also by the fact that, in this study, the social elite stood out because their giving was virtually exclusively concentrated on culture and education.

Up to now, the focus has been on the prestige derived by elites from organizations, but the relationship also works the other way, with nonprofits deriving prestige from associated elites. Nonprofits seek prominent board members with valuable names in order to retain their own stature and thereby attract other donors.[29] This is why boards will sometimes accept a relatively uninvolved board member if his or her name carries enough weight. Thus, when she tried to resign from a board, one donor was told, "We want your name," even though she made it known that she would not be active. A donor who told me that she believes board members should work, explained that nonetheless, "I have had people . . . who have wanted to get off, but their names are so important to me, I've said, 'I won't allow you to go off.' Even though they do nothing. I think when you're doing a benefit and they see that name on the letterhead, it's important."[30] As with organizations, members of the elite differ with respect to their prestige, as well as in terms of the other resources they can bring to an institution. Furthermore, as the example indicates, the donor with one resource (such as a "name") may not have (or be willing to share) other desirable resources. The multiplicity of potentially important resources, as well as the fact that they may belong to different people, are among the factors that contribute to status competition in philanthropy.

PHILANTHROPY, STATUS COMPETITION, AND STATUS BOUNDARIES

In light of the links between involvement with nonprofits, prestige, and elite interaction, it might be anticipated that philanthropy would become the scene of status competition. This should be particularly true in the case of organizations with the greatest prestige. And it should be particularly intense with respect to board membership, which is such a highly valued sign of elite status. As new individuals and groups accumulate wealth, they will want to associate themselves with the nonprofits,[31] while those who were formerly associated will not want to give up the association between the organization and their own circles and will resent newcomers.

As discussed in the previous chapter, conflicts can arise from the relationship between nonprofit institutions and elite groups, specifically between upper-class status goals of exclusivity and the economic interests of organizations.[32] This tension was expressed well by the observation of a woman who is a member of the social elite and had recently organized a large charity benefit. She was critical of an attitude she had heard from fellow members of the elite, and expressed a view more in keeping with the organizational perspective when she made the following comment about organizing charity benefits: "It's a business. . . . Some people don't want the price to go too high, because they want all their friends to be able to attend. But that's not the point. It's a business, and it really has to be looked at that way."

The combination of new millionaires and mounting financial needs on the part of organizations suggest that such tensions would indeed arise in New York philanthropy during the 1980s. Indeed, many donors spoke about a desire of those in control to maintain their position, of newcomers to associate themselves with the organization, and of the organizational need for money. The view was repeatedly expressed that New York philanthropy had changed during the past twenty to twenty-five years, so that one could now "buy in" to a position of prominence. One person said that there used to be a tight circle, but "what blew that apart were the [Xs] and people like that coming in who nobody knew . . . what we call nouvelle society. It did change things. All of a sudden these people started giving huge amounts of money. You had to notice. But it also made people look bad who were moderate donors and they didn't like losing their position."

The thing that people were "buying," according to donors, were seats on nonprofit boards.[33] One donor, a trustee of a major New York cultural institution, felt that things have changed over the past twenty years so that "money now buys anything," including board membership. When asked about social exclusivity on the part of boards on which she serves, she said, "That has broken down tremendously, because all those people they wanted to be snobbish towards are now very rich, so they're no longer snobbish towards them." Similarly, another social elite trustee, who serves on another prestigious arts board, said that board recruitment has changed since she first joined, so that now, people are told to "sign on," donate, and buy a seat to become socially acceptable.

A trustee of a different prestigious art institution, and a member of the social elite, told me that he has personally "struggled" to keep his board from admitting new members on the basis of their ability to contribute, but added that it is very difficult to say no to someone capable of contributing enormous sums, "no matter what their personal qualifications are." He added that specified levels of donations have also increasingly become a prerequisite for serving on other bodies associated with the institution. Though he finds it troubling in some ways, he acknowledged that this trend has helped the organization, for "the result has been that more money is coming in, and that, of course, is something that they very much need."

A broader variety of donors also made a link between giving large sums and getting on boards. Some spoke about the "price" associated with particular boards. One donor said that a certain organization has a "$100,000 board . . . almost like a bill." Another told me that a board she serves on expects annual contributions in the low five figures, and contrasted that with the amounts expected by other boards. One woman told me, "I don't give [thousands of dollars] to [Organization X] not to be known." She explained that she wanted the current trustees to be aware of her gift because she would like to have the honor of serving on that board and feels that giving will help her to achieve that goal. It may well have done so, for she has indeed joined the board since the time of the interview.

As noted earlier, those who view themselves as members of the "old group" (of people in philanthropy) might be expected to take a negative view of the changes they described, and their remarks revealed that this was indeed the case. Comments revealed a particular tendency of this group to portray themselves as the "true guardians" of the organization, and to stress the importance of time given and the spirit in which giving was done, while contrasting this with the crassness of the "new donors," who "only" give money.[34] By distinguishing philanthropy from the concrete act of giving money and identifying it with a particular style or attitude, it can still be presented as associated with the "old guard" and not the new, although the latter may make larger donations. In this regard, philanthropy shares characteristics of other marks of class status, such as aesthetic appreciation, which involves not only "consumption," but a style of appropriation, such as the correct posture when listening to a concert.[35]

One social elite donor, for instance, distanced herself from the "new rich," whom she portrayed as giving for status, implying that she herself did not. Asked about any snobbery connected with philanthropy, she said, "They say now there's a whole bunch of new rich that you read about and so forth—you do see at benefits. I don't think that's necessarily bothersome. . . . You certainly wish they'd do it for reasons other than their own aggrandizement. But if they do it, they do it. Let them do it. They should do it."

Another member of the social elite believes that while boards used to invite members to serve because they were responsible and worked hard, they have lowered their standards to accommodate the newly rich who seek social acceptance. In her view, the world has become "more crass." Needless to say, from the point of view of those who view themselves as outside the old group, such "higher standards" may appear more like in-group exclusiveness.[36] From a sociological perspective, such comments reflect the tension between the ability of individuals to establish prestige through philanthropy, and the ability of groups to monopolize identification with particular organizations as a source of collective status.[37]

It is important to stress that donors did not say that giving large sums of money was the sole path to board membership. The ability to raise money from other sources (such as corporations) was also seen as a route. Personal and family prestige and being known by current trustees were also seen as valued characteristics. Rather, the point that donors were making was that the ability to contribute large sums had become an increasingly important factor.

In sum, the material from the interviews leads to the conclusion that the 1980s did indeed witness a greater openness on nonprofit boards with respect to members of the elite. Serving on a prestigious board, therefore, is not so clearly or directly a reflection of membership within the social elite, because an individual, by virtue of having money, now has greater access to board membership. Status boundaries, these findings suggest, did indeed appear to have weakened in elite philanthropy.

Are actual patterns of board membership consistent with this conclusion? To answer this question, let us analyze actual patterns of board membership, comparing the results with donors' comments.

The Determinants of Board Membership

During the interviews, donors were asked to identify the boards on which they serve. These data were used to examine the correlates of board membership, with particular attention to the factors on which we have focused. The results of a regression analysis revealed that three factors were associated with serving on more boards. These were membership in the social elite,[38] the total amount of money contributed by the donor during the past year, and having an association with a business (see Table 1.4).[39] In other words, members of the social elite do have an

TABLE 1.4
Determinants of Board Membership: Ordinary Least Squares and Logistic
Regression Results

Independent Variables	Dependent Variables			
	A No. of Boards	B Culture Board	C Col./Univ. Board	D Hospital Board
Total $ Donated/ (Area)[a]	.004** (.001)	5.8*	.7	8.3**
Largest Gift Area (1 = Yes)	NA	8.1**	5.9*	.06
Social Elite (1 = Yes)	1.3* (.50)	5.0*	2.9	.02
Business (1 = Yes)	1.1* (.52)	.17	3.9*	.24
Ethnicity/Religion (1 = Jewish)	.55 (.51)	.04	7.8**	.24
Gender (1 = Female)	−.38 (.51)	.51	see [b]	.65
Adjusted R-square	34	NA	NA	NA
N	73	63	69	70

Note: Column A presents parameter estimates and standard errors (in parentheses) from ordinary least squares regression. Columns B–D present chi-squares from logistic regression analyses. For logistic regressions, the dependent variable is coded 1 if the donor is on a board in that area and 0 otherwise.

[a] For analyses of numbers of boards and whether the donor sat on any board, the variable used is the total amount of money contributed during the past year. For analyses by area, the variable used is total dollars contributed to that area during the past year.

[b] The logistic regression could not be estimated with the inclusion of the gender variable, which was therefore excluded. Separate analyses (using subsets of variables) indicated that the gender variable was not significant once controls were added.

* $p < .05$.
** $p < .01$.

advantage, independent of other factors. Yet competing with this group principle is an individual principle. The decision to contribute large sums of money will give someone an advantage as well, regardless of the donor's affiliation with the social elite.[40]

Up to this point, I have discussed only numbers of boards. What about the kinds of boards on which donors serve? Additional analyses examined the determinants of serving on boards of institutions in different areas. The results reveal that the sole area in which social elite membership offered a clear advantage was culture. Yet even here, two other variables were significant as well: the total dollars contributed by the donor to culture during the previous year, and whether or not one of the donor's largest gifts went to a cultural institution (see Table 1.4).[41] These results also highlight my view that philanthropy must be analyzed as a heterogeneous phenomenon, for giving and volunteering in different areas can respond to distinct influences.

There has, it seems, been an evolution in the determinants of board membership, or at least in their relative importance. We thus find that one enclave, cultural boards, stands out as a remaining area where the social elite have an advantage simply because they are the social elite. Why should this be the case? Perhaps cultural institutions today remain more dependent on their patrons, including their board members, for their own prestige.[42] By contrast, the prestige of institutions in other areas, such as universities, may be less influenced by the social standing of board members, and rooted to a greater degree in the reputation and stature of the organization itself.

In light of these findings, we can understand the changes that have occurred in the composition of some of New York's major cultural boards over the past twenty years. Today, the Metropolitan Museum of Art, for instance, has a far lower percentage of board members listed in the *Social Register* than it did twenty years ago. While fully 67 percent of members were listed in 1972, the figure dropped to 44 percent in 1982, and then to 33 percent in 1992. The comparable figures for the Metropolitan Opera during the same time periods were 48 percent, 30 percent, and 22 percent. Lincoln Center's board offers yet another example, with the percentage of members in the *Social Register* dropping from 36 percent to 24 percent and finally to 18 percent. Carnegie Hall showed a dramatic decrease over the entire period as well. Interestingly, however, while trustees in the *Social Register* on the Carnegie board dropped from 21 percent in 1972 to 7 percent in 1982, they actually increased slightly in 1992, to 11 percent.[43] Taken together, the analyses, then, do support the idea that status boundaries in philanthropy have indeed been weakened.

CONCLUSION

As visible and public as its consequences may be, philanthropy develops from, occurs within, and serves to sustain, the relatively closed boundaries of elite life. This does not mean that donors are unconcerned about the particular causes they support or their social consequences. As we have seen, they are often deeply involved with these and committed to them on a long-term basis. It does mean philanthropy and nonprofits have a special place within the elite that goes beyond the particular services of the organizations. Attending a museum benefit could be important to a donor for its social value, or because a friend is being honored, or because there is peer pressure to go—regardless of how many times that donor attends an exhibit at the museum.

This, in turn, helps us to answer the question posed earlier concerning whether, and how, exclusivity coexists in elite philanthropy under changed organizational circumstances. Through charity benefits, board memberships, private events open only to large donors, and related mechanisms, elites carve out a separate world for themselves through philanthropy. In this way, a sense of a distinctive and exclusive relationship to organizations they value is maintained, regardless of who else may have access to the organization's services. DiMaggio and Useem observe that elites have historically resisted the extension of cultural organizations' services even to the upper middle class.[44] As we can see, philanthropy permits the re-creation of a relatively homogeneous elite environment even under such circumstances. An implication of this discussion, however, is that any efforts to make boards more heterogeneous with respect to class should meet with considerable resistance by elites, for it would threaten philanthropy's very functioning as a mark of class status and separate arena.

From an intra-elite perspective, however, the philanthropic world is anything but homogeneous. To say that elite philanthropy is a closed world does not mean that it is composed of any single, tightly integrated group. It is useful to conceptualize philanthropy in terms of the idea of a hierarchical field of institutions and actors, developed by the sociologist Pierre Bourdieu in relation to other areas. Within social fields, individuals compete to position themselves, drawing on the different types of "capital," or resources, at their disposal.[45] In philanthropy, such capital includes personal prestige, money, time, and connections. At various periods, not only those who possess these resources but also the value of different resources themselves can change. The events of the 1970s and 1980s witnessed changes favorable for the entry of new, or even previously excluded, millionaires to rise to prominence in philanthropy. At the same time, they provided circumstances favorable to individual attributes as determinants of prominence, as boundaries based on status group membership within philanthropy weakened. Social elite membership continues to function as a valuable asset in the philanthropic world, but members of the social elite must increasingly share coveted positions with others and may indeed even find themselves outnumbered on any particular board. At the same time, however, the opening up of philanthropy generates new sources of support and thereby strengthens and sustains its meaning and role within the elite as a whole.

This chapter began our examination of the weakening of status boundaries within philanthropy. Another important aspect of this issue concerns the erosion of an ethnic/religious boundary in elite philanthropy, which is the subject of the next chapter.

Chapter Two

RELIGION, ETHNICITY, AND JEWISH
PHILANTHROPY

RELIGION, especially the distinction between Protestants and Jews, has been a major source of differentiation among elites in the United States.[1] Furthermore, religion, or ethnicity,[2] has served as one of the boundaries excluding Jews from the Protestant-dominated social elite and its institutions.[3] As with other intra-elite divisions, this ethnic boundary should not be thought of in absolute or static terms, for it has varied in strength over time. Thus, relatively greater acceptance of Jews was replaced by considerable barriers and anti-Semitism in the late 1800s and early 1900s.[4] Indeed, although a Jewish man was among the founders of New York's elite Union League Club during the Civil War, by the 1890s the son of this same man was denied membership because of his Judaism.[5]

What is the relevance of religious differentiation for elite philanthropy today? That is the question posed by this chapter, which extends our analysis of continuity and change in contemporary philanthropy to the subject of Jewish participation in elite philanthropy. Paralleling the changes already described, it shows that the 1980s were a time in which the boundaries against Jewish participation in prestigious, nonreligiously affiliated, elite institutions had weakened.

Compared with the previous chapter, the present discussion of boundaries has an added dimension, because the subject of Jewish philanthropy involves not only the relationship of Jewish donors to a set of elite institutions but also to the highly developed world of Jewish philanthropy, which has its own norms and prestige processes. Indeed, the existence of a distinctive Jewish philanthropic subculture was recognized and discussed by both Jews and non-Jews during the interviews.[6] This chapter thus addresses two interrelated topics. It examines how philanthropy among elites responds to another kind of group identification (religion) in addition to class, particularly in the case of Jewish donors. It also considers how distinctive subgroup patterns of philanthropy, linked with religion, relate to the general and dominant pattern of elite philanthropy that has been our focus to this point.

An ongoing theme of this book has been that philanthropy is an expression of group identity among elites. A focus on ethnicity introduces the consideration that elites can participate in multiple group identities. Accordingly, this chapter examines the impact and relative strength of alternative identities and affiliations on members of the elite in their philanthropy. It particularly examines the impact of acceptance into the social elite on religiously linked patterns of philanthropy among Jewish donors. The discussion of the distinctive characteristics of Jewish philanthropy permits us to assess not only whether such an impact exists, but also the substantive consequences that result when the philanthropic values of the subculture are overshadowed as a consequence of class assimilation.

Before turning to the discussion itself, an important note about what is not included in this chapter: Successful Catholics in the United States have also faced barriers from the social elite and its institutions,[7] and it would have been of interest to conduct parallel analyses for Catholics and Jews. Unfortunately, as discussed in greater detail below, this was not possible because of the small number of Catholics in the present sample. It should also be noted that this chapter is not meant as a comparative analysis of religious philanthropy among wealthy Jewish, Protestant, and Catholic donors, or even as an analysis of the complicated subject of Jewish philanthropy per se. Such analyses, while of considerable interest, would require a sample and data that this research was not designed to collect.[8] Rather, this chapter addresses religiously linked philanthropy in the specific context of a study of elites. It is meant to explore one distinctive subculture and pattern that emerged among this group of wealthy donors, which sheds light on the complex relationship between typical and alternative forms of philanthropy among the elite.

THE RELIGIOUS AFFILIATION OF DONORS

The religious composition of the sample is itself of interest for the questions and suggestions it raises concerning the characteristics of wealthy donors. The highest percentage of donors in the sample were Jewish (59.1 percent), followed by Protestants (26.1 percent), Catholics (10.2 percent), and those with no religious affiliation (4.5 percent).[9] Particularly striking is the high number of Jews in the sample.[10] Statistics on the religious composition of large donors (or wealthy individuals) in New York as a whole, which could be used for comparison, are lacking. However, available information does indicate that at least one reason for this high percentage of Jews is that Jews are in fact large contributors to philanthropic causes. This information comes from a telephone survey of giving among a random sample of 2,759 New Yorkers conducted by Sirota and Alper Associates. The study found that being Jewish was one characteristic associated with being a large donor, or someone who contributes 5 percent of income or more. Similarly, it found that Jews gave a two-and-a-half times larger proportion of their income than did others.[11]

Particularly relevant are the findings from the Sirota and Alper survey concerning their seventy-eight respondents with incomes of more than $100,000. Among these donors, 2 percent of Protestants, 11 percent of Catholics, but fully 37 percent of Jews had contributed $5,000 or more during the previous twelve months.[12] Although caution must be exercised given the small size of the sample, the findings do support the conclusion that the strong Jewish presence in this study reflects their high level of giving.[13]

At the same time, the Sirota and Alper survey raises questions concerning the relatively low percentage of Catholics in the present sample. Their sample of respondents with incomes of more than $100,000 included twenty-six Catholics, twenty-three Jews, thirteen Protestants, and fifteen respondents not classifiable as one of these. Moreover, a larger percentage of Catholics than Protestants had contributed more than $5,000, raising the question of why the present sample has so far fewer Catholics than Protestants?

Although no conclusions can be drawn, given the limited material available, certain possibilities may be suggested. First, the Sirota and Alper survey was confined to New York City residents, while my study sampled donors who work or live in New York, thus including people who live in the suburbs. Since there is some reason to believe that affluent Protestants are concentrated in the suburbs,[14] the percentage living in the New York vicinity may exceed the percentage whose primary residence is in the city.

It is also possible that affluent Catholic donors are less likely than Protestants and Jews to contribute to the organizations from which donors for this study were sampled, the major nonprofits in New York City. Their contributions may go more exclusively to other kinds of beneficiaries. For example, the Sirota and Alper research found that among people who made contributions, affluent Catholics gave a larger percentage of money to religious organizations than did affluent Jewish or Protestant donors. Since the definition of "religious organizations" was left to respondents, this finding is difficult to interpret, but if respondents interpreted it in a fairly restrictive way (i.e., to mean churches or temples), then it would provide one potential reason for the low number of Catholics in this study, which did not include churches and temples in the sampling base. Regardless of which, if any, of these reasons are true, the sample composition suggests that an important difference in the nature of philanthropic activity and participation in nonprofit organizations may exist among Catholic members of the elite. Although it is beyond the scope and data of this study to consider this possibility any further, the topic of philanthropy among wealthy Catholics (and indeed studies of this group as a whole) is one of great interest on which additional research is clearly needed.

RELIGIOUS AFFILIATION AND DISTINCTIVE PATTERNS OF GIVING

With respect to their largest gifts, Protestants, Catholics, and Jews each exhibited a distinctive, religiously linked pattern of giving (see Table 2.1). For Protestants, religious affiliation was tied to making major donations to a church. Fully 31.8 percent of Protestants, as compared with 9.7 percent of other donors, had made one of their largest gifts to a religious congregation.[15] This marked difference primarily reflects the contrast between Protestants and Jews, only 8.2 percent of whom had contributed to a religious congregation. Among Catholics, the religiously linked pattern is found in giving to schools at the precollege level. While 44.4 percent of Catholics had made one of their largest gifts to such an institution, only 18.2 percent of Protestants and 8.2 percent of Jews had done so. All the gifts made by Catholic donors went to schools with a Catholic affiliation. Finally, Jewish donors contributed at a far higher rate (40 percent) to the social services than Protestants (13.6 percent) or Catholics (none). This high level of giving among Jews is due to major giving by Jews (34 percent) to a Jewish-affiliated federated fund.[16] Indeed, so many donors made a gift to this one organization that it warranted being put into a category of its own. As we shall see, this institution occupies a central position in the Jewish community. It's stature was further confirmed when, on several occasions, Jewish donors who did not make a major gift to it spoke of why they did not, without being asked.

At the same time that distinctive religious patterns exist, culture and education, the leading overall recipients of major donations, are frequently chosen by Protestants, Catholics, and Jews alike. This underscores the fact that it is legitimate to speak of a widespread "elite pattern" of giving among donors, who share a general orientation and way of life as members of the elite. This pattern, however, coexists with divergent patterns related to donors' other affiliations and organiza-

TABLE 2.1
Donors' Religious Affiliation and Area of Giving (Largest Gifts)

Religion	No. of Donors	Percentage of Donors Making a Largest Gift in Area			
		Culture	All Educ.	Univ., Rltd.[a]	Schools, Rltd.
Jewish	49	38.8	61.2	53.1	8.2
Protestant	22	50.0	78.3	69.6	18.2
Catholic	9	44.4	77.8	66.7	44.4*
None	4[b]				

		Soc. Serv.	All Health	Hosps. Only	Other Health
Jewish[c]	40.0**		38.0	26.0	22.5*
Protestant	13.6		27.3	22.7	9.1
Catholic	0.0		11.1	11.1	0.0

		Youth (n.e.c)	Church/Temple	Anim./Env.	Rights/ Advocacy/Policy
Jewish	2.0		8.2*	8.2	16.3
Protestant	13.6		31.8*	13.6	0.0
Catholic	11.1		22.2	22.2	11.1

Note: For tables of all health, hospitals, and social services, the number of Jewish respondents is fifty. For tables of all education and universities, the number of Protestants is twenty-three.

Significance levels are reported for tables of dichotomized religion variables (e.g., Jewish vs. others) by each area of giving. For the relationship between being Jewish and making a largest gift to education (all categories), to all health, and to rights/advocacy/policy, $p \leq .10$. For the relationship between being Protestant and making a largest gift to rights/advocacy/policy, $p \leq .10$.

Since data are based on multiple (three) largest gifts made by donors, the percentage of gifts made to each area does not sum to 100 percent for each religion.

[a] On the "related" organizations included in this and the following category, see Table 1.3, notes a and b.

[b] The breakdown of gifts for those with no religious affiliation is not presented due to the small number of respondents in that category.

[c] For Jewish donors, the percentage contributing to the Jewish-affiliated fund is 34 percent. The percentage contributing to other social service organizations is 10.2 percent.

*$p \leq .05$ for table, Fisher's test or chi-square.
**$p \leq .01$.

tional involvements. As we can see, then, conformity in giving in certain areas coexists with variations in others. In addition, the difference in the percentage of donors making largest gifts to culture and education as compared with largest gifts to other areas varies among subgroups, reinforcing my earlier caution not to draw conclusions about concentration of giving to particular areas based on patterns of giving among elites as a whole.

Donors often related their gifts to churches and Catholic schools to their personal involvement with the organizations, as they did for gifts of other kinds. One man supports his church and the other organizations that received his largest gifts because "I've been very much involved with all of them—forever." Another explained that he made his three largest gifts, including one to his church, because "I'm indebted to all three of these organizations, in the sense that I feel a personal involvement with all three." In giving his reasons for a major donation to a church, another donor included his membership in the church, as well as his friendship with the clergyman, and the fact that the church does "wonderful work."[17]

All the gifts made to Catholic schools went to institutions attended by the donor or a relative. Speaking of a gift he made to a Catholic school, one donor explained, "That, of course, has very deep roots as far as my life is concerned. We got an excellent education there." He spoke of his gratitude to the school and interest in contributing "to help others get what you received." Another man gave to a school used by his family "more or less on the ground that education does need support. Not that I'm terribly religious, but what the hell? I felt they needed it more than [Ivy League Schools X and Y]." Asked about his gift to a school, another Catholic donor said he had "a personal association with the place," which he had attended and with which his family had long been involved. He went on to stress his commitment to Catholic schools, explaining that "I very much wanted to have those values and that doctrine, and so forth—at least my children exposed to them. I feel that it's very important we have those kinds of schools, so it means a lot."

As these comments highlight, donors become involved with organizations affiliated with their religious group, as well as with their class. Just as various cultural nonprofits are linked with prestigious social circles, other organizations are linked with membership in, and a sense of belonging to, particular religious groups. When asked whether he felt pressure to give to any particular organizations, a donor who is active in his church replied, "I can't imagine being in the Church and not giving. It would be a feeling of ostracism. Few people would know, but it would be."

The religiously affiliated pattern of giving among Jewish donors, however, diverged from the situation found elsewhere. As we saw in the previous chapter, the personal involvement with organizations that so often accompanies other largest donations (whether religiously linked or not) did not characterize giving to the Jewish-affiliated organization. The Jewish pattern was also unusual in other ways. It involves huge sums of money contributed to a federated fund, although major elite philanthropy virtually never goes to umbrella organizations. Indeed, apart from the Jewish-affiliated federated fund, only one other combined appeal received a largest donation, and this was only from one donor.[18] It also represents huge sums of money directed toward the social services, not otherwise a typical recipient of largest gifts. Furthermore, giving to the Jewish-affiliated fund diverged in terms of the very rationale for philanthropy employed. Donors viewed these contributions in a different fashion from their other gifts, and employed a different language when speaking of them.

PARTICIPATION IN JEWISH PHILANTHROPY

Interestingly, donors themselves were aware of the unusual nature of their gifts to the Jewish-affiliated fund, commenting often on their lack of personal involvement with the organization. One person said this gift is her only major contribution that is unaccompanied by a personal involvement, but that it would be "unthinkable" not to contribute. Another explained that she and her husband make an annual contribution, "and it is an enormous gift," but added that it was the only one of their large gifts that is "without connections," and is made as a "matter of mechanics." As these comments indicate, donors simply accounted for and discussed these donations differently from their others.

Donors spoke of this gift as an obligation they felt they had as Jews. In doing so, their emphasis was on a sense of ethnic identity and membership in a particular community, rather than religiosity.[19] Indeed, as we have seen, Jewish donors were less likely to have made a largest gift to a temple than were Christian donors to a church. Speaking of her own gift, one donor explained, "But that's not religion. That's sort of—Judaism is more than a religion, I think. Philanthropy is a tradition of the Jewish religion, and obviously I give to Jewish causes."

The rationale for contributing to the Jewish-affiliated fund was posed in communal, rather than individualistic terms. People spoke of giving to the Jewish affiliated fund as a "tax" that you simply pay as a member of the community. One donor told me that "not to participate in that particular philanthropy is not to be a member of the Jewish community." He said, "Now, you can be a member of a synagogue or not be a member of a synagogue. Do as you please. . . . But you can't be a citizen of New York and of the Jewish faith and not feel that you have an obligation to support [the fund]. It's as simple as that to me. It's as if it were a tax." Another emphasized that these donations are not a question of interest but of "obligation—if we don't support it, nobody will." Yet another said that she does not really care much about the organization, but continues to give because "I would feel as though it was being against motherhood not to give anymore." And still another contributor called giving to various Jewish charities "a must."

The subject of Jewish philanthropy was brought up even by donors who had not made a largest gift to a Jewish-affiliated organization. Some Jewish donors raised the topic on their own and explained why they did not contribute, or why they did not contribute more. The fact that they did so underscores the visibility and prominence of philanthropic organizations in the Jewish community, as well as donors' awareness that they are expected to support them. For example, after describing the causes he supports, one donor volunteered, "I do not give, although I am Jewish, to [the Jewish-affiliated fund]." Another person explained that she came from a family where there was "fierce devotion" to the organization, but did not wish to make contributions there, so she had worked out a compromise by selecting an organization that receives support from the larger fund and giving to it directly.

Donors also indicated that visibility and peer pressure play a role in contributions. One woman said that as established members of the Jewish community, her family has to give to numerous Jewish causes "or it would just be remiss. It's an expectation. . . . I'm not anonymous." Such donations become intertwined with business as well. A donor whose office is "predominantly Jewish" explained that their giving "has to do with the stature of [the organization] in the community. . . . How could you be [an organization] of stature and not give?" Another donor, who described how solicitations for donations are done by business and social peers, explained that "you're either in the club or not in the club." As such comments indicate, making contributions to Jewish charities is seen as part of what it means to be a member of the Jewish community. These comments further illustrate how Jewish giving functions as an alternative, organized philanthropic subculture.

Donors discussed the success with which Jewish organizations raised money, emphasizing the skillful use that was made of visibility, peer pressure, and social networks. Said one, "They know all the techniques." Indeed, one Christian donor described the success with which fundraising was carried on in the Jewish community, laughed, and said, "I'm going to adopt those principles!" People described how charity benefits would be organized along industry lines. One donor explained, "You try to identify the person within the . . . industry who is not only most prominent . . . but is the person to whom others . . . will be particularly responsive." Thus when this person is honored at a benefit, "everybody" comes and contributes. Several donors also described the well-known practice of "card calling" whereby someone is called upon to publicly announce a donation at a fundraising event. One woman, who "couldn't believe it" and "was frightened" the first time she attended such an event, described the practice as "very clever." Said she, "You get up and they want you to stand up and say you are giving so much in honor of someone. They hope that once at the benefit, you will give more . . . and often you do. . . . So giving is done in a group." She added that she had never seen this done at a non-Jewish fundraiser. Similarly, another donor explained that people go with the understanding that there is a minimum contribution, but then when called "sometimes they'll say, 'I was going to give $5,000 but the speaker moved me so much, I'm adding another $1,000.' That's the way it's done." Even some donors who said they personally disliked the fundraising techniques thought they were successful. Thus, one donor who does contribute but "just won't go to a card-calling dinner" added that "I know it's good for them, because they make a lot of money out of it."[20]

The issue of social pressure and fundraising in Jewish charities, however, is a complex one. In particular, while it might be tempting to conclude that Jewish philanthropy is the product of social pressure, such an explanation would be oversimplistic and indeed misleading. As we have seen, donors readily discussed the role of visibility and peer pressure in fundraising techniques. And one donor did say that he made his donation because "it's a Jewish thing" and because a good friend whom he "respects" told him that he "really has to give." What is striking, however, is that so many did not experience their own particular gift as a response to social pressure. Rather, anecdotes about peer pressure and fundraising techniques were offered to explain the success of Jewish philanthropy or to describe how that world operates. Furthermore, some donors spoke of these fundraising techniques as the reason they did not contribute (or contribute more), thereby suggesting that social pressure alone does not result in donations. This was true, for instance, of a donor who does not support the Jewish-affiliated fund, although she gets a lot of "flak."

It appears that those who participate to the extent of making their largest gifts to Jewish philanthropy generally view it as an obligation themselves, and thus do not feel they are responding to an externally imposed pressure—even when they say they believe the pressure exists. One donor, for example, said, "The Jewish organizations put you under a lot of pressure. But since I give anyway, and generally give in advance and a reasonable size, I don't feel any pressure."

In other cases, donors said they did feel external pressure, but added that they view giving to the organization as something they ought to do themselves. One man said that he felt pressure to give from "People.

Not business, but people in the charity call you up. Your friends call you up and say, 'Hey you've got to do something.' I agree with them, so I do it." In speaking of her gift, another donor said, "You can't not do it—they'd kill you. So I just do it." Yet this was the same donor who felt that it would be "like being against motherhood" not to contribute. Someone else said that the only place pressure could have been a factor was when he was working, because of the practice of fundraising by industry. Yet he added that he contributed irrespective of that pressure, a claim supported by the fact that he continues to contribute although he is now retired. Such comments underscore that by participating in Jewish philanthropy, donors meet a set of social expectations that they find legitimate as members of a particular community.

As we have seen, religious differentiation does indeed have an impact that is reflected in distinct, religiously linked patterns of giving. In the case of Jewish donors, moreover, we have traced the connection between religious or ethnic affiliation and participation in a separate philanthropic subculture. These religiously linked patterns do not preclude, but coexist with, other philanthropic giving. It is important to note as well that at least half the donors of any religion did not exhibit the distinctive pattern associated with their religious subgroup in their major donations. This indicates that variations within, as well as between, religious groups must be explained, a subject to which we return later in this chapter.

I have thus far focused on alternative, religiously linked patterns of giving. The opening of this chapter also raised questions concerning the relationship between Jewish donors and nonreligiously affiliated elite nonprofit institutions. I now turn to this second topic and the relationship between the two subjects.

Jewish Donors and Ethnic Boundaries in Elite Philanthropy

The relationship of Jewish donors to nonreligiously affiliated philanthropy brings us again to the subjects of intra-elite boundaries and board membership. Donors' comments revealed that while ethnicity remains a salient distinction within the elite, it is one that has decreased in importance with respect to philanthropy. Many donors told of how Jews formerly faced exclusion from New York's prestigious nonprofit institutions, but indicated that these boundaries had been weakening. In making these comments, they referred to involvement with the organizations, especially to that highly valued form of participation, board membership. The point was made in a particularly dramatic way by a Jewish donor who served as a major officer of one board. Noting that discrimination against Jews had lessened over time, he said, "I'm an example. Fifteen to twenty years ago it would be unheard of for a Jew to be the [officer] of [Organization X]."[21] Another explained,

> The cultural arenas had been barred to Jews. Just as Jews in general were kind of barred from some of the top universities and executive suites of some of the major companies, so they were barred from some of the socially oriented charitable enterprises. . . . So they were kind of, by implication, barred from being welcomed into the circles that were running these enterprises, which have, as I say, a kind of social backdrop to them. As a consequence, Jews tended to move their philanthropy into Jewish-oriented, rather than secular activities. That's been changing.

Yet another Jewish donor said, "There were certain institutions that were Jewish and there were certain institutions that were Christian and it didn't really mix. . . . It still exists, but I think the gap is much, much narrower." Significantly, however, she did not attribute the evolution to changing attitudes or greater acceptance of Jews, but to the need to raise contributions from Jewish donors: "In order to survive they had to open up the doors." Similarly, another Jewish donor believes that barriers to Jews eventually weakened because "money gives power." As these and other similar comments demonstrate, formal admission need not be experienced as social acceptance.[22]

Moreover, this perception was not limited to Jewish respondents. A woman who was not Jewish told of a major cultural organization that formerly refused to admit a Jew to the board but eventually had to "because he gave so much money." She said that "they've had to change," in addition to which "the strong Christian organizations realized the best thing they could do is to get Jews because Jews had a great tradition of giving."

Analyses of the actual determinants of board membership discussed in chapter 1 are indeed consistent with donors' comments about access to boards. As was noted, Jews were not at a disadvantage with respect to serving on boards. Of particular importance was that this held true for cultural boards, to which donors so often referred when speaking of organizations where former barriers had weakened. These findings, in turn, raise questions about the relationship between participation in Jewish philanthropy and nonreligiously affiliated nonprofits. Philanthropic decisions may be viewed as a response to both opportunities and constraints.[23] Accordingly, a sense of exclusion from other nonprofit institutions and affiliated groups, as well as the draw of values and traditions associated with the Jewish philanthropic subculture, may contribute to sustaining involvement with Jewish organizations. Indeed, as we have seen, this connection was made by some donors themselves.[24]

The case of a Jewish donor in this study illustrates these points, highlighting the potential impact of greater access to prestigious, nonreligiously affiliated institutions on participation in Jewish philanthropy. When this donor first became involved in New York philanthropy many years ago, he was quite active in various Jewish-affiliated institutions. This, however, is no longer the case. Explaining why, he said, "Those organizations I reduced my interest in, mostly because these other things, like [Cultural Organizations X and Y] are much more interesting. And the Jewish leadership in those organizations has increased enormously. You have a Jewish [officer] of [Organization X]. That would have been inconceivable thirty years ago." His major financial commitments, as well as his time, also went to such organizations, with all three of his largest gifts going to cultural institutions. It should be noted that his changing priorities involved a shift in substantive areas as well as a move away from religiously affiliated organizations. Thus, for instance, he reduced participation in one Jewish-affiliated social service agency in favor of greater involvement with cultural organizations.

The relationship between greater access to such organizations and donations to Jewish-affiliated causes is not lost on fundraisers in the Jewish community. One fundraising consultant wrote an article in which he observed that even when barred from the boards of cultural and educational organizations, Jews still supported them generously through financial donations. He went on to add that "if the Jewish rich were generous when treated as inferiors, think of the possibilities when they were actually seated on boards of major universities, symphony orchestras, museums, and opera companies."[25]

Do actual patterns of giving among Jewish donors support the idea of a relationship between greater access to such organizations and donations to Jewish-affiliated causes, as I have suggested? To examine this question, Jewish donors were distinguished according to whether they serve on the board of a nonreligiously affiliated university or cultural board. Comparing the two groups reveals that 35 percent of Jews on such boards, as compared with fully 78.6 percent of other Jewish donors, had made a largest gift to an organization with a Jewish affiliation.[26] These findings indicate that while access to valued, nonreligious nonprofits does not eliminate major giving to Jewish causes, it certainly appears to considerably weaken the draw of such causes for Jewish donors. Apparently, for many Jews who do become involved with them, the status or values associated with universities and cultural organizations overshadows those associated with philanthropic support for Jewish causes. Earlier, I noted the need to address variation in philanthropic giving within religious groups. At least in the case of Jewish donors, we now see that one key to understanding such variation comes from considering the relationship and access donors have to institutions outside their ethnic community.

This discussion raises more general questions about the relationship between, and the relative importance of, class and ethnic identity as influences on philanthropy. These may be addressed by analyzing the consequences when Jewish donors are assimilated into the social elite itself.

JEWISH PHILANTHROPY AND MEMBERSHIP IN THE SOCIAL ELITE

As noted at the outset, Jews have experienced exclusion from both the social circles and institutions associated with the social elite. Indeed, Digby Baltzell observed that the social elite in the United States had evolved into a closed caste that was dominated by white Anglo-Saxon Protestants and closed to successful Jews.[27] Looking at the donors in this study, we find that fully 73.9 percent of Protestants, as compared with 25 percent of Catholics and only 19.2 percent of the Jews, were in the social elite. Such figures indicate that the social elite in New York certainly retains its Protestant character. They further show that while affluence and social elite membership usually go together for Protestants, this is not true for Jews.[28] At the same time, the frequency of Jewish membership, close to one in five, does indicate a Jewish entry into the social elite that clearly goes beyond exceptional, isolated cases. In short, the figures suggest that a process of assimilation of Jews into the social elite is occurring even as broader ethnic boundaries persist.

We have already seen that incorporation into nonreligious institutions tends to erode support for Jewish-affiliated causes. What, then, becomes of those Jews who are incorporated into the social elite itself? Do they continue to exhibit a religiously linked pattern of giving? A hypothesis is suggested by Baltzell's famous thesis that "class tends to replace religion (and even ethnicity and race) as the independent variable in social relationships at the highest levels of our society."[29] Extending this argument to philanthropy, we would expect religiously linked patterns of giving to be weaker or nonexistent among members of the social elite. In short, class identity should overshadow ethnic affiliation with respect to philanthropy.

Looking within the social elite, the distinctive Jewish pattern of philanthropy disappears—precisely as anticipated by the hypothesis developed from Baltzell's thesis. Indeed, none of the Jews in the social elite had made a largest gift to the Jewish-affiliated fund.[30] Accordingly, the differences in giving to the social services between Jews and non-Jews disappears within the social elite. While these findings do not mean that religion has no impact on philanthropy in the social elite, they do show that its relative importance, or the nature of its impact, changes.[31] They further suggest that major philanthropy in the social elite is relatively more insular and closed in nature, being less responsive to multiple influences. Consistent with this interpretation is the fact that a lower percentage of Protestants in the social elite had made a largest gift to a church than had other Protestants.[32]

The idea that class identity overshadows ethnic identity with respect to major philanthropy is further supported when we expand the analysis of giving among Jews in the social elite to include largest donations to any organization with a Jewish affiliation. Using this broad category, we still find that only one (or 11.1 percent) of the Jewish members of the social elite had made a largest gift to such an organization. By contrast, fully 69.4 percent of other Jewish donors had done so. These findings, as well as those just discussed, indicate that membership in the social elite provides one key to understanding variations in religiously linked giving among members of the same religious group.[33]

Yet at the same time that we find this greater conformity in giving among members of the social elite, a new and striking difference between Jews and other donors also emerges in that group. The contrast is in largest giving to organizations in the area of rights, advocacy, and policy. Fully 44.4 percent of Jews in the social elite, but no other donors in that group, had made a largest gift in this area. The difference was not present outside the social elite.[34] Apparently, although major giving to organizations with an explicit Jewish affiliation disappears among members of the social elite, religious affiliation still continues to exert an influence on the selection of beneficiaries in this general area, albeit in a less visible fashion.

A consideration of the rights, advocacy, and policy organizations receiving support from Jews in the social elite suggests an explanation. A high percentage addressed issues of human rights and freedoms, and had a liberal orientation.[35] Affluent Jews are relatively more liberal and more likely to support the Democratic party than are their non-Jewish counterparts,[36] an observation that certainly applies to the present sample. While other members of the social elite were generally Republicans (80 percent), the overwhelming majority of Jews in the social elite were Democrats (77.8 percent), none were Republicans, and the remainder were Independents.[37] The contributions of Jewish respondents to rights, advocacy, and policy organizations, then, reflect the generally less conservative nature of these donors. Furthermore, the kind of activities supported suggests that giving in this area responds to similar values and concerns about discrimination that motivate political attitudes and behavior among affluent Jews.[38] Thus even in a closed and relatively well-defined elite group—the social elite—we must continue to approach both elites and philanthropy as heterogeneous phenomena.

CONCLUSION

New York philanthropy during the 1980s was a scene of both continuity and change. The very factors that served to encourage the entry of new, or previously excluded, millionaires also served to weaken barriers against Jewish individuals based on their ethnic affiliation. While ethnic barriers might be consistent with a status-based logic protective of group exclusivity, they are inconsistent with an organizational logic that addresses the functional needs of nonprofit institutions.[39] This is clearly true with respect to Jewish members of the elite, who form such a large pool of donors, and who were in fact the majority of donors in this study.

The situation described in this chapter is well illustrated by the transformation of the New York Public Library. Faced with financial crises during the 1970s, the organization launched an effort to increase its funds. In the course of this successful effort, as one researcher notes, the Library took steps to overcome what one newspaper called its image as a "private refuge for the old Wasp establishment." This included expanding and diversifying its board. Indeed, the man recruited to chair the board in 1977 and help lead the fundraising effort was himself a Jewish business executive.[40]

The changes in philanthropy that we have been considering bolster a larger continuity—namely the culture and practice of elite philanthropy itself. In this respect, it is important to emphasize that there was a pool of people to draw on who shared certain philanthropic values or priorities[41] with the very groups whose exclusionary practices had made it difficult for others to gain access. The point is an important one because just as boards and established elites must incorporate outsiders to sustain themselves, these outsiders must also be interested in being incorporated and in dedicating their money and time to those particular institutions. The fact that they are willing to do so may indicate a desire to associate with the social elite. I believe, however, that it also has to do with the fact that the organizations themselves have a stature and meaning that goes beyond their association with the elite. As Marcus observes, the values of an elite can live on in its institutions even after the elite itself has declined.[42] If, as Baltzell believes, the Protestant Establishment is a class in decline,[43] the extent to which organizational prestige is independent of the social elite may be a critical future issue.

The discussion of ethnic boundaries in philanthropy raises the question of how donors relate to multiple—and potentially alternative—philanthropic cultures and group affiliations in their philanthropy. Whether we consider integration of Jews into nonreligiously affiliated institutions or into the social elite, the conclusion that must be drawn is that the weakening of ethnic boundaries has a negative effect on major gifts to the alternative philanthropic subculture. Among those who simply participate in such institutions, we find lower levels of major giving to Jewish institutions. Among those who both participate in such institutions and are members of the social elite, it virtually disappears.

The fact that Jews in the social elite did not participate in the Jewish-linked pattern of giving with their major gifts supports my observation that philanthropy reflects elite organization, for when we consider Jewish donors who are associated with different social groups, their philanthropic giving varies as well.[44] Since giving to churches among Protestants was lower inside than outside the social elite, the greater influence of class over religious identity within that group is apparently not confined to Jews. Taken together, the findings reveal that philanthropy within the social elite is more insular in nature, responding more exclusively to class-based identity. Accordingly, even where the alternative philanthropic subculture is a majority subculture, social elite membership tends to overwhelm that identity.

At the same time, we have seen that even within the social elite, we cannot dismiss the importance of ethnicity or religion as an influence on philanthropy. Most Jewish members of the social elite did support the Jewish-affiliated fund, but not with their major gifts. Furthermore, differences in giving to rights, advocacy, and policy organizations in the social elite reveal that ethnic affiliation does continue to play a role, albeit in a different and less visible fashion. Thus the influence of social elite membership overrides, but does not eliminate, ethnic identification. Moreover, the findings show that ethnic affiliation can be influential in nonvisible ways, perhaps even to donors themselves, who did not speak of their gifts to rights groups in terms of their ethnicity. Perhaps it also indicates that Jewish members of the social elite at one and the same time prefer to view themselves as thoroughly fitting in as part of the group (and thus not making major gifts to an organization that is explicitly Jewish), and yet remain cautious about the stability of that acceptance. Alternately, it may be that although they feel secure in their own situation, their background sensitizes them, more than other members of the social elite, to the precariousness of the rights of others. Regardless of which is the case, the point is that ethnic affiliation continues to exert an influence.

An important finding has been that different group identifications have substantive consequences for the kinds of causes supported by the wealthy. Participation in a particular ethnic community spurred Jewish donors to make gifts to an organization with which they had little personal involvement—one that channels gifts to other organizations with which they have little involvement, such as agencies in the social services.[45] As respondents readily acknowledged, their gifts had to do with the prominent position of the particular organization within the Jewish community as a whole. Thus, giving is directed by elite donors to various causes through an intermediary organization, which has the standing within the community that the agencies who are the ultimate recipients may themselves lack.[46]

By contrast, cultural and educational organizations are the privileged recipients of nonreligious elite philanthropy. In short, the group with which a donor identifies will have substantive consequences for who receives major gifts. These findings suggest that research is needed on why particular elite groups become associated with one particular kind of institution rather than another, so that individual members express their group affiliation by giving to a social service, cultural organization, school, or church. That is, attention must be given to the particular attitudes and organization of elite subgroups, as well as to relationships between donors and beneficiaries, and to the motives of individual donors.

With respect to Jewish donors, one generalization (perhaps more appropriately called a prejudice) that these findings clearly contradict is the idea that Jewish philanthropy essentially benefits Jewish organizations and people. Such, for instance, was the attitude expressed by one Christian donor in this study, who complained that Jews give all their money to the Jewish-affiliated fund. He said that while he is "the most non-racist, non-anti-Semitic person you'll meet," he believes that "the Jewish community in New York City has some obligation, which . . . I don't think they face up to this responsibility." In reality, the overwhelming majority of Jewish donors in this study (94 percent) gave largest gifts to causes outside the Jewish community, and many (41 percent) made no largest gifts to any Jewish organization. Furthermore, the fact that integration into nonreligious nonprofits and the social elite erodes support for Jewish causes reveals that it is support for nonreligious causes that overshadows giving to Jewish causes, and not the reverse. In addition to all this, of course, many Jewish-affiliated causes (such as hospitals) receiving support clearly provide services that are not limited to the Jewish community. Indeed, the more typical comments of donors in this study indicate that the willingness of Jews to support nonreligiously affiliated causes has become evident to others in the elite and has led to their increasing incorporation into such causes. As a further thought on this subject, however, I would argue that Jewish giving to Jewish causes may, ironically, be more universalistic than their giving to nonreligiously affiliated causes that comes with assimilation—because the Jewish causes are more likely to offer services cutting across a broader class spectrum than the kinds of prestigious nonreligious institutions to which Jews have been gaining greater access.

My findings suggest caution in generalizing from the experience of Jewish donors to other groups that have experienced barriers in philanthropy. Donors' comments suggest that the Jewish community was viewed as an important source of funds, at a time when the need for additional funds was acute. Had one of these factors been lacking, the outcome might have been different. This indicates that the diversification of nonprofit boards needs an external prompting that leads current trustees to believe that in order to maintain the organization they must open it up to others. The particular prompts involved, and the specifics of the assimilation of various groups, however, must be studied individually, and are an important area for future research. Bear in mind as well that the people enjoying greater access to boards I have discussed are all wealthy. Certainly, then, we should avoid any inferences about a weakening of boundaries toward those outside the elite based on the results of this study.

Furthermore, my findings suggest that boundaries within philanthropy are more fluid than boundaries within the elite itself. Barriers to prominence in philanthropy, such as boards, may weaken more readily or be less rigid in general than those to the social elite. While Jews may have faced fewer barriers from prestigious boards in the 1980s, for instance, one study found that during this same decade, they continued to be systematically excluded from the *Social Register*.[47] In this respect, it should be noted that a higher percentage of Jews served on cultural or university boards alone than were members of the social elite.[48] As I discussed in chapter 1, many members of the social elite reacted negatively to the increased access to nonprofits enjoyed by the newly wealthy, indicating that acceptance into nonprofit institutions was not paralleled by acceptance into their social class. This has important consequences for Jewish philanthropy, for the evidence indicates that integration into such institutions is associated with lower levels of making major gifts to Jewish organizations.

The relatively more fluid boundaries in philanthropy, I believe, reflects its contradictory nature as a basis of elite status. Philanthropy is particularly susceptible to just the sort of economic influences that, as Max Weber observed, are in conflict with status group exclusivity.

> [A]ll groups having interests in the status order react with special sharpness precisely against the pretensions of purely economic acquisition. . . . Precisely because of the rigorous reactions against the claims of property *per se*, the "parvenu" is never accepted, personally and without reservation, by the privileged status groups no matter how completely his style of life has been adjusted to theirs. They will only accept his descendants who have been educated in the conventions of their status group.[49]

Philanthropy holds prestige among the elite, but it is intrinsically difficult to separate from its material, economic basis, because nonprofit institutions must have money to survive. Thus, there will always be pressures to admit those who might otherwise be excluded, if they have sufficient funds. Without doing so, the very organizations that provide status cannot be maintained. Although this poses a challenge to the ability of the social elite (or any particular elite subgroup) to maintain dominance in philanthropy, it contributes to the ongoing strength of philanthropy as an elite institution. While the fortunes of any individual elite subgroup may decline, philanthropy and the organizations themselves can persist, replenished by association with new members of the elite capable of providing the necessary funds. At the same time, the fact that this process happens slowly, that boards do not simply take anyone with money, and that they continue to recruit various people shows that a balance is maintained between the economic and status dimensions.[50] For were board seats truly to become seen as mere goods to be bought, they would lose the very ability to confer the prestige that makes them so desirable. While philanthropy needs money to survive, it needs status to attract money.

Chapter Three

GENDER, MARRIAGE, AND PHILANTHROPY

THE RELATIONSHIP between gender boundaries and philanthropy is a complex one. It involves the connection between philanthropy and gender arrangements in the elite, as well as the place of gender as an organizing principle within philanthropy itself. Women occupy an ambivalent position as members of the elite, which combines both power and powerlessness. Although they are members of society's most privileged class, they generally do not hold the positions of economic and social authority occupied by their male counterparts, on whom they generally depend for their resources.[1] In fact, women are virtually absent from top institutional positions of economic power in the United States.[2] Class norms and attitudes as well as formal, organizational barriers have reinforced women's distance from the business and professional world. An heiress in this study for example, explained that while her family expected her brothers to join the family business, the idea of her doing so, "would have been anathema to them." For female members of an elite organized around traditional gender roles, philanthropic activities have served as a socially acceptable avenue for the exercise of leadership and public participation.[3] As Kathleen McCarthy has observed, "Unlike men, who enjoyed a host of . . . options in their pursuit of meaningful careers, women most often turned to nonprofit institutions and reform associations as their primary points of access to public roles."[4]

As we shall see, elite philanthropy continues to operate in a fashion that is in many ways consistent with traditional gender arrangements. Thus, one goal of this chapter is to assess the similarities and differences in the philanthropy of men and women and to understand how these, in turn, relate to gender roles within the elite. Furthermore, this chapter explores the impact of women's position within the elite on their contributions. Given their relatively dependent position on others for their funds, are women able to support causes of their own choosing? Do their donations bring them privileged positions and prominence within the philanthropic world, as is true for men? To what extent are women assigned to "women's boards" or "women's committees," and to what extent do they join the main boards of organizations? Such are the questions to be addressed.

The relative openness of philanthropy to women has not meant that women have always enjoyed a stature equal to that of men.[5] We must therefore be interested not only in how broader gender divisions are reflected within philanthropy, but also the extent to which gender functions as a dividing line or barrier within philanthropy itself, and how the situation has evolved. In addressing these issues, I focus once again on access to nonprofit boards. Evidence will be presented to indicate that, as with other barriers already discussed, gender barriers to prominence in elite philanthropy in New York were also weakening during the 1970s and 1980s. Where these trends appear to be weaker or stronger, and why, will also be considered.

GENDER, MARRIAGE, AND PHILANTHROPIC PARTICIPATION

The observation that female members of the elite generally remain outside the economic sphere inhabited by men certainly applies to the donors in this study, as illustrated by the occupational patterns of the fifty-nine men and twenty-nine women interviewed. Among the men, 17.2 percent of donors were retired, 25.9 percent were managers in financial establishments, 29.3 percent were other managers, 19 percent were attorneys, and 8.6 percent worked in another professional occupation.[6] By contrast, fully 69 percent of women did not work, 24.1 percent worked in a cultural or human service profession, and 6.9 percent were managers (in cultural or service organizations).[7]

Accordingly, an initial issue for this discussion concerns the potential impact of women's economic dependency on their ability to financially support causes of their choosing. Specifically, did these women feel they could and were they able to support such causes? It should be noted that women's own comments during discussions of money expressed an awareness of their economic position. When asked what percentage of her donations were made jointly, one woman said, "It's all his [her husband's] money, though he refers to it as 'our' money. It's his money. [It's] just that some of them say my name on it—that's all." At the same time, other comments made by this donor illustrate that such feelings about who money "really belongs to" must be sharply distinguished from women's actual and perceived control over wealth. Thus, this same woman decides on her own about contributions involving huge sums of money, and feels free to give to causes of her own choosing. Indeed, she indicated that two of her largest gifts were made by her alone, and that the third was given because of her interests, although it was made in both her and her husband's name. Only when issues of money per se came up did the distinction about who really has the money emerge, along with the conclusion that ultimately it was "all his."

Similarly, another woman, who had funds of her own to contribute, also received money from her husband. She had been "a bit timid" about asking him for help, but he was "very generous," and supplemented her contributions with his funds—he "nicely thought of them as ours." Again, she explained that these funds were used to support her interests and that her husband was "always very helpful to me in my choices."

Giving patterns among male and female donors also testify to women's ability to contribute to causes of their choosing. With similar frequency, married men (50 percent) and women (43.7 percent) directed largest gifts to organizations where the donor served as a trustee (an indicator that the gift was going to one of "their" causes). Furthermore, the high percentage among married women was not a result of their having access to inherited wealth independent of their husbands, and was comparable to the percentage for unmarried women.[8] Taken together, both donors' comments and observed patterns of giving indicate that, while financially dependent, married women felt, and were, able to direct donations to causes they support.[9]

The interviews also support a more general observation concerning philanthropy and married couples. Philanthropy, including both giving and volunteering, tends to be an interest and a value that is shared by the couple. The character of philanthropy as a shared priority is seen in patterns of volunteering among donors and their spouses. Those who volunteer more time tended to be married to people who also volunteer more time.[10] Donors often referred to the philanthropic endeavors of husbands and wives as well. Some discussed how both had a background in philanthropy prior to the marriage. Others told of how a wife or husband had encouraged their philanthropy, or of how they had encouraged or supported the philanthropy of a spouse. And in a case where a woman had been married to a man who did not share her philanthropic values, she reported that this had been one of the things they argued about.

For many donors, philanthropy as a whole was seen as a joint activity and priority of the couple, within which husband and wife might have different, individual philanthropic involvements and interests. This explains the otherwise puzzling fact that many donors regarded all their donations as having been done jointly with a spouse, but also clearly differentiated particular causes and gifts as "belonging" primarily to one member of the couple. Indeed, one donor even viewed gifts that she never discusses with her husband as part of the couple's joint philanthropy. Said she, "I consider them all made with my husband. I don't ask him. I just do it. Then he has some of his own that he does." Men and women were equally likely to regard all or most of their philanthropy as done jointly with a spouse, highlighting again that it is an activity viewed as a shared value of the couple.[11] The fact that philanthropy is a priority shared by members of a couple reaffirms this book's ongoing theme that philanthropy is not merely an isolated activity, but part of a way of life for donors.

Reviewing the discussion to this point, we have seen that despite their financial dependency, women were able to allocate considerable funds to philanthropic causes they value. This was reflected in their comments as well as in their largest donations.[12] With this background, we now examine the similarities and differences in how men and women did in fact allocate their contributions.

GENDER AND PATTERNS OF GIVING

The impact of gender on philanthropic choices is most apparent in women's greater emphasis on the social services. A far higher percentage of women (46.4 percent) than men (21.1 percent) made one of their largest gifts to the social services (see Table 3.1). A comparison of the position of the social services in relation to other areas also illustrates its prominence in women's philanthropy. Both men and women most frequently gave largest donations to education and culture. In the case of women, however, the social services were chosen with similar frequency, whereas among men, the differences between those supporting education (75.4 percent), culture (39.3 percent), and the social services (21.1 percent) were quite large. By comparison, while 57.1 percent of women made a largest gift to education and 50 percent made one to culture, the social service area, receiving gifts from 46.4 percent, was not far behind. In short, the social services were one of the more typical philanthropic choices for women, but not for men.[13] Overall, the comparison between men and women reaffirms the prestige of culture and education as popular choices among many subgroups, while showing how other areas of giving enjoy equal prominence among particular subgroups. It also reveals a similar emphasis on the social services in the giving of female and Jewish donors, to be considered at the end of this chapter. It is important to emphasize that being female and being Jewish each have an independent association with support for the social services.[14] Accordingly, women's giving in this area, like that of Jewish donors, must be understood in its own right.

In their social service giving, women dedicate major gifts to causes that enjoy less prestige within the hierarchy of the elite and are more distant from the life and concerns of their class, but that are related to

TABLE 3.1
Gender and Area of Giving (Largest Gifts)

Area	% of Men	% of Women
Culture	39.3	50.0
Education	75.4	57.1
Colleges/Universities, related[a]	64.9	53.4
Schools, related	16.1	10.7
Social Services	21.1	46.4*
Jewish Affil. Fund	15.8	28.6
Other	8.9	17.9
Health	29.8	32.1
Hospitals	21.1	25.0
Other	14.3	17.9
Animals/Environment	7.1	17.9
Rights/Advocacy/Policy	14.3	3.6
Youth (n.e.c.)	7.1	3.6
Church/Temple	17.9	10.7

Note: The number of men is fifty-six for the areas of culture, youth, animals/environment, and rights/advocacy/policy. It is fifty-seven in all the other categories. The number of women is twenty-eight.

For the combined education category, $p < .10$ for the difference between men and women.

[a] On the "related" organizations included in this and the following category, see Table 1.3, notes a and b.

*$p \leq .05$, chi-square.

the life, concerns, and priorities of these women as women. There is a historical continuity in women's current support for the social services. Within the philanthropic world, women have traditionally donated time and money to support causes of concern and interest to them as women. Social service organizations run the kinds of programs (provision of services), for the kinds of clientele (such as children) that are consistent with traditional female caretaking roles, and historically women's philanthropy has been concerned with such groups.[15] This observation applies to the social service gifts made by the women in this study. All but one of women's largest social service gifts (outside of those made through the Jewish-affiliated fund) went to organizations with a distinct focus on providing services for youth and women. A gender connection was also present in the remaining case, in that it was a woman's service organization. Indeed, the variety of women's service organizations that exist within different ethnic, religious, and class affiliations testifies to the prominence of providing social services in women's philanthropic culture. One longtime member of a woman's service institution interviewed in this study stressed the importance of such organizations for addressing issues of children's welfare and encouraging progress in such areas as assistance for victims of domestic violence.

An emphasis on wanting to support the provision of services also emerged when women discussed their gifts. One donor explained, "I like programs," adding that she derived particular satisfaction from her gifts to fund services for children and mothers. Another makes her largest gift to a particular social service organization because "they provide services for kids that never had a service before." In this respect, it is of interest that women were more likely than men to have had direct personal experience as providers of services to beneficiaries of philanthropy. Some, for example, worked directly with patients in hospitals, and others with needy children. Reflecting on her philanthropic career, one woman said, "When I started, there wasn't a man around. It was the women who worked—not to say men didn't contribute. Rather [it was] their position in the community rather than service for men." She added, "I think a lot of men are involved because it looks good on the CV and corporations want it. It's a prestige thing for men—more than it ever was for women. . . . In the [social service] field there wasn't a man who gave a hoot."

Social services were the area in which gender differences in giving were most clear and direct. The area of educational giving is also of interest because it reflects an indirect influence of gender on giving. A somewhat higher percentage of men (75.4 percent) than women (57.1 percent) had made a largest gift in this area.[16] The difference, however, proved to be a result of the generally higher educational level of men in this sample.[17] Among those with a college degree, the percentage of men (74.4 percent) and women (70 percent) making a largest gift to education were essentially equal. This illustrates how gender-related experiences and opportunities in the broader society—here, educational level—have an impact on philanthropic choices. It also suggests that education may well assume a more prominent place in women's major giving as younger women in the elite increasingly earn higher degrees.

By way of concluding this section, I would like to offer some more speculative observations concerning gender differences in another area, that of animal and environmental causes. Few men or women interviewed made a largest gift to such causes. A different source of data, as well as donors' comments, however, lead me to believe that there may be gender-related differences in this field as well, though not necessarily at the level of largest gifts. As will be recalled, data for this study were collected on gifts of $1,000 or more made to a set of large New York nonprofits in seven areas of activity. These data may be used to compare

TABLE 3.2

Gifts of $1,000 or More Received from Men, Women, and Couples by Large New York Nonprofits in Different Areas of Activity

| Area | No. of All Gifts | Percentage of Gifts in Area | | | |
		Men	Women	Couples	Other
Culture	5,924	26.8	26.6	45.3	1.3
Education	2,226	68.7	14.6	16.4	.4
Hospitals	905	47.9	19.2	31.5	1.4
Other Health	239	46.4	32.2	20.9	.4
Social Services	510	35.3	33.7	30.0	1.0
Youth (n.e.c.)	308	86.0	10.1	3.9	0.0
Animals/Environment	1,169	29.3	37.2	32.2	1.3
Total	11,281	39.4	24.7	34.8	1.1

Note: Table includes gifts received by 37 of the 48 New York nonprofit organizations for whom donor lists with a baseline of $1,000 or more were available (in the remaining cases, the baseline was higher than $1,000). Excluded are 175 gifts where the gender of the donor could not be determined. Analyses were also done using data from all 48 organizations, which resulted in identical conclusions.

The "Other" category refers to gifts made by combinations of individuals other than couples (e.g., siblings).

$p < .001$ for table, chi-square.

($p < .001$ for table with men and women only, chi-square.)

the percentage of an area's gifts that are received from men, from women, from couples, or from other combinations of individuals. Only in the area of animal and environmental causes did the percentage of gifts received from women (37.2 percent) exceed the percentage received from men (29.3 percent), with the balance received from couples and other combinations of individuals (see Table 3.2).[18] I suspect the reason for the prevalence of women in this area is related to the fact that elite women have generally remained outside the business positions occupied by men of their class. Animal and environmental causes are often perceived as antithetical to business interests (e.g., as supporting costly antipollution measures or conservation over development). The fact that women do not have the same direct personal involvement with business as men may make such perceptions less of a deterrent to them, or even lessen the likelihood of their viewing animal and environmental causes from this perspective at all. Interest in such causes would also be consistent with women's traditional caretaker role, as is their giving to social service causes. When asked if he had given any money to a cause related to animal or environmental protection, one businessman interviewed said he had, because his wife "goes in for some of that nonsense."[19] These observations about the connection between gender and animal and environmental philanthropy can only be offered as hypotheses at this point. The connection, however, is one that presents a fruitful area for additional research.[20]

CONTRIBUTIONS TO CULTURE: GENDER, MARRIAGE, AND PHILANTHROPY

The focus up to now has been on differences in patterns of giving among men and women. This discussion offers suggestive evidence that couples also function as a distinct unit of donor whose importance varies in different areas of philanthropy. In addition, marriage itself has an impact on women's philanthropy. To illustrate the first part of this argument, let us return to the 11,281 gifts of $1,000 or more received by a set of large New York nonprofit organizations (see Table 3.2). The area of culture stands out because it is dependent to an unusual degree on gifts from couples. The percentage of all cultural gifts received from couples (45.3 percent) was higher than in any other field. Culture was the sole area that received a higher percentage of its total gifts from couples than from either men (26.8 percent) or women (26.6 percent).[21]

Comments made by donors allow us to formulate hypotheses about why culture should be a focus of couples. For one thing, cultural institutions are likely to be currently used by donors. Attending arts events becomes part of the ongoing shared social life of couples, which is then reflected in their philanthropy. One donor said a reason for one of their largest gifts to a cultural organization was that she and her husband "love" the institution and enjoy the atmosphere there. Donors often mentioned becoming interested in a particular art form or cultural organization through their spouse. One man had made a largest gift to a performing arts organization with his wife, because "my wife is a great [music] lover, so it's something that we both enjoy doing." He added that his wife also contributes additional funds to the institution on her own. Similarly, another man reported a largest gift to a performing arts organization that he and his wife attend on a regular basis. He explained that his wife, who is "crazy about singing," had brought him around to enjoying music as well. While a spouse might certainly be supportive of a husband's or wife's other philanthropic involvements, there is less of an impetus to become personally involved or identified with these than there is in cultural interests. It may also be relevant that performing arts organizations tend to have especially visible listings of donors, placed in playbills distributed at performances. Accordingly, there is a greater likelihood that people will be aware that their donations to such causes are listed and visible to others. As one donor said, "I mean, if we're going to a theater and it's one of the theaters we do support, we look to see if it's listing people in a certain category, just out of curiosity. [And we] look to see if we're there." Under such circumstances, donors may take greater care to ensure that both members of the couple are listed. The comment of another woman suggests an additional, pragmatic reason for making gifts jointly to culture: these institutions often offer membership benefits to donors. As she indicated, "If you give in two people's names, it actually makes a difference." While suggesting that the issue may be one of mechanics rather than how the gift itself is viewed by the couple, this comment still highlights the fact that arts organizations are used by both members of the couple.[22]

One reason for discussing couples' involvement in cultural philanthropy is to propose that they be examined as a distinct kind or group of donor. It also helps to explain a striking difference between the giving of married and unmarried female donors who were interviewed for this study. Married women (75 percent) were far more likely than unmarried women (16.7 percent) to have made a largest gift to culture.[23] Indeed, more married women gave to culture than to any other area. Among unmarried women, the most common choice was the social services (58.3 percent).

As we can see, marriage itself has an impact on giving among women.[24] Married women more frequently make a largest gift to the very area of philanthropy associated with the giving of couples. This indicates that their philanthropic giving is likely to reflect the interests and activities of the couple as a couple.[25] The process does not appear to be a self-conscious one in which women purposely adapt their philanthropy to the couple's priorities. Furthermore, cultural philanthropy does not monopolize married women's major giving, or eradicate their support for the social services, although it does surpass it in frequency.[26] The donor list data on gifts of $1,000 or more to large New York organizations also support the idea that, in the area of culture, married women's individual donations reflect their giving as part of a couple. Those cases in which both the couple and an individual member of the couple had made such a gift were extracted from the larger database to permit a comparison of giving by couples and individual members of the couple. In 78.6 percent of the 112 cases where women had contributed to culture as part of a couple, they had also given to a cultural organization alone. The comparable figure for men was 54.5 percent (of 299 cases). Thus, even when couples make cultural gifts together, the woman typically has independent cultural commitments, and has them more frequently than men.[27] Taken together, these findings lend support to the idea that married women's perspective on, and approach to, philanthropy is shaped by their identification as part of a couple. To further scrutinize and extend this idea would require information on how the philanthropy of the same women evolved following marriage, to see whether it did in fact shift in the expected direction. Such material would also allow us to understand the process through which marriage influences giving. The entire subject of how philanthropic interests shift as donors move in and out of marriage is a large one, warranting additional research.

GENDER, VOLUNTEERING, AND BOARD MEMBERSHIP

Although there are many similarities in the volunteer work of men and women, it holds a different meaning for the two groups, which in turn is linked to the organization of gender roles within the elite. This emerges through a consideration of the amount of time spent, board membership, and the meaning of volunteering to participants.

On average, men volunteered 30.6 hours a month, and women 38.5 hours a month.[28] The source of this difference is that a higher percentage of women volunteer any time. Volunteering is virtually universal among women (96 percent) in this study, although it is also engaged in by the vast majority of men (80.4 percent). Among those donors who do volunteer, the average hours per month spent by men (38.1) and women (40.1) were close.[29] With respect to volunteering per se, then, men and women are quite similar.

Volunteering, however, includes a variety of activities, which are ordered hierarchically in the eyes of donors. As we have seen, board membership is held in particularly high esteem. Given that men of the elite generally hold the top positions in other valued spheres, such as business, it was of particular interest to compare women's and men's access to the top positions in philanthropy, namely board membership. Equal percentages of men (74.6) and women (75.9) served on any boards, and comparable percentages of men (62.7) and women (58.6) sat on multiple boards.[30] These figures, it should be emphasized, represent membership on organizations' main boards, and therefore indicate that women were not restricted to separate, "women's boards."[31]

Notable differences between men and women with respect to volunteering do begin to emerge, however, when considering how men and women understand, experience, and discuss volunteer work. Indeed, the differences in how they do so provide one of the more striking instances of how gender arrangements and roles within the elite shape philanthropic activities. The characteristic involvement of affluent women in volunteer work has been viewed as interconnected with the fact that they do not work and remain outside of economic positions.[32] This was a connection made by female donors themselves.

Some women discussed volunteering as an alternative to "doing nothing." A woman who volunteers between twenty and thirty hours a week explained, "I was brought up in a family that had quite a social consciousness . . . and [I] never—I'm not sure if it's fortunate or unfortunate—never had to work. And [I] felt that I have to give something back. I'm also not the kind of a person who can sit around doing nothing. I adore playing bridge and socializing, but I couldn't do it all day, day in and day out." Similarly, a woman who volunteers twenty hours a week said, "I don't mind if you play bridge every day. But I couldn't do that. It would bore me out of my wits. So you know, if you have the time and energy to do something, and you're doing it for something worthwhile—wonderful!" Yet another donor explained that she began to volunteer, "when I was first married. Before I was married I was in [a profession] and I had a child, so I retired. . . . I'm a failure at tennis, I can't play bridge, and I wanted to do something meaningful and challenging." While some expressed regret over not having held a job, others expressed sorrow over the negative consequences they believe the trend toward working has had on women's volunteer activities. Said one, "I'm a feminist. [The women's school I attended] makes you that way. [But] the women's movement has played hell with philanthropy. You can't get a woman who's not working full time now. . . . They were lifesavers. They still exist but their time is limited. . . . Young married women just don't have service." She offered her granddaughter, who is married and has children but continues to work, as an example.

The above comments reveal that these women view volunteering both as an alternative to work and an opportunity to do something they consider to be worthwhile and valuable.[33] The nature of their comments also clearly reveal that while men and women volunteer, the pathway to, and meaning of, volunteer work for women is related to their distinctive situation as women.

Among men, volunteering was not viewed as an alternative to paid work or "doing nothing," but as a further option and additional activity. Men often conveyed a sense of continuity between their paid and volunteer work. A characteristic example of this was when men pointed to similarities in the skills that both required. For instance, a man who had built his own business described how he had helped to organize fundraising efforts for one nonprofit organization as follows: "It's management. The same as you build your business through good management. You delegate, and you give authority. It's what I learned at [business school]. . . . It's what I experienced in my own business." As noted in the discussion of pathways to philanthropy,[34] some men become engaged in volunteer work through business. Men in top business positions frequently receive invitations to serve on boards. As the head of one large business who serves on many boards explained, "In the position that I'm in, you just get asked to do these things all the time."[35]

Men often viewed their business skills and experience as a major source of their qualification and desirability as volunteers. This is seen in the following account of how one businessman came to serve on a particular board: "I went on the board because my [relative] had a good friend [on the board] and they were looking for someone with financial experience who was interested. . . . I was always interested in [the area] . . . so I went on the board. The reason I was asked to go on was because I was younger and had some financial experience."

Some men drew an even more direct connection between their professional skills and volunteering, offering monetary estimates of the value of the skills they had donated to various organizations. After discussing his donations, one man noted that volunteering also represents a form of giving money. By way of example, he pointed to financial services he has provided for one nonprofit, giving an estimate of the thousands of dollars the organization would otherwise have been required to pay. A similar estimate was offered by an attorney who emphasized the value of the professional services he and his firm have provided free of charge to nonprofit organizations. After men retire from business, volunteer work offers them a chance to continue to use such skills and background in another setting.[36]

The continuities men saw between business and volunteering should not be interpreted to mean that they viewed their volunteer work as an extension of business. Many viewed volunteer activities as offering satisfactions and experiences not available in their paid careers. A man who earned his fortune in the financial world said that although he does not believe his business activities are "detrimental," he also does not feel they are of any benefit to society. By contrast, he believes that it is through his philanthropy, to which he devotes considerable time, that he does contribute to society. Another said that he has reached a point where "I've done all I want on Wall Street," and now puts his energy into philanthropic activities because "they are more important." Indeed, a few men spoke of structuring their business and professional lives to permit them more time for involvement with nonprofits. One man said that a factor in starting his own business was that it would permit him to devote more time to philanthropic activities. Another had joined a particular organization for this same reason.

The analyses of contributions of money and time complement one another. In volunteering, as in giving money, women and men exhibit both similarities and differences. Whereas the analysis of contributions of money highlighted differences in behavior, this discussion of volunteering illustrates that even comparable philanthropic activities can assume a different meaning to men and women. For that reason, volunteering contributes in an important way to our overall view of how philanthropy is shaped by the differential roles, opportunities, and constraints facing men and women in the elite.[37]

SHIFTING GENDER BOUNDARIES IN ELITE PHILANTHROPY

An ongoing focus of this book has been on shifts in subgroup boundaries within elite philanthropy. In the previous shifts considered, donors themselves expressed an awareness of internal boundaries within philanthropy and the fact that these had evolved. By contrast, the existence, nature, or evolution of gender barriers within elite philanthropy was not a subject discussed by donors.[38] Yet gender barriers might be expected to respond to the very factors that were also eroding other boundaries. Additionally, pressures toward, and calls for, greater inclusion and equality for women being raised during the 1970s and 1980s would also encourage weakening of gender-related barriers.[39] The fact that women and men in this study enjoyed such comparable access to boards further suggested that such a weakening had occurred.

I therefore examined the percentage of women on the boards of a group of major New York City nonprofit organizations in 1972, 1982, and 1992. The results indicate that gender barriers to board membership, so highly valued among members of the elite, were indeed weakening during the 1970s and 1980s. In many cases, the percentage of women on a board nearly doubled, did double, or more than doubled. For example, between 1972 and 1992, the percentage of female trustees grew from 21 percent to 38.8 percent at the Metropolitan Museum, from 20 percent to 37.8 percent at the Metropolitan Opera, from 14.3 percent to 34.2 percent at the New York Public Library, from 9 percent to 18.9 percent at Lincoln Center, from 10 percent to 20.3 percent at the Memorial Sloan-Kettering Cancer Center, and from 10.5 percent to 22.7 percent at New York University. Increases were also found at other organizations, including Carnegie Hall, New York University Medical Center, St. Luke's-Roosevelt Hospital, and Presbyterian Hospital.[40] Thus we find developments with respect to gender that parallel the weakening of boundaries we have seen in other areas.

This weakening of gender barriers, however, should not be equated with a disappearance. In some cases, the percentage of female and male trustees did become nearly equal over this time period. Yet in other cases, the initially low percentage of women on the board meant that

TABLE 3.3
Percentage of Women on Large New York Nonprofit
Boards by Area of Activity

Area	Mean (Standard Deviation)
Animals/Environment	25.7 (15.2)
Culture	29.3 (7.8)
Education	17.3 (5.9)
Hospitals	21.7 (10.1)
Other Health	20.0 (9.5)
Social Services	34.2 (20.0)
Youth (n.e.c.)	29.1 (40.5)
Rights/Advocacy/Policy	23.6 (19.6)

Note: Based on fifty-six boards.

even after a large increase, women remained considerably in the minority. Both the growth in the percentage of women on boards and the actual size of the percentages must therefore be taken into account.

A comparison of the percentage of women on boards in various areas indicates that gender boundaries have weakened unevenly in different fields, as illustrated by another set of data, on the board membership of fifty-six of the largest New York nonprofit organizations in various areas of activity during the mid-1980s (see Table 3.3).[41] These data reveal that women are a considerable, but minority presence as board members in all areas. The social service field, however, stands out for the higher presence of women on boards. On average, just over a third of these boards were composed of women. The comparatively high representation of women on social service boards provides a further illustration of women's particular involvement in this field. By contrast, with women constituting an average of only 17.3 percent of board members, educational boards had an unusually low representation of women.

Viewed in relation to one another, the organizational data on boards and the interview material on board membership pose an apparent discrepancy. The women interviewed were as likely to serve on boards as men. Furthermore, this was true across many areas, including culture and hospitals, which have the highest numbers of board members. Yet organizational data reveal that women constitute a minority of trustees. To reconcile these facts, we must return to the earlier observation that the subject of gender and philanthropy involves both barriers within philanthropy and ways in which philanthropy reflects broader gender arrangements and roles in the elite. The women interviewed for this study were affluent donors and were therefore in a position to be considered for board membership. Yet there were fewer women in this study than men. Indeed, women also constitute a minority of donors to the large New York nonprofits we have examined. This is particularly true of larger donations.[42] Taken together, these considerations suggest that for those men and women who command the requisite resources, access to valued boards is not dependent on gender. Being in a position to command those resources, however, clearly remains so in our society. The gender composition of boards reflects these wider gender inequalities in access to elite positions. To the extent that such inequalities persist, and that access to these other elite positions continues to be so closely tied to attaining elite position within philanthropy, women are likely to remain in the minority.

CONCLUSION

The analysis of gender complements and extends our discussion of religion and philanthropy. In both cases, we find subgroups of donors with distinctive patterns of giving. In both cases, the specific nature of that pattern relates to an identity held by donors that exists in addition to their class identity. Women's gifts to the social services are consistent with traditional female concerns (e.g., caring for children) and with conventional gender distinctions that emphasize women's role as caretaker within the home and family. In the case of both women and Jews, donors' distinctive pattern of giving resulted in major gifts to causes that are relatively low in prestige in the elite hierarchy. In both cases, an alternative framework or identity exists whereby such causes are considered important and assume a personal significance to donors. I would thus conclude that a major factor in donors' willingness to deviate from the prestige hierarchy of their class with respect to major giving is precisely the presence and strength of such alternative identities.

The strength of these identities, in turn, are related to donors' own position within the elite, and are affected by shifts in that position. When Jewish donors were assimilated, class identity overshadowed ethnic identity with respect to major giving. Women's barriers within the elite, on the other hand, have not been in relation to social prestige. Their position has been partially defined in terms of their distance from the core economic institutions of their class, which have been dominated by men. The question that arises is whether women's distinctive pattern of giving will persist as they gain admittance to the corporate world, or whether, as they move out of traditional female roles, their philanthropic interest in female concerns will diminish. Of course, it is possible that increased economic independence will lead women to develop new distinctive patterns of giving. As such questions indicate, the movement of women into traditionally male occupations may have significant consequences for philanthropy that bear watching over the next several years.

The fact that women in this study were not currently in such occupations raises a further issue about the relationship between elite status, gender, and philanthropy. During the 1970s and 1980s, gender barriers in philanthropy were weakening. In this respect, philanthropy was moving far in advance of other sectors. The percentage of women on nonprofit boards, for instance, has far outpaced that of corporate boards. Thus there is a continuity with philanthropy's past role of providing opportunities for leadership and authority to women that are less readily available elsewhere. This has occurred, however, within the traditional boundaries of elite philanthropy. I believe that the weakening of gender barriers largely reflects greater access being enjoyed by a distinct set of women, those who are affluent by virtue of either inheriting or marrying into wealth. Without their connection to men who earn wealth (either in the present or the past, as is the case for widows), it is doubtful that the women I met with would enjoy comparable access. Until more women assume the very highest corporate positions, or until prestigious nonprofit boards exhibit greater willingness to cross class barriers in selecting trustees, women's access to the most prestigious nonprofits will continue to be dependent on their relationship to men of wealth—whether that be a husband or a male ancestor. I think it is more likely that women will ultimately be drawn from top corporate positions than that class barriers will be crossed.

This discussion raises an important point about the diversification of nonprofit boards. While the homogeneity of boards contributes to their prestige among elites, they do not exist in a vacuum. Rather, the organizations they oversee are often visible, and must deal with constituencies outside the elite. Accordingly, boards are subject to the same calls for diversification that have been made in other contexts. With respect to women, such calls are readily satisfied without essentially challenging the elite composition of the board. One can, for example, ask the wife of a business associate, instead of the business associate himself, to join. Or one can increase the number of daughters, rather than sons, of wealthy families invited to join a board. It is also important to note that gender barriers in philanthropy can weaken without any fundamental challenge to established gender roles within philanthropy or the elite. Philanthropic participation has always been among the acceptable—and even expected—activities for affluent women. Accordingly, enhancing access to nonprofit boards represents an extension of a traditional role. For an affluent woman to go on a nonprofit board does not challenge basic gender arrangements in the way that, for instance, her assuming control of the family business would.

These observations may explain why the gender shift in philanthropic institutions was so rarely discussed by donors, while shifts involving Jews and the newly wealthy were frequently raised. The increased presence of Jews and the newly wealthy were viewed as representing a basic change in the philanthropic elite. This is not only a question of serving on boards but also of who is at charity benefits and other functions associated with philanthropy. Women may simply not have been experienced as representing a new or outsider group, and thus their presence may not have been perceived as representing a comparably basic change. Indeed, apart from any specific pressures for enhancing the representativeness of nonprofit boards, weakening gender boundaries within philanthropy may simply illustrate how the elite is influenced by, and responds to, changes in broader societal norms involving women's rights.

As women gain increasing access to top positions in business and related fields such as law, it will be crucial to chart the evolution of boards, to see whether these women are also selected for membership on nonprofit boards. It will be equally important to see whether and how their emergence affects the extent to which women from the more traditional pool continue to be drawn onto boards.[43] Although gender barriers in philanthropy have been weakening, women remain a minority as both donors and board members. A major issue to be followed in the future, therefore, is whether an increase in the number of women in business and related fields will result in an overall increase in the numbers of women on boards, and if not, why not. The relationship between those women who remain in traditional roles and philanthropy may continue to evolve as well. Interviews uncovered some rather surprising adaptations to conventional volunteer roles among women. For instance, two women had pursued graduate degrees to develop skills and knowledge they planned to use as volunteers. Said one woman, "One of the problems was people kept saying, 'Oh, you don't understand, you're not a professional.' So I thought, Oh, to hell with that. I'll go back to school." Such cases show that new and unexpected adaptations can take place as the institution of philanthropy is maintained. In short, there is every sign that, both internally and in relation to the broader society, the issue of gender relations, giving, and volunteering may be among the most dynamic and significant in philanthropy in the years to come.

Chapter Four

EDUCATION, CULTURE, AND THE

INSTITUTIONALIZATION OF

PHILANTHROPIC VALUES

A S WE HAVE SEEN, education and culture hold a particularly favorable position in elite philanthropy. Organizations in these areas command great prestige in the eyes of affluent donors, and they are the frequent recipients of largest gifts made by members of numerous elite subgroups. This chapter focuses on these two important philanthropic areas, expanding our discussion of the factors that contribute to their popularity and prestige. Although both education and culture are prominent, there are differences as well as similarities in the involvements and attachments that donors develop in the two areas. Moreover, while education and culture both command prestige, differences and similarities also exist in the reasons for their stature. The chapter goes on to connect, in terms of the overarching relationship between philanthropic and elite hierarchies, the prominence of education and culture to the philanthropic values of the social elite. I argue that these values, in turn, have been institutionalized and accepted beyond the social elite to elite donors more broadly.

The analysis of culture and education is of further interest in exploring the relationship between donors' experience of their philanthropic involvements as individuals, and the philanthropic patterns that emerge in a sociological analysis of the elite as a social group. In recounting how they became associated with particular organizations, donors naturally make reference to the circumstances of their individual lives. It is striking how often their accounts also portray their philanthropic involvements as the product of coincidental or fortuitous circumstances. One woman said she first became involved with a cultural organization she has enthusiastically supported for over twenty years as a result of "timing." She explained that she happened to run into an acquaintance at an event sponsored by the organization, was recruited, and things "jelled." Although that meeting may have been coincidental in one sense, that this woman would have friends engaged in cultural philanthropy, that she and her friends would meet at cultural events, and that she would find philanthropic involvement with a cultural organization appealing, are all typical for a member of her class. Such stories reveal the day-to-day individual processes behind the larger patterns of educational and cultural philanthropy among the elite as a group.

They also illustrate an important point concerning the relationship between individual incentives for giving and the class outcomes of philanthropy. In cultural and educational philanthropy, we find individuals supporting organizations that have a significance for the maintenance and reproduction of their class. Yet we need not attribute any conscious intention to attain class ends to individual donors to understand why they participate in cultural and educational philanthropy. Loyalty to one's school, an interest in the arts, or a desire to advance one's own social position will do. In short, we see how choices with significant class consequences can evolve at an individual level simply through the course of donors pursuing their personal lives and concerns—for these are in turn deeply shaped by the class context in which they exist.

SUPPORT FOR EDUCATION AS A NORM AMONG ELITES

Major giving to education was a norm among this elite group of donors. Virtually everyone had contributed some money to an educational cause, with 92 percent having donated to universities or colleges alone. Moreover, during the previous twelve months, 69.4 percent of donors had made at least one of their largest gifts to education, exceeding the percentage for any other area. Their emphasis was primarily on higher education. Indeed, were we to confine the education category to colleges and universities, we would still find that 57.1 percent of donors had made a largest gift in this area.[1] This high level of donations reflects donors' desire to support the specific schools they or a family member attended. Of all largest gifts made to colleges and universities, 80.9 percent went to such a school.[2]

Donors view certain institutions as having a greater claim on their donations, and schools are among those privileged in this regard. Graduates' feelings of indebtedness and loyalty to their alma mater contribute to sustaining broad support for higher education. As one avid supporter of his college explained, "The thing I think it's easiest to do is the university, because people feel that they've got to plough some money back into their educational background." Another donor said, "I give to [my alma mater] because I really feel a sense of obligation. I had a wonderful experience there, and had such good teachers. I wanted to [contribute] the cost of maintaining another student." One man said he gives because "that's where I went to college and law school, and I believe that I owe some responsibility to see that the education of the young ones now are continued with help." Even some donors who were ambivalent about their schools had given them a largest gift. One woman gave to her college even though she does not "feel good about it," because her family "strongly believe that if we as graduates don't support our schools, who then will?"

Sometimes donors interpreted their debt to their school quite literally. Thus one woman said that "when you go through, you know, you don't pay in full, so you sort of owe something." Similarly, when explaining his support for his school, another donor said, "I consider that not to be generosity; I consider that to be almost an obligation. It's like repaying a student loan. . . . You really should do something if you can."[3] Some donors had received scholarships, contributing to their sense of gratitude. One man supports his school because he is "grateful" for the "liberal scholarship" he received as a student. Another said he was happy to make a very large gift to his alma mater, which he attended for free.

Donors' feelings of gratitude also derive from the belief that their schools contributed to their success and shaped the development of their personal and professional lives. Although his primary philanthropic interest is in culture rather than education, one donor made largest gifts to his schools out of a sense of "debt." He explained that he has been successful, and thinks that "I ought to share some of that success, for which they are in no small way responsible, and pay them back so that other people can take advantage of what they offer . . . especially in a time when it's difficult for educational institutions to run." Similarly, another man gave to his alma mater to "show my pleasure at a university that is responsible for my career. I appreciate their help." One of the female donors who works in a paid occupation also made a largest gift to her school, because "a lot of what I am now is due to education, and they were very generous to me at a period of crisis." She believes that her life would have been very different had she done the "normal thing" by staying home and attending the local, public college. She and her husband also support his alma mater for reasons that include the school's contribution to his career.

While discussing their reasons for making larger gifts to their schools, some people also spoke of the enduring, personal relationships they formed as students. These relationships perpetuate their sense of involvement and attachment to their school. One man, for example, explained that he met his best friend at college, and got to know his wife through another school friend. Similarly, one woman said that she derives a lot of satisfaction from giving to her school because she and her husband met as students there, her children attended it, and she formed a number of longlasting friendships there. Because of the connection between family, friends, and school, donors may be asked to give by someone they know well, a further encouragement to contribute. For instance, one donor told me "strictly confidentially" that he did not like to support his college, and disliked the institution. Yet even he contributes, because a family member also attended the school and is an active fundraiser, so "it was very hard to say no . . . and you really can't be capricious about it [and not] choose some things because you just don't like them."

Educational experiences may initially appear to differ from other influences on philanthropy such as gender or ethnicity. Yet there is a similarity, related to donors' viewing their schools as central to making them who and what they are. The common link is that educational background also becomes connected to donors' sense of identity, which in turn is reflected in their philanthropic priorities. Indeed, particular schools are sometimes incorporated into the identity of entire families. This is seen in comments made by some who decided not to attend the traditional family college. One man thus described his selection of one Ivy League school over another attended by family members as a form of rebellion, which he did "sort of out of spite." Another characterized his choice of school (Harvard), rather than the traditional family college as a "leftist move on my part."

An important characteristic of educational philanthropy is that it reflects donors' desire to support specific, individual institutions. When explaining why they made donations in this area, donors generally did not express a general interest in, or desire to support, education per se. Indeed, we saw that one donor made largest gifts to his schools despite the fact that education is not his primary interest. Another said he could not imagine contributing to a school other than his own unless he were married, in which case he would also support his wife's alma mater. Expressing a similar sentiment, one woman said, "I don't think anyone gives to a school they didn't go to unless they have some family connection, or enormous amounts of money to throw away."[4]

This discussion is not meant to imply that donors do not believe in the value and importance of education. Rather, it is meant to emphasize that an important foundation of education's popularity as a recipient of major gifts consists of donors' commitments to individual institutions they have attended rather than to a general area per se. This conclusion will receive further support in a later section on cultural philanthropy, when we see that donors frequently do express such broader interests in discussing other kinds of gifts.

EDUCATIONAL BACKGROUND, PRESTIGE, AND VARIATIONS IN EDUCATIONAL PHILANTHROPY

Given that a considerable portion of gifts to education represent donors' wish to support their schools, we would expect college graduates to make largest gifts to education more frequently than other people. Indeed, a higher percentage (73.3 percent) of college graduates than other donors (40 percent) had made such a gift.[5] Donors also develop ties with schools through children, and a higher percentage (73.3 percent) of those with children than other donors (40 percent) made a largest gift to education.[6] Most of those interviewed for this study were highly educated and did have children.[7] Thus the characteristics associated with higher levels of support for education were common, contributing to the widespread pattern of giving in this area.

As common as it was for donors to make largest gifts to their schools, not all had done so. Thus, it is of interest to ask what differentiates college graduates who made a largest gift to their alma mater from those who made no such gift. An important key lies in the prestige of the schools they attended; graduates of more prestigious colleges and universities were more likely to have made a largest gift to their alma mater. This conclusion is based on an analysis of levels of donor giving according to school rank, as indicated by the Astin Index of Selectivity, which ranges from 1 (least selective schools) to 7 (most selective).[8] Among graduates of the most selective institutions, fully 57.1 percent had made a largest gift to their school. The figure drops considerably, to 25 percent, among graduates of schools ranked 6, and falls to 15.4 percent among graduates of schools rated 5 or less.[9]

These figures dramatically illustrate the importance of institutional prestige as an influence on alumni giving among this group. They also show that a considerable portion of educational philanthropy by these elite donors is directed at schools that are also elite, in the world of academic institutions. We have seen that donors derive personal prestige from association with institutions that are prestigious in the eyes of their peers,[10] and we may connect the influence of institutional prestige and identification with schools as influences on alumni giving. Specifically, graduates of more prestigious colleges are likely to have a greater interest in retaining their connection and sense of identification with their alma mater because they derive gratification from being a graduate of such a prestigious school.

It is interesting to note that schools favored by members of the elite, such as those in the Ivy League, have retained their prestige in the eyes of the elite even as they have become more diverse with respect to their student body and selective with respect to academic (as opposed to social background) criteria.[11] Similarly, schools' prestige within the elite have been retained even as the basis of their prestige has come to depend more on their position in an academic hierarchy than on their association with traditional upper classes. Donors themselves made reference to this evolution. In speaking of his (formerly all male) Ivy League alma mater, one member of the social elite said, "My father went [there]. My brother went [there]. My daughters are too old to have gone. My granddaughter wasn't smart enough. . . . I couldn't get into [the school], today, that's for sure." Nonetheless he continues to contribute and volunteers for the school.[12] Another member of the social elite said that one reason he contributes more to his college than his prep school is precisely because the former changed. He believes that his college decided, "we want the best students in," while the prep school has remained "a pretty privileged place." Although he is not against privileged prep schools, he thinks that institutions like his college have a greater social impact on society, another reason that he prefers to give the college more money.

In concluding this section, I would like to offer a more preliminary discussion concerning the potential influence of another institutional characteristic, namely a school's status as a public or private institution. Public colleges and universities, like private ones, do solicit and receive large private donations.[13] One reason a difference might be expected is that graduates of public schools may believe it is less vital to make sizable gifts to their alma mater, feeling that alternative (public) sources of funds make such gifts less important. One donor gave this as the very reason he and his wife contribute less to her state school than to his private school. Another donor similarly observed that she and her husband do not give large gifts to the state schools they attended. And a man who does enthusiastically support his state school believes that its public status is a "hurdle" in terms of fundraising, because people believe the state provides the necessary support. Said he, "I think Yale and Harvard have an edge on the public institutions. They can plead that they need private support." Furthermore, given that donors believe philanthropy serves an important role by sustaining private organizations, they might simply be less receptive to using it to support public ones.

In fact, a far lower percentage of public college graduates had made a largest gift to their alma mater. Only 9.1 percent of these donors had made such a gift, as compared with 47.5 percent of those who attended a private college.[14] As it turns out, however, the public/private distinction among schools was correlated with their prestige ranking. Donors who graduated from private schools were also more likely to have attended more selective schools.[15] Analyses to disentangle the effects of the two institutional characteristics, moreover, confirmed the impact of prestige but not public/private status.[16] The results suggest that public college graduates less frequently made largest gifts to their schools because they had less prestige, not because of their public status per se. Yet given that only a few of these donors had attended a public college, and none had attended one with the highest ranking, a final conclusion cannot be drawn.[17] Particularly in light of qualitative materials that indicate public/private status to be a factor in donors' thinking, it is an issue that warrants future research on a larger group that would include greater numbers of affluent graduates from public and private schools of all selectivity levels.[18]

CULTURAL PHILANTHROPY AND ITS ROLE

Virtually everyone in this study had contributed some money to a cultural cause. With respect to largest gifts, culture was second only to education, receiving these from 42.9 percent of those interviewed. Furthermore, culture and education garnered large total contributions from a comparably high percentage of donors.[19] And when we compare donations to a group of New York City's largest nonprofit organizations, we find that cultural and educational organizations received more gifts of $1,000 or more than organizations in any of the five other areas.[20] Although similar with respect to the prominence and prestige they enjoy, there are also differences between educational and cultural philanthropy.

More than any other area receiving philanthropic support, the cultural arena stands out because of its integration into the ongoing lives of donors, both as individuals and as members of their class. An initial indicator of the distinctive character of cultural philanthropy is illustrated by the pattern of overlaps among donors to the large New York City nonprofits in different areas of activity. Examining 1,077 people who had contributed $1,000 or more to at least two of the organizations included, an analysis was performed to examine whether donors to each area (such as health) were any more or less likely to have contributed to organizations in each of the other areas. To the extent that such relationships exist, they were overwhelmingly negative, and usually involved culture. Donors to culture were less likely than others to have been contributors to all six of the other areas.[21] Since all these people had contributed to multiple organizations, this indicates that the major cultural institutions that did share donors with other large New York nonprofits tended to share them with one another.

As this finding suggests, gifts to particular cultural organizations tend to be part of a donor's overall interest and involvement in the cultural field as a whole. This was also evident in the way that donors who had made largest gifts to cultural institutions discussed their donations. In describing the reasons for these gifts, donors repeatedly made reference to their interest, enjoyment, and concern for culture as a field. To explain the reasons for two largest gifts she had made to cultural organizations, one woman said that she is an artist, loves the arts, and believes they have an important role in New York society because "they keep life balanced." She contrasted her feelings about supporting culture with those concerning her involvement with a social service organization, which she finds of interest, but about whose mission she does not feel as "passionately." Similarly, another donor explained that she had made her gifts because "I love and adore classical music." Yet another accounted for his cultural gifts in terms of "a real commitment to music, and to the cultural life of this city and the nation." One donor supports a performing arts company because he is concerned that the performing arts in this country are in a relatively "sad state." One man said that he started to support a particular musical form because, as his wife pointed out to him, "You really like that, and think that's something worthwhile, and have strong feelings about it." Another donor supports an arts organization because he enjoys going there, and "it's an institution I believe in, and a vital part of the culture of New York City, and the country, and the world." One man explained that he supports a museum because "I believe in what they're doing," and added,

> Whenever I go [to the museum], I'm amazed at what they have. The culture that's there. The opportunity for learning that's there—both by the patrons and people that come in off the streets, the visitors to New York. Part of it is—one of the . . . things that man has going for it is appreciation for the arts. I think it's a really good thing.

Donors' repeated references to their interest and enjoyment of culture when discussing individual cultural gifts contrasts with what we saw in the case of educational donations, where donors typically accounted for gifts in terms of their feelings and support for specific institutions, namely their schools. Donors certainly develop close ties to specific cultural institutions as well, but they placed these within the context of a larger desire to be associated with the cultural field (or a subfield, such as music). Their comments imply that had they not formed a relationship with the particular cultural institutions that they did, they would have formed one with another cultural one. On the other hand—and although there were certainly exceptions—the comments of donors to schools more generally left the impression that without a compelling reason to support the specific schools that they did, they might not have made a largest gift to education at all. In this respect, it may be recalled that although educational institutions were more frequently recipients of donors' largest gifts, the fields of education and culture received large total contributions from a comparably high percentage of donors. This indicates that donors to education were focusing their gifts on an individual organization to a larger extent than donors to culture, who were allocating their gifts to a greater number of institutions.

As donors' comments also illustrate, cultural pursuits form an important part of the social and recreational activities of many members of the elite. Indeed, one man said that he supports a musical organization for "selfish" reasons, because "I like good . . . music, and I like for it to be varied, and I think that's what they do." Similarly, another gives because "I like music and it's in a selfish way, because the more you give them, the more one assumes they will be producing." One donor made largest gifts to "cultural organizations which have given me and my wife pleasure." Another supports a museum that he loves to visit, explaining, "I could move in there. After a bad day, a few hours [there] will change your whole perspective."

The enjoyment of cultural activities is more than an individual pursuit. Performances and exhibitions also provide settings in which members of the elite come together with their peers. To recall an earlier discussion,[22] privileged access to cultural settings and events, such as attending a special viewing of an exhibit, is one of the benefits of giving to arts organizations. Thus, artistic events are often engaged in by the elite in exclusive settings restricted to their peers. Cultural organizations themselves also become the setting for dinners and parties, as well as for various artistic events. These organizations and events, both social and artistic, become a meeting ground where the elite interact with one another. Cultural organizations and settings associated with the arts also enjoy enormous prestige among these donors. Involvement with culture is one of the characteristic activities of the elite, and this is reflected in their philanthropy. Donors themselves were well aware of the social dimensions of involvement with cultural causes. For instance, one woman volunteered that people often go to performances at a particular organization because "it's fashionable."[23] With respect to the group of cultural donors in this study, however, I do not see aesthetic and social motives for cultural participation as mutually exclusive. Many of these donors clearly have an interest in the arts, and even engage in some form of artistic activity themselves, sometimes professionally.[24] This is one measure of the prestige and value of the arts in the eyes of the elite.

The particular role of culture as an arena of elite interaction is further illustrated by network data indicating that larger donors to culture were in fact more likely to know one another socially. The level of acquaintanceship among donors is provided by a measure of network "density," the number of social ties actually present among donors divided by the total possible number of ties.[25] The figure (.16) was four times as great among larger culture donors (those with total giving to culture of more than $25,000 during the previous twelve months) than for donors in general (.04). It was also four times as high as the figure for large donors to universities and colleges (.04), and over twice as high as the figure for large donors to hospitals (.07). Taken together, this finding, along with the overlap in donors to New York's large cultural institutions, the prestige of culture for donors, and their enthusiasm for associating with arts organizations, testifies to the fact that cultural philanthropy reflects, and contributes to sustaining, the distinctive role of culture among the elite.

Another indicator of culture's status is that donors repeatedly pointed to major cultural institutions as exemplifying organizations whose boards command the greatest prestige, because of the status of both the institution and its trustees. Moreover, comments about newcomers "buying in" were often made by people involved with cultural boards.[26] Donors often pointed to cultural organizations as targets of those seeking to establish their status. The fact that cultural organizations were particularly likely to become the focus of status competition and concern about "outsiders" testifies to the exclusive and prestigious nature of culture among the elite. In this respect, it should be added that a higher percentage of donors (33.7 percent) served on cultural boards than on boards in any other area.[27] This shows that donors particularly seek to become personally involved with the cultural world and its institutions as philanthropists in this area. As we saw earlier, culture was also the one field in which members of the social elite enjoyed an advantage in gaining access to boards, indicating that the cultural arena retains its unique identification with elite status and upper-class identity.

EDUCATION, CULTURE, AND THE SOCIAL ELITE

Philanthropy is patterned according to a prestige hierarchy, with one determinant of an organization's ranking being its area of activity. The philanthropic hierarchy parallels a status hierarchy within the elite itself. Just as the social elite exists as the central status group within the elite, educational and cultural causes valued by this group enjoy a privileged and widespread status in elite philanthropy. The fact that cultural and educational institutions enjoy such widespread esteem among multiple subgroups of donors is indicative of how the values of the social elite continue to serve as a reference point for philanthropic behavior within the broader elite, even as the relative position of the social elite itself undergoes change.

Culture and education are distinctive because they enjoy prestige and are so frequently chosen as recipients of largest gifts across diverse subgroups of donors. At the same time, however, we have seen that within individual subgroups of donors, such as women and Jews, giving to culture and education coexists with alternative patterns of giving associated with that subgroup. By contrast, the social elite exhibits a more insular pattern of giving, focused far more exclusively on culture and education. The contrast between the social elite and other donors is illustrated by the overall distribution of largest gifts. Members of both groups most frequently allocated largest gifts to education and culture. Thus, 66.7 percent of those outside the social elite made a largest gift to education, and 39.2 percent made one to culture. Yet fully 35.3 percent had also made a largest gift to health, and 35.3 percent had made one to the social services. Thus, after education, three areas received largest gifts from a sizable and relatively close percentage of people. A different picture emerges when we look at the social elite. Here, 75.9 percent made a largest gift to education, and 50 percent made one to culture, but the figure then drops to 17.9 percent in the next area, which was health. These figures clearly confirm that major giving by members of the social elite is far more exclusively focused on the prestigious areas of education and culture.

Major giving to culture was particularly high among members of the social elite who belonged to exclusive clubs, with fully 61.1 percent of these donors having made a largest gift in this area. Club membership and cultural resources, like cultural philanthropy, are associated with elite interaction.[28] Members of clubs were generally from the business world, and their club membership and cultural philanthropy may both reflect the larger phenomenon of their participation in networks associated with the broader business community.

The importance of the social elite as an economic and political class has been a longstanding source of debate, and differences of opinion continue to be expressed concerning its evolution and current role. Baltzell has argued that this Protestant Establishment is a class in decline, increasingly replaced by an atomized corporate elite.[29] He attributes this decline, in part, to an unwillingness to assimilate new members, such as Jews, to its ranks, thereby revitalizing and sustaining the class. Yet revisiting this thesis in the early 1980s, Zweigenhaft and Domhoff argued that the Protestant social elite remained strong, and that assimilation was occurring even though prejudice persisted.[30]

With respect to philanthropy, the influence of the social elite does endure, reflecting the group's continued preeminence with respect to status.[31] The values of this group have retained their force, even as the group itself has increasingly been forced to share coveted, influential positions in philanthropy with those outside its ranks.[32] I believe that with respect to philanthropy, the social elite, or at least its core members, have been willing to accept the involvement of others in order to perpetuate their prized institutions. It is my impression and hypothesis that as the process of broadening has occurred, it has become more difficult for the less affluent members of the social elite to gain access to the most prestigious boards, and that they are more frequently relegated to second tier boards that are well regarded but not at the very top of the hierarchy. The shifting position of the social elite has been discussed previously.[33] The point to be emphasized here is that the values of the social elite continue to orient behavior within the broader elite, even as the relative position of the group itself shifts. Indeed, at this point, the value accorded to culture and education appears to have become so widely entrenched outside, as well as inside, the social elite, that donors contribute independently of a desire to gain entrée into the social elite itself.

Thus, even if the social elite is in decline with respect to philanthropy, there are ample numbers of people coming to replace it, who have taken on their values. Accordingly, there was a continuity in elite philanthropy during the 1980s in New York, even as many new individuals joined the ranks of the wealthy. This is also well illustrated by comparing the largest gifts made by donors who inherited no wealth with those made by donors who inherited considerable sums ($1 million or more). Of the various lines of differentiation among the wealthy, the distinction between those of inherited wealth and those of self-made wealth is one that comes quickly to mind. It is one that many wealthy individuals themselves emphasize. The distinction, however, was simply not associated with the kinds of causes supported by donors through their major giving. Similarly high percentages of donors from both groups made largest gifts to education and culture. Furthermore, in both groups, these areas were the two most frequent recipients of largest gifts.[34] This lack of variation shows that the newly affluent do indeed share the philanthropic values of more established groups and continue support for their institutions.

The assimilation of new members into the social elite itself further strengthens the ability of the social elite to perpetuate its philanthropic causes and values, as seen in the case of Jewish donors. Although Jewish donors constituted less than one-third of those in the social elite, they represented over half of the largest donors in that group. Furthermore, Jewish members of the social elite had social acquaintanceships within the social elite as well as with donors outside of it. At the same time that they were socially integrated within the social elite, their social networks appeared to be less insular than those of non-Jews in the social elite, which were more exclusively confined within the social elite.[35] These findings indicate that with respect to philanthropy, the social elite has indeed revitalized itself through incorporating new members. They also suggest that Jews within the social elite may well serve as a bridge between the social elite and the larger elite community, encouraging others to support their causes. Thus we can see that while in one sense the social elite is in decline, its values live on.

CONCLUSION

Nonprofit institutions are an important part of the milieu in which elites live. They provide an organizational basis to social and cultural life among elites analogous to the basis for economic life provided by business organizations. A considerable portion of elite philanthropy grows out of donors' involvement with particular kinds of nonprofit organizations, a fact that is especially clear in the case of cultural and educational institutions. In this respect, elite philanthropy may well resemble giving among other social groups, but with different consequences. A great deal of philanthropic giving by individuals in the United States goes to churches.[36] Perhaps the support given by the wealthy to cultural and educational institutions is analogous to other people's support for their religious congregation, which to congregation members may represent not only a religious center but also a social or community center, and an institution that serves as one of the focal points of their identity as a member of a community.[37]

Gift exchange has been interpreted as a symbolic representation of the relationships among the individuals who exchange gifts.[38] Philanthropic gifts are also expressive of relationships, but they express the individual's relationship to, and identification with, particular social groups. This identification is expressed through support of the group's organizations. I believe, however, that the relationship between individual donors, social groups, and particular organizations is becoming more complex as nonprofit institutions become increasingly detached from particular, integrated, local upper classes who may have founded them. Nevertheless, it appears that the same elite institutions continue to attract major support, even as their status shifts to a more autonomous organizational basis.

As this chapter has also shown, there are differences in the basis of education and culture's prestige to donors and in the reasons that people contribute. Thus, while major gifts to educational institutions reflect donors' assessment of their prestige within an academic hierarchy, cultural institutions were more tightly bound to the prestige hierarchies within the elite itself. While educational giving was so often bound to supporting a specific organization, cultural philanthropy grew out of a more general involvement in the area as a whole. In this respect, it may be recalled that although educational institutions were more frequently recipients of donors' largest gifts, the two fields received large total contributions from a comparably high percentage of donors. This indicates that the money that donors give to culture is spread out among a larger number of institutions than the money they give to education. A common thread, however, is that whether giving to culture or giving to education, elite donors exhibit a preference for supporting those organizations that are among the elite in their fields. They select those institutions that, to their mind, represent the best in their respective areas.

Perhaps the popularity of educational institutions as recipients of largest gifts is indicative of a more intense and more personal involvement that donors develop with such organizations. At one point, after all, they actually lived (when students) as members of the institution. Cultural institutions respond to donors' aesthetic interests and are one vehicle for participating in the social life and identity of their class. Educational organizations, however, are viewed by donors as responsible for their very material ability to participate in the elite at all. Donors accordingly express a sense of dependency on educational organizations, and these institutions' advantage may also derive from their closer connection to such basic material concerns.

This chapter has also underscored an essential continuity in elite philanthropy. The values of the social elite have been institutionalized within the elite more broadly. Whether or not people seek entrée to the social elite itself, its values exert a unifying influence on elite philanthropy more generally. Even as members of other subgroups differentiate themselves through distinctive philanthropic choices that assume significance within their own subgroup, they come together to perpetuate a distinctively elite pattern of philanthropy by sharing these other, common philanthropic values. The commonality in giving among those of self-made wealth and those of inherited wealth further testifies to the readiness of new elites to take up and support traditional causes. For many donors, particularly members of the social elite, the appearance of many newly wealthy people brought a sense of disruption and change. From the point of view of philanthropy, however, it represented a guarantee of continuity—that there would be an elite there to sustain it, even though the contours and composition of that elite might undergo change.

Chapter Five

ATTITUDES TOWARD INHERITANCE AND
PHILANTHROPIC BEQUESTS

ALTHOUGH MOST of the donors I spoke with planned to do the bulk of their giving while alive, most had also made provision for philanthropy in their wills. Philanthropic bequests are of interest as more than just an alternative mechanism for making donations. They warrant attention because they allow us to extend and expand our discussion of the influences shaping philanthropy among affluent donors, by explicitly looking at donations in relation to alternative uses of wealth. Donations are influenced by the availability and desirability of alternative options for disposing of wealth, namely passing wealth to children or to government through taxation. Thus, contributions result from donors' ambivalent and even negative evaluations of other options, as well as from the positive values associated with philanthropy. The assessment that donors make of the various options, moreover, brings us to consider the ideological assumptions and cultural attitudes that underlie and foster elite philanthropy, focusing primarily on those attitudes concerning inheritance and wealth holding.

Up to this point, we have concentrated on the relationship of philanthropy to internal elite culture, identity, and organization. Decisions about philanthropic bequests also occur against the backdrop of a tax structure that encourages donations, an ideological framework that discourages letting wealth pass to government, and a culturally defined set of attitudes concerning wealth, success, and inheritance. The analysis of giving by bequests highlights the fact that elites' philanthropy is also guided by cultural and institutional influences in the wider society. Indeed, the presence of such wider societal support contributes to the persistence of philanthropy as an institution among the wealthy, even as elite groups themselves undergo change.

Many donors are deeply concerned about what will happen to their wealth upon their death. Their concern is of particular interest, moreover, because it is not merely expressive of personal considerations. Donors' comments bring to mind C. Wright Mills's observation that the absence of a feudal epoch in the United States has been decisive for the development of elites in this country. Among other things, he said, it has meant that "no set of noble families has commanded the top positions and monopolized the values that are generally held in high esteem;

and certainly that no set has done so explicitly by inherited right."[1] The absence of a framework providing for a hereditary or natural right of children to inherit can be seen repeatedly in donors' comments. By contrast, their comments are reflective of the distinctive issues and tensions concerning inheritance that arise for an elite based in a capitalist system, who live in a society that values individualism and private initiative. As we shall see, these issues and tensions bear on donors' decision to use philanthropic bequests as one option for distributing their wealth.

One thing that donors clearly do not want is to see their wealth pass to government through taxes. Money that goes to government is seen as taken away, while money donated to philanthropy is seen as money given away. Wealth that is taxed is perceived as going to an entity and purposes with which the donor feels no connection. By contrast, philanthropic gifts permit donors to direct their funds to institutions and causes with which they identify and which they feel are expressive of their priorities. We can thus see how the sense of identification that donors develop with recipient organizations during life has consequences for the disposition of their wealth at death. At the extreme, an identification with the recipient organization literally becomes a way to perpetuate the donor's own name and identity after death. One man, who said that a desire for immortality plays a role in his thinking, spoke of giving "a wing in a hospital, a gallery in a museum" as a way of leaving "footprints on the sand of time." Another told me that his works of art would be going to museums upon his death, and "I am thrilled at the idea that in the future I'll be associated with them." In cases such as these, philanthropy becomes a vehicle for attaining stature after death, as well as during life.

Although donors themselves may be influenced by concerns about the fate of their own individual fortune, name, and favorite causes when making bequests, the class consequences of their decisions should also be emphasized. Philanthropic bequests represent a potential vehicle for passing wealth on to support institutions and values central to the elite, thereby preserving these for future generations. Accordingly, from a sociological perspective, philanthropic bequests also deserve our attention as one way in which elite groups maintain their culture, organizations, and cohesion over time.

LIFETIME GIVING VERSUS PHILANTHROPIC BEQUESTS

The majority of donors (59.7 percent) planned to do more of their giving during their lifetime. By comparison, 7.8 percent planned to do more giving by bequest, and 10.4 percent planned to do comparable amounts or had no particular leaning. A number of donors (19.5 per-

cent) did not yet know.[2] People offered various reasons for their preference for lifetime giving. Some emphasized that they enjoy giving, want
to be involved in their philanthropy, and wish to see the benefits that
result from their contributions. One woman feels that "the time is
now—to really live while you have a life." She is one who enjoys the
involvement and does not want her gifts to be "in name only." Furthermore, although she and her husband made a large bequest in order to
stop one organization from "breathing down our neck," she finds it
"spooky" to know an institution is out there waiting for them to die.

Another donor said, "You get more gratification from lifetime. What
do I care if they stick up a brass plate after I'm dead?" Similarly, one
donor explained, "I feel that it's important to do it while you can enjoy
doing it. To give to something [where] you can enjoy seeing the people
helped, or whatever it is. When I'm gone, it won't matter to me." Such
comments, and the general preference for lifetime giving, are consistent
with our earlier observations concerning the involvement that accompanies contributions of money.

Some donors also expressed concerns about how their money might
be spent after their death. As one explained, "I wouldn't leave it to a
foundation. . . . I have a feeling that the people who eventually became
trustees, say in twenty-five years, would be doing things—that I just
would be horror struck. I'd rather give while I'm still alive."[3] Another
prefers to know where the money is going, rather than have it distributed by some "functionary." Similarly, a donor who has been a very active volunteer said, "on the theory that since I know something about
these things," he wants to be part of the decision, which would not happen if he gave by bequest.

Various other reasons were offered as well. One donor thinks lifetime
giving is preferable because it allows him to learn from experience and
make better decisions about future contributions. Some argued that it
was unfair or wrong to defer donations until death. A donor who favors
lifetime giving, "can't imagine doing it any other way—you can't expect
them to sit around and wait until you die." Another believes it is
"chintzy" to give by bequest.

There were, however, an unusual few who plan to do the bulk of their
giving by bequest. A striking feature of these six donors is that half of
them had no children. Indeed, donors who had no children were more
likely (37.5 percent) than others (4.4 percent) to do most of their giving
by bequest.[4] Donors themselves drew connections between their not
having children and leaving wealth to philanthropy.[5] The relationship
between having children and giving by bequest illustrates well how philanthropic bequests can be influenced by the availability of other options.
So, too, did some of the stories donors told of wealthy people they knew

who died without children. Some attorneys, for instance, had been left responsibility for distributing their estates. In one case, the person who left the wealth indicated no preferences whatsoever about how the money should be spent or what organizations should receive the funds. She simply had no children, little family, and thus wanted all her money to go for charitable causes.

Although donors generally planned to do more of their giving while alive, the majority (59.2 percent) had also made provisions for philanthropy in their will.[6] Furthermore, those who do have bequests had left an average of 33.4 percent of their estate for philanthropic purposes (the median was 23.8 percent). Thus, while these donors may generally prefer to give during life, giving by bequest is also clearly a widespread and significant component of elite philanthropy, by no means confined to those without children.[7] Accordingly, we turn to consider other influences leading donors to make philanthropic bequests.

DONOR ATTITUDES TOWARD ESTATE TAXATION

One option that donors clearly do not want is for government to tax the bulk of estates. The vast majority of donors (73 percent) believed that individuals should be allowed to decide what will happen to most of their wealth after they die.[8] Moreover, among the few (9.5 percent) who favored heavy government taxation, half volunteered that allowing wealth to be left for philanthropic purposes should be an acceptable alternative.

Donors explained their opposition to heavy estate taxation in various ways. Some maintained that high estate taxes are a form of double taxation. One donor objected that "we pay during life" and asked, "How many times do you have to tax?" Another donor does not oppose the estate tax "because it is needed to protect against too much concentration of wealth." Yet he believes that high rates represent "double taxation" because "you've been taxed all of your life on your earnings." He went on to say,

> Usually people screw it up themselves badly enough. You leave it to the spendthrifts in society and they'll burn through it pretty quickly. . . . And the other thing, I don't approve of giving it to the government to spend willy nilly. I would rather have it under private control. And if it's my giving it to my kids or my giving it to charity, that is a private decision that I exercise, which I think is overall better for society than to automatically take everything that I earned . . . and have it distributed through a public overseeing. I think independent, individual decision is much more important to what goes on and is successful in the world.

As this comment suggests, donors also expressed doubts about the use of money collected by government. Another man said that the untaxed portion of the estate is capital, "and I think capital is a very important part of our economy. If the government takes it all, then it's all spent and goes down the drain somehow." He also warned that "as soon as the government takes more than 50 percent of anybody's income or wealth, you do run into problems. You want to avoid paying those taxes."

Some donors expressed particular concern about the impact of inheritance taxes on the continuity of a business. Thus, one donor who generally favors high rates of taxation qualified his view by saying, "It would be stupid to have the inheritance laws cause a business to be broken up or disposed of because . . . a profitable business is not a purely personal thing. . . . Society has an interest." Another was particularly against any tax that would cause a family farm or business to be sold because "you lose a certain amount of continuity and tradition. That is harmful to society as a whole."

As we have seen, those opposed to higher estate taxes defended the right of individuals to allocate their funds as they please. By contrast, those unusual donors who favored high tax rates raised questions concerning who, if anyone, has a legitimate claim to the money other than the original person who earned the wealth. One person said,

> It's really a funny question—who owns it in a society in which help comes from all directions. But you know, it's a good thing to accumulate. But whether it should pass to a person . . . most of the time I just think not. . . . [The] person accumulating it is probably a good person to decide how to use it, but after that it becomes just a consumption pattern.

Another donor, who had amassed a fortune through a business he built, believes that

> any inheritance that goes beyond providing for the basic security, not the luxury security . . . of the next generation should either be taxed . . . or provide for giving. I see no justification for self-respecting people to expect to survive on what their forbears have done. . . . I'm not interested in endowing the ability of my children to live on Fifth Avenue or have Rolls Royces. That would not be a popular view. Well, it is a popular view. But people just talk about it because it makes them feel noble. But in practice, they don't do it.

Both of these donors felt people should be allowed to leave wealth for philanthropic purposes.

As we have seen, however, the vast majority believe the individual should be allowed to decide what happens to most of his or her wealth and do not wish to see most of it pass to government. What then do these donors believe should happen to the estate? How do they view the institution of inheritance? And how do their views relate to giving by bequest? It is to these questions that we now turn.

DONOR ATTITUDES TOWARD INHERITANCE

Although donors generally believed individuals should control the disposition of their wealth, there was less agreement and confidence about having individuals inherit estates.[9] In speaking of the positive aspects of inheritance, donors emphasized that it motivates people to work and save. Thus, one woman said that the issue of estate taxes "sounds like an ethical question, but it's an economic question. Ideally, people shouldn't inherit money. The world is not ideal, though, and many people wouldn't contribute to the economic aspects of society if they couldn't control their wealth." Another believes that when estate taxes become too high, "that gets rather ominous-sounding in terms of the implications of incentive." One went so far as to comment that "if you deny inheritance, you deny the laws of human nature." Some donors also felt that without the ability to leave wealth as they choose, people would try to spend all their money while alive, thereby using it "foolishly" or making "frivolous" expenditures.

One man said that a desire to leave a large estate for his children had been a strong motivating force for him, even though "in theory" he believes that it is probably bad to leave children money. Nonetheless, he wants to leave his own children a large estate, "so that they can do all the things I couldn't do—just like my parents sent me to school, which they couldn't do. I in turn want to leave the luxury of idleness, having worked hard all my life, on the theory that they can then do what they want to do, and not what they have to do." He believes that the possibility of leaving money to charities of interest also serves as a motivator for work and savings.

It is important to note that in these discussions of the positive consequences of inheritance, donors focused on the person accumulating the wealth. By contrast, discussions of the negative consequences focused on those who inherit wealth, bringing us to the issue of donors' attitudes toward passing wealth on to children. During the interviews, it became apparent that the issue of leaving wealth to children was of deep personal concern to many donors. When asked about her views on the subject, one donor said, "It's a debate that goes on in this house all the time, and frankly we have not come up with a satisfactory answer. . . . We certainly believe that an awful lot of money should be given away. How much one should leave for one's children, and what the ramifications of that are, are very problematic." Another donor told me, "I struggle with it every day. You came in just when I was talking to my lawyer about this problem." And one man said, "I'm wrestling with that right now. It's a very difficult problem if you have a good deal of money. . . . There's so many aspects to that question, that I could keep you here all day, because I've been working on that for two months." To illustrate, he explained that he knows that if he treats his children equally, some will squander their money while others will use it well. Nonetheless, he has decided it would be wrong to differentiate. He also said that leaving wealth to his grandchildren was problematic, because their parents might object to having them made independent by inheriting large sums. Others brought up similar concerns.[10] Some donors referred to other wealthy people who are known (through media reports) for their views against leaving children great fortunes, indicating their own concern with the issue.

The ability to bequeath wealth is seen as encouraging work and achievement, but inheriting great wealth is viewed as a threat to incentive, thus donors' attitudes toward inheritance pose a dilemma. On the one hand, they believe that individuals, not government, should determine what happens to most of an estate. On the other, they question the legitimacy and benefits of allowing individuals to inherit large estates. A donor who has amassed a large fortune, illustrated this tension when discussing estate taxes:

> It's two edged. Government should not be taxing wealth people want to leave heirs. . . . People should be permitted to do what they want with the money they earned during their life. They paid tax on it. It isn't as if the money wasn't taxed. . . . But [I'm] not sure we do good by leaving money to children. The greatest joy in my life has been earning money, and I would hate to deprive my kids of that. They've already been deprived of a certain amount of that because they didn't have to work their way through school. They're starting life out with a base so [they] don't have to worry about starving to death, which I had to worry about. Maybe it was a stimulus, although there are examples of kids from better families who do pretty good on their own. But if you give them too much, there's a worry about them becoming wastrels. And I'm not going to take that chance.[11]

Interestingly, some donors who had grown up in wealthy families also expressed such suspicions. One donor said that although she would feel like an "ingrate" if she said that children should not inherit too much, she does believe that wealthy children "are usually a mess."[12] A donor who is active in a profession said that in her family, the children "were programmed to believe they would never have to 'worry.' I think a little worry is maybe a good idea." Yet another such donor felt that "if you're born with too much money, it undermines the necessity to take care of yourself. And of course that's one of the great motivators in life."[13]

In response to these concerns, some arranged their estate so that children would not inherit most of their money until reaching a certain age. Thus, one donor plans to leave her children a lot of money, but will not allow them to use the money until they reach their mid-thirties so that it will not be "undermining." Similarly, another donor does not believe in giving children "a dime" before their mid-thirties because they "should know that life is hard." And one person reported that she and her husband did not give large amounts to their children, "until we found out they could be good citizens." Restricting funds left to children about whom the donor has doubts served as another option. This was done by one donor who told me, "I have [some] kids that I will sew up everything for and from, and [other] kids that I will give as much as I can to loose and free." Yet another option taken by some is to leave wealth for philanthropic purposes, while giving children a role in deciding how the money will be distributed.

THE LEGITIMACY OF WEALTH

Donors' comments with respect to inheritance bring to mind Max Weber's observation that people are not content to merely have good fortune, but want to feel that their fortune is deserved.[14] For many donors, wealth that is deserved is wealth that is earned. It was clearly not seen as legitimate for children to stop working or worrying about caring for themselves because of their money. In this respect, these wealthy individuals share an attitude found among other members of American society, that "it is only insofar as they can claim that they have succeeded *through their own efforts* that they can feel they have deserved that achievement."[15]

The connection between earning and deserving wealth was also seen in the responses given by donors when asked whether they felt at all uncomfortable or guilty about the amount of money they had or how it was made. One donor had no such feelings because "I got it through plain, hard work." He added that he would be "very surprised" if anyone thought he did not deserve his money after doing his work for a few weeks. Similarly, another donor felt quite comfortable with his wealth because "I earned it myself."[16]

Furthermore, such responses were also given by some who had inherited considerable amounts of wealth. While they acknowledged that they had inherited funds, there was some tendency for inheritors to stress their own accomplishments or to downplay the importance of what they had inherited. One donor said he had inherited wealth but not until he was older, so that the amount was not "meaningful." Another emphasized that he had greatly increased the worth of a business interest he had inherited and thus has no "guilt complex" about his wealth because "I worked for it."[17] Such comments illustrate responses to a situation in which many wealthy individuals clearly do pass on privileges to their children, while at the same time being disposed toward a meritocratic and individualistic ideology that holds that individual rewards should reflect individual achievement. Accordingly, for those who did not work to earn the wealth, it is viewed as important to at least show that they work to deserve the wealth.

ATTITUDES TOWARD INHERITANCE: CONSEQUENCES FOR PHILANTHROPY

Donors believe individuals ought to be able to dispose of most of their estate as they choose, and do not wish their wealth to pass to government. At the same time, some express reservations about leaving wealth to children, and some have no children. Under these circumstances, it is hypothesized, philanthropy will benefit. While money paid in taxes is experienced as taken away or gone, philanthropic donations are seen as furthering the interests and goals of the donor. Philanthropic bequests are also viewed as socially beneficial by donors, and thus enjoy a legitimacy that gifts to children may not share. For instance, one donor noted that one of the ways that people seek immortality is through philanthropy, "fortunately, to everybody's advantage."

A set of analyses permits us to examine the connection between the percentage of the donor's estate left to philanthropy and the availability and assessment of the alternatives that have been discussed. Table 5.1 presents the mean and median amount of their estate that donors plan to leave for philanthropic purposes,[18] breaking these down according to whether the donor has children, and attitudes toward inheritance. These figures are given first for all donors, and then only for those making philanthropic bequests (right-hand columns).

The percentage of their estate that donors plan to leave as philanthropic bequests does indeed vary sharply among the different subgroups. Among all donors, those with children plan to leave an average of 20.6 percent of their estate for philanthropic purposes (median = 7.5), while the figure jumps to 50.4 percent among those without children (median = 33). Even when we exclude those donors leaving no bequests, striking differences remain. Among this group, donors with children plan to leave an average of 29.2 percent of their estate (median = 20) as

TABLE 5.1
Percentage of Donors' Estate Left to Philanthropy: Means and Medians

	All Donors			Donors Making Bequests Only		
	No.	Mean (Std. Dev.)	Median	No.	Mean (Std. Dev.)	Median
All	58	24.2 (31.3)	8.8	42	33.4 (32.4)	23.8
Donor has						
No children	7	50.4 (44.0)	33.0	6	58.8 (41.6)	60.3
Children	51	20.6 (27.8)	7.5	36	29.2 (29.2)	20.0
Donor believes inheritance has						
Negative conseq.	7	52.8 (38.6)	50.0	7	52.8 (38.6)	50.0
Positive conseq.	19	10.4 (15.5)	2.5	11	17.9 (16.9)	7.5
Both	9	16.6 (28.4)	1.5	6	24.9 (32.3)	17.5
Neither	4	38.3 (43.3)	26.5	3	51.0 (42.9)	33.0
Don't know	1	—	—	1	—	—
Depends	10	22.6 (25.6)	17.5	7	32.2 (24.9)	25.0
Donor view on leaving children wealth						
Leave as much as possible	10	9.5 (12.9)	5.8	6	15.8 (13.4)	8.8
Should not get too much	13	44.0 (38.3)	40.0	12	47.7 (37.6)	45.0
Depends on child	14	20.6 (29.5)	5.0	9	32.1 (31.6)	20.0
Don't know	6	12.1 (13.3)	11.3	3	24.2 (1.4)	25.0
Mixed/moderate	8	29.4 (33.9)	20.0	7	33.6 (34.3)	25.0
Other	3	44.2 (48.5)	20.0	3	44.2 (48.5)	20.0

Note: The first three columns provide figures for all donors. The second three repeat the analysis, excluding those sixteen donors making no bequests.

Fifteen donors, who do not know what they will leave for philanthropy, are excluded from the analysis, as are three other donors whose answer could not be categorized for this analysis.

compared with an average of 58.8 percent (median = 60.3) among those without children.[19]

The percentage of their estate dedicated to philanthropy also varies among those holding different attitudes toward inheritance. While those who believe inheritance has positive consequences plan to leave an average of 10.4 percent of their estate (median = 2.5), the figure jumps to 52.8 percent among those who believe it has negative consequences (median = 50). Similarly, those who wish to leave children as much as possible, plan to leave an average of 9.5 percent of their estate for philanthropic purposes (median = 5.8), as compared with an average of 44 percent among those who believe children should not be left too much (median = 40).[20]

TABLE 5.2
Percentage of Donors' Estate Left to Philanthropy:
Regression Analysis Results

Independent Variable	Coefficients (t statistic)
Asset level (1 = Top)	21.5* (2.2)
Children (1 = Yes)	−38.3** (3.4)
Marital status (1 = Married)	23.3* (2.6)
Inheritance has negative economic consequences (1 = Yes)	34.4** (3.3)
Intercept	30.8** (3.0)
Adjusted R-square	.45
N	37

Note: Coefficients are unstandardized. Absolute value of t statistic is presented.

Dependent variable is the percentage of his or her estate the donor plans to leave for philanthropic purposes.

The top asset level includes those with $20 million or more in assets. Collapses of variables into dichotomous categories are based on exploratory analyses.

* $p \leq .05$.
** $p \leq .01$.

To simultaneously examine the effects of multiple influences on the percentage of the donor's estate left to philanthropy, ordinary least squares regression analysis was employed (see Table 5.2). The results reveal that whether or not the donor has children, believing that inheritance has negative consequences, being a top asset holder ($20 million or more), and being married each have a significant relationship with the percentage of the donor's estate left for philanthropic purposes.[21] Moreover, taken together, these variables explain 45 percent of the variation in the percentage of the estate left to philanthropy.[22] The importance of the belief concerning the negative consequences of inheritance was further emphasized when the regression was performed excluding that variable. The R-square for that regression dropped to 28, fully 17 points lower than when that attitudinal variable was included.

CONCLUSION

Among the donors in this study, philanthropy is widely seen as an acceptable and even natural option for disposing of wealth. For many as well, it is one of the priorities taken into account in making plans for the ultimate disposition of wealth. As one donor said, "I think it's nice to leave a reasonable amount to one's children or grandchildren, but I do think that people should leave something to some good causes." Yet another donor plans to provide for her children, but added that her children also know that she will make philanthropic bequests because "I have a responsibility both ways." The fact that so many donors made provisions for philanthropy in their wills is further testimony to the attachments and interests that they develop with nonprofit organizations during their life.[23]

While recognizing the positive value donors place on philanthropy, this chapter has expanded our analysis by emphasizing that donations also result from ambivalent or negative evaluations of other alternatives. It more generally calls our attention to the fact that decisions about philanthropy do not necessarily stand alone, but may well be influenced by decisions concerning other uses of money. The chapter has further shown that donors' evaluation of available alternatives is deeply shaped by cultural and ideological conceptions about wealth and inheritance. Donors' comments reflect the nature of the American elite as a business-oriented, capitalist class. They also indicate that in this area, affluent donors share broader American social values concerning individual accomplishment and success. Although such values are readily drawn on to legitimate the privilege of individuals who accumulate wealth and to argue that these individuals, rather than government, should be able to determine the fate of most of their fortune, they do not provide a ready justification for retaining wealth in the family. Indeed, from the framework within which donors operate, we can see that philanthropy as a vehicle for disposing of wealth enjoys a rather distinctive legitimacy.

While the tensions in donors' attitudes toward inheritance are both important and consequential, the fact remains that these donors (or at least many of them) are transmitting privilege to their children. It is interesting to note the presence of a set of rituals that serve to justify this in the eyes of both donors and children. Examples include keeping wealth in trust for a longer period so that children can "prove" themselves, and having a child start out at the bottom of the family business. Indeed, training children to be philanthropic itself provides another example. Such practices allow parent and child to feel that, even if not earned, at least wealth is deserved. Perhaps most extreme, however, is the way in which heirs virtually redefine themselves as "self-made" by emphasizing their role in expanding the family fortune. From such examples, we see yet again how, as Weber observed, the well-off are not merely content to enjoy their good fortune, but they want to feel that it is deserved.[24]

In this discussion of wealth and inheritance, I have expanded my overall analysis by highlighting the presence of ideological attitudes and assumptions that influence elite philanthropy. While noting that donors did not wish to see their wealth go to government, I did not delve further into the nature of donors' thinking about government. Indeed, so central and extensive are the issues in this area, that this discussion has been reserved for a separate chapter, to which we now turn.

Chapter Six

GOVERNMENT AND PHILANTHROPY:

ALTERNATIVES OR COMPLEMENTS?

THIS CHAPTER examines donors' conceptions of the nature, roles, and relationship of governmental and philanthropic activity. Donors hold strong and impassioned views in this area that relate to the very cultural and political foundations of philanthropy. They defend a complex position that legitimates philanthropy and nonprofit organizations as institutions whose mission is "public" but carried out under private auspices. Distrust and skepticism toward government are integral components of this position, yet donors' outlook cannot be understood as an expression of antigovernmental sentiments alone. Rather, they assert a pluralistic view of society in which power is dispersed among governmental and private parties.

Despite the strength of donors' views, issues pertaining to government and philanthropy seldom arose before I explicitly raised them. The lack of reference to government was particularly surprising during the late 1980s, given the emphasis on private initiative as an alternative to government in political discourse during the Reagan era. A consideration of why the issues were not raised before is itself revealing. Earlier portions of the interviews focused on donors' own philanthropic involvements, their history, and their meaning. Respondents rarely connected their own giving to governmental activities and programs. Indeed, they seldom discussed their philanthropy in ideological terms or spoke of gifts as a means of attaining broad social or political goals. Rather, as we have seen, they typically thought in terms of personal considerations, social and familial networks and identifications, and attachments to specific organizations. Once questions concerning government and philanthropy were raised, however, donors responded with fervor. Their responses revealed that there is indeed an underlying ideological framework that informs their basic understanding of philanthropy as a social institution. This did not emerge earlier, however, because donors do not draw on this framework in thinking about their own particular philanthropy. Thus, the ideological character of philanthropy as an institution must not be generalized to the actual conduct of philanthropy, such as the kinds of areas chosen or their meaning to donors. At the same time, the factors involved in individuals' philanthropic decisions must not keep us from considering the underlying ideological framework in terms of which philanthropy per se appears as valuable and legitimate. That framework is the focus of this chapter.

A discussion of attitudes toward philanthropy and government complements my earlier analyses in an additional way. Having highlighted the differentiated nature of the sources (such as gender and ethnicity) and the character of distinct kinds of philanthropy (such as cultural or social service), one might well ask what basis there is for considering "philanthropy" a unified activity at all. This chapter illustrates the presence of a set of political and cultural attitudes that do give a common foundation to the diversity of philanthropy. Indeed, I believe that these attitudes contribute to explaining why donors themselves categorize varied types of giving and volunteering as different forms of the same activity, philanthropy.

This chapter also extends the previous analysis of how elite philanthropy responds to elites' participation in a wider culture and society. Many attitudes expressed by these donors, from suspicion toward governmental power and bureaucracy to high regard for private, individual initiative, are not unique to members of the elite. They reflect broader themes, concerns, and values in American society. An understanding of elite philanthropy must analyze its sources both within and outside a specific class context. A consideration of attitudes toward government and philanthropy furthers that aim.

GOVERNMENT AS A SUBSTITUTE FOR PHILANTHROPY: DONOR VIEWS

It would be hard to find a set of issues that elicit such uniform and impassioned comments as those concerning government and philanthropy. For instance, donors emphatically rejected a hypothetical proposal that would eliminate the tax incentive for giving, and have government use the increased revenue to support the types of cultural and welfare activities that have benefited from philanthropy. Virtually everyone (90.4 percent) expressed opposition, adding such comments as, "I'd absolutely hate that," "that would be awful," "I think it would be sad," and "that's socialism."[1] One woman exclaimed, "If I wanted to live that way, I'd move to Sweden!"

Donors offered various reasons for their opposition to substituting government for philanthropy. Some simply felt that this scenario was unrealistic and could never happen. A donor who had been in government replied, "If we wait for government to do everything, we will be waiting for a long, long time!" Another person maintained, "History proves that doesn't happen. . . . The Olympics is a good example. We're the only country in the world where the Olympics is supported by private donations or corporate donations." Other donors observed that government should not—and perhaps could not—support certain kinds of causes. A man whose philanthropy is focused on religiously affiliated organizations suggested it might even be "unconstitutional in some respects" for government to fund the nonprofits he supports.

Donors objected to far more than the perceived impracticality of the proposal. Donors believe that one strength of philanthropy is that it allows individuals to support causes they value. They felt that government would not support the causes of interest and importance to them and would generally be unresponsive to the concerns and needs of individuals. One donor asked, "How can you expect government to know what organizations [people want to support]? It doesn't make sense. . . . How could the government satisfy everyone?" Similarly, another donor believes the opportunity for individual involvement is the most important feature of philanthropy, but "if government took it over, then unless I become a legislator, how can I have a say?" One man objected that an expanded government would "set its own standard, and then we'd have the 'official art' and so on. That is exactly what this country is not about!" Rather, he added, "It is about freedom of choice." Even one unusual donor, who was less opposed to an increased governmental role, said she still could not really support the idea because "if I were president of the U.S., I wouldn't support the fundamentalist churches, but clearly they have a vital role to play in the lives of many American citizens."[2]

As we can see, donors argue that the fact that philanthropy places a measure of influence in private hands and outside the governmental domain is appropriate and desirable. They value the individualism, in terms of choice, initiative, and impact, that they believe the current system respects. Largely for these reasons, philanthropy represents more to donors than a mechanism for channeling money to worthy causes. Rather, it is seen as representing some of the most valuable and even defining elements of American society. Thus, for one woman, philanthropy is "the idea of giving and citizen participation—and I think that's what America's all about." Another donor objected that were we to eliminate private input, "we wouldn't be following the American precept." One man felt that private initiative is "the whole difference between our system and the European system, [where] the government fills that gap and the people don't do anything." And a donor who was born in another country regards "voluntarism" and the "multifaceted" American system that allows individuals to participate as "fantastic," and what is "distinctive about the United States." Donors view philanthropy as important to sustaining a set of organizations. But they also view it as important because it sustains a set of values and a relationship between the individual and society that donors believe epitomizes the "American way." As we shall see, donors also believe that philanthropy and nonprofit organizations work better than government in many respects.

Donors' preference for the private sector is seen as well in their opinions about how governmental funding should be administered. I asked whether they believed that government spending should be increased, decreased, or continued at present levels in health care, the arts, higher education, social services, and environmental and animal protection. A majority believed that government spending should be increased in each of these fields.[3] I then asked those who favored an increase whether they felt government should channel these funds through private nonprofits or administer programs directly. Although a number of donors exhibited a willingness to see government take some direct role, virtually no one said the money should be administered entirely under government auspices. By contrast, the highest percentage felt the money should be channeled through private nonprofit organizations in each of the areas.[4]

DONOR PERCEPTIONS OF THE LIMITS OF GOVERNMENT

Donors believe that governmental actions are prone to weaknesses that do not characterize private donations or nonprofit organizations. They systematically disagreed when asked to react to a set of statements proposing that positive outcomes might result if the United States government were expanded to assume more responsibilities, as in certain European countries. They overwhelmingly agreed, by contrast, that negative consequences would result from such a change. The vast majority thus rejected the idea that centralization under government would allow for better coordination among programs and produce a more reasonable use of money, or that government would distribute funds more fairly because of greater accountability.[5] The great majority did agree, moreover, that enhancing government's role would reduce social variety, because government would not respond to the range of values and problems addressed by donors. They also agreed that funds would be used less efficiently because of the red tape involved in governmental administration.[6] To understand the reasoning behind donors' views and the aspects of government they find problematic, we may turn now to consider the points they raised during discussions of these subjects.

Donors' accounts do not depict governmental action as the result of a process in which decisions are made on behalf of a public. Rather, they range from portrayals of government as a bureaucratic monolith that pursues its own interests, to an arena in which decisions are highly politicized, based on "special interests," and influenced more by politicians' desire to advance their own careers than what is socially necessary and desirable. In keeping with this basic viewpoint, donors argue that governmental allocation of funds would suffer from being highly politicized. For example, they objected that as political administrations shifted, causes would alternately gain and lose funding, rendering their existence precarious. One person warned that you might get a different policy every four years. Another said, "I can imagine what would happen to the funding of either certain right-wing church organizations or Planned Parenthood. They might not get a cent, depending on how the vote went." One donor objected that in government, "everybody's so busy protecting themselves, nothing happens." Some emphasized that they had experiences with government activity in areas of their own philanthropic interests that confirmed their views. One was a donor with cultural interests, who was critical of what government has done in the arts because "it's political, like everything else that comes out of Washington."

Donors also pointed to the politicized nature of decision making in government in rejecting the idea that government would be more accountable. One donor drily observed that "if you pump everything in before an election, that isn't going to be very accountable." Similarly, another asked, "Where's the accountability?" He then proceeded to mention various government officials facing charges of unethical or illegal behavior at the time. One woman argued that government would not be more accountable because for that, "you need one-on-one contact, and bureaucracies don't allow that." And another donor simply expressed astonishment that anyone could say government would be more accountable, joking that anyone who did "must have been running for office."

Donors' critical comments about government often focused on its large size and bureaucratic structure, which they viewed as a source of both inefficiency and a potentially dangerous concentration of power. This was illustrated by the comments of one man who described himself as "bitterly opposed" to transferring philanthropic funds to the government, because they would then be in the hands of "bureaucrats" who would spend it improperly, due to waste and corruption—which he thinks is already happening with tax money. Another donor simply "would not trust that much control in government, or any big organization." A number of people believed that bureaucracy and large size made it too difficult for government to get things done. One man said he is not "antigovernment" but just feels that "between the red tape and all the rest of it . . . it just goes through too many people, too many committees, too many—too many everything! And when it does, it's not too great. I'm against it." Similarly, another observed that when government administers something, "you have to wait so long to get anything done, that nothing ever gets done."

Donors widely believed that philanthropy produces a level of diversity and innovation that would not be sustained by government. Some observed that government would always make cautious funding decisions. This was the view of one donor, who works in a health field. Although he regards government funding as "mostly good" and important in his field, he also believes it is dominated by "a certain ingroup" and "mainline thinking" that would prevent a researcher with a "crazy idea" from obtaining funds. He thinks that private funders have been an important source of support for newer, more offbeat ideas in the field, "so that if you eliminated private funding, you'd have a lot of trouble." Another donor said that "it just boggles the mind that there should be no more private philanthropy if you expect a diversity of opinion."

Donors do not only believe that government would reduce diversity because of particular preferences in its funding patterns (e.g., for "safe" causes). They also believe it would be a result of centralizing decision making in a single source. The opposition to such centralization is basic to their objections to increasing government's role at the expense of philanthropy. For instance, one donor believes, "It's the same thing for charity as it is for a socialist country like Russia, where the government controls all the economy and it becomes stagnant. No new ideas. No new incentives." He went on to point out that it was just that situation that Gorbachev was trying to correct. Donors believe that philanthropy works well, and produces socially desirable outcomes, such as greater diversity, because it puts decision making in the hands of many individuals. Expressing this widespread view, one explained, "The sum total of individuals, when they have an individual incentive to pursue things of their own choosing, produces more variety. So anything having to do with consolidating would decrease variety." As illustrated by these last quotes, donors discuss philanthropy in terms similar to capitalism, as a system that derives its strength from encouraging and relying on individual initiative and incentive. Indeed, they drew an equation between eliminating philanthropy and shifting to socialism, which they argued would stifle individual incentive.

Finally, some pointed to the caliber of the people employed as one of the weaknesses of government. One believed that because of the personnel making the decisions, government "would kill a lot of the entrepreneurship and the new developments," in the arts, elaborating as follows:

> When you say the government, you've got to think who you're dealing with . . . a group of people who are probably medium to low paid . . . who aren't as intelligent about things as are the people who run the philanthropies. Because you've got people who run the philanthropies, and most of them are way up in the cultural and business world—knowledgeable—and that you won't find in government.

Some said it is more reasonable to leave things to government in Europe because they believe their personnel are of a higher quality. One respondent thinks that "they have a more honest and better civil service. . . . It's got a certain social value, status. . . . Government service is looked down on as a lower form of activity in America."[7] A somewhat different criticism was offered by a man who attributes the weakness of government personnel to the fact that as bureaucracy builds up, "you get people who avoid the conflict of the marketplace and out of the [habit] of being valued and revalued." Some donors view governmental solutions as more workable in Europe than the United States for additional reasons. The large size and diverse population of the United States were cited as making it particularly difficult for a central government to administer programs. One woman observed that "countries that can do that are the countries that are much smaller." What was clear, however, was that donors did not believe that enhancing government at the expense of philanthropy was best for this country.

GOVERNMENT OR PHILANTHROPY, OR GOVERNMENT AND PHILANTHROPY?

The character and fervor of donors' comments might suggest the conclusion that they are antigovernment and pro-philanthropy. Yet such a conclusion would be misleading, for it would overlook additional components of their views. Despite their lack of enthusiasm for government, donors conceded, if sometimes regretfully, that government is better suited than philanthropy for handling certain tasks. This attitude was not unique to unusually liberal respondents, as evidenced by the comments of both Democrats and Republicans.

Most typically, government was identified as necessary for responding to large-scale social problems and tasks. For instance, a Republican who generally opposed enlarging the role of government, felt that it did need to be more active in creating and administering health programs because of the size of the problem and the population requiring services. Similarly, a Democrat described AIDS as "such an enormous problem, it obviously must have government support. For private enterprise to try and find a solution is like trying to brush the sand away from the beach. It's a hopeless adventure." Magnitude of the undertaking and special issues of oversight were cited by some who discussed the need for a governmental role in addressing environmental concerns. Thus a Democratic respondent believed that because of "the accountability factor," government should spend more on the environment and administer programs directly, noting that "if you give money for environmental concerns to the NRA, you can imagine what might happen to the animals!" A Republican donor acknowledged the need for a government role in this area, explaining his view as follows: "I'm sure there's the lunatic fringe at the EPA, but I think that those are important governmental duties. . . . It's like the police. We have to have police for law and order. You need the EPA for making sure the pollution is not out of gear."

Further discussion with donors reveal that when they object to substituting government for philanthropy, they do so on the assumption that certain tasks are already part of government's responsibility. This underscores the importance of understanding how donors themselves define "philanthropy" and its scope. Some, for example, distinguish welfare from philanthropy. One man believes that his tax dollars go to buy food and clothes for people in need, which he regards as a government responsibility. By contrast, he said, "Philanthropy to me is the support of institutions, rather than life-or-death issues—the richness of one's life." Another donor emphasized that "welfare programs" are not the same thing as philanthropy, observing:

> I think they [government] have a very important place in welfare programs. There's no way private philanthropy can sustain the needs of our society. I think we're just supposed to fill in for the government. The government should take care of people's health. They should have minimum standards of housing, transportation, the supplying of vital services. They're too big even for cities and states.

This donor was no advocate of substituting governmental for private organizations, but thought that certain large-scale problems must be attended to by government.

On the other hand, donors felt it was important to take care that philanthropy not be used to address problems that exceed its capacity. The ability to "make a difference" was a guiding factor in the philanthropic choices of many donors. This reflects the greater sense of personal fulfillment such giving brings them, as well as their view that it represents the most efficient and wise use of philanthropic resources. Thus, one donor likes to give "where I can accomplish something," and another follows the principle, "Don't intrude into a field into which you can make no effective contribution." One man explained,

> I've always felt it was the right thing to give back something of the largesse that you make in this country. And so the most important thing is the sense of fulfillment that you are, in fact, doing something. That translates into particular ways of giving, which allow you to have the most effect with the money that you've got available to give.

A donor who likes "to get the biggest bang for my buck," reduced his donations to an organization when he became convinced that his gifts were no longer effective. He explained, "They're becoming so institutionalized in their fundraising that what I was giving had become irrelevant." In general, he avoids giving to large institutions he feels spend a great deal on bureaucracy and fundraising. In addition to being wasteful, he feels "no matter how much I give to them, it doesn't matter. It's just too unimportant. And there's just no way I can contribute anything to their purpose, or what they do, or the way they do it."[8]

As we have seen, donors want their philanthropy to make a difference. Furthermore, as much as they value philanthropy, they also recognize that it has its limitations, and that some tasks are so large that they are beyond its reach. Although they might wish it were otherwise, donors acknowledge that government is needed for, and better suited to dealing with, certain social problems and fields. Thus, donors do not advocate eliminating or even necessarily reducing government in favor of philanthropy. Rather, they object to a scenario in which government would become an exclusive source of authority and funds, and maintain the desirability of encouraging private involvement through philanthropy. As one respondent put it, he opposes putting all the money in "one pot."

Many others made similar comments, such as the donor who explained, "I like the interweaving. I don't like all the power being in the hands of a few people. It's best to have a balance. Government gets wicked, too." Another believes that the "American system is the best" because it combines philanthropic and governmental involvement. And one man thinks it is fine for government to initiate programs and organizations, but that it would be "terrible" to leave everything to government, adding that "our social system contravenes that completely." Another said, "It's important to have individuals in society making philanthropic decisions as opposed to a bureaucracy. . . . They can make them too. I'm not proposing to close the NIH or the cultural affairs committee. . . . There's a public and a private role. But I think the private role is very, very important."

Advocacy for having private and public involvement also emerged during discussions of corporate philanthropy. One donor felt that corporate giving is positive because "multiple donors" are needed, rather than having the government adjudicate everything. And another explained, "I think government and corporate giving have a joint responsibility. . . . I can't make that kind of distinction where corporations don't give at all and government takes full responsibility, or vice versa."

CRITICISMS OF PHILANTHROPY: DONOR REACTIONS

The historian Robert Bremner observes that Americans have traditionally exhibited mixed reactions to philanthropy among the wealthy. He writes,

> There is something about philanthropy that seems to go against the democratic grain. . . . We expect rich men to be generous with their wealth and criticize them when they are not; but when they make benefaction, we question their motives, deplore the methods by which they obtained their abundance, and wonder whether their gifts will not do more harm than good.[9]

We have already seen that donors recognize limitations in the scope of philanthropy, and we may now examine how they assess and respond to criticisms of elite philanthropy. The takeoff point for donors' comments was a series of negative statements about philanthropy that I presented to them. Their responses underscore how positive a view they hold of philanthropy. Anticipating that most would not wholeheartedly agree with the criticisms, I also asked whether they would even "agree somewhat" with each. Regardless, the majority of donors simply disagreed with most of the negative characterizations. A number, though, did feel there was some element of truth to them, usually in a modified or qualified form. None, however, accepted that any of the criticisms cast doubt on the basic character of philanthropy as a valuable social institution. The extended comments that donors made in connection with these statements are particularly informative. They show that although donors view negative traits as basic and defining characteristics of government, negative aspects of philanthropy are seen as exceptions or corruptions of the institution, reflective of individual donors rather than philanthropy itself, and are never regarded as overwhelming its basically positive consequences. A consideration of donors' reasoning on this subject provides further insights into how they understand and legitimate philanthropy.

Donors most widely and thoroughly rejected the notion that philanthropy discourages people from working and supporting themselves, and encourages idleness and dependency.[10] They dismissed this view with such responses as "gibberish," "idiotic," "sounds like a Reaganite," and "nonsense." One woman said she associates this outlook with attitudes from three hundred years ago. Some believed that this was merely an excuse given by "tightwads" to rationalize their failure to contribute. As one donor said, "I don't buy it. . . . It's a sop to their conscience. They are guilty because they don't give and so they say this."

For some, the organizational character of contemporary philanthropy made the criticism inapplicable. One woman responded that "philanthropy in New York doesn't give to people as much as to organizations. . . . It doesn't go directly to the person as a stipend." Another man argued, "That's Scrooge's argument! That's so old-fashioned people would laugh. Anyway, it's not realistic anymore. . . . You're not giving to the person who's actually going to use it, you're giving to these great corporate causes, with the idea that they're developing some enterprises. Getting people off the dole, rather than on it."

Similarly, other donors noted that they did not understand how the particular things supported by philanthropy could possibly have such deleterious effects. Some asked how contributing to a library or the arts could foster idleness or dependency. One man observed that scholarships, which he often supports, have just the opposite effect. Others said that criticism brings welfare to mind more than philanthropy. One donor felt, "That's more welfare giving than anything else," and another said, "Sounds more like government handouts or something. I can't think of a philanthropy that would produce that effect." And even a donor who believed the criticism has some truth, said, "You can't spend your life making rules for yourself based on a few who violate."

Donors were also asked to respond to the criticism that philanthropy is used as a cover for highly questionable and fraudulent activities. Most disagreed completely, but a number thought there was some truth to this, although they view it as the exception.[11] A number emphasized that donors have a responsibility to inform themselves about causes they support. Donors generally had few suspicions concerning the legitimacy of the organizations they personally support. Indeed, some of their impressions concerning the existence of fraud appeared to come from newspaper articles, particularly those concerning accusations of abuses of church funds by "televangelists" that were receiving considerable publicity at the time. In some cases, however, donors described personal experiences with fraudulent appeals. This was true of one man, who received a phone solicitation for an organization that sounded worthwhile. He decided not to contribute because the person requesting funds turned down his request for a brochure, and he later learned that it had not been a legitimate appeal. Another donor said he often requests a soliciting organization's Internal Revenue Service number to verify its authenticity, and "in some of these cases you don't hear from them again."

Donors, including those who agreed somewhat with the statement, believed that such cases were not characteristic. As one put it, "I'm sure it happens from time to time. But as a blanket statement, it's stupid." Some observed that reporting requirements and the attorney general's monitoring authority helped protect against abuses. Still others noted that some instances of fraud occurred in philanthropy, just as they occur in any area of social life, but did not see this as a particular problem of philanthropy. And one felt that this was yet another criticism used by people who do not contribute in order to "avoid their obvious responsibilities."

The other two criticisms presented to respondents focused on donors rather than recipients. The first was that philanthropy is closely associated with social snobbery. This was the sole criticism the majority of donors believed had some truth, even though they did not accept it as a general characterization.[12] Most who expressed some agreeement with the statement did so because they felt it was applicable to "glizty" fundraising benefits. One donor thought over the criticism and said, "Those who give by buying benefit tickets, yes. Those who give to general support of an organization, absolutely not." Another expressed it this way: "There is something to that. These big parties that some institutions run, where everybody comes dressed to his eyeballs and so on . . . what can you say? I think there's something to be said for that last thing, but I think it's a small percentage." After an initial hesitation, another donor agreed, because "just look at all the benefits and all the fancy dresses," which then appear in the paper "and people love it."

Some donors acknowledged the basis for the criticism, but maintained that this sort of giving is not "real philanthropy." One donor, for instance, knows someone who fits the criticism "perfectly," but believes that this is "a corruption of philanthropy." Another replied, "I would define philanthropy as the giving of money and time towards the accomplishment of a goal, not getting into shoes that hurt and [going out]."

Although many said they think it is unfortunate when philanthropy is done for status-related reasons, they clearly viewed the desire for prestige and social entrée as a useful mechanism for raising funds.[13] One donor said, "You work on that human failing," while another observed that "social snobbery is a device of fundraising." Similarly, many said it is better to give for other reasons, but thought it was fine if a desire for prestige encourages contributions, because the outcome is beneficial. One donor expressed a common perspective when she said, "Anything that motivates people to give is OK. If they wouldn't give otherwise, get 'em." Similarly, another believes that, "Whatever the motivation, if the end result is a good one, I would think that would be a perfectly fine motivator." Others contended that even people who are most identified with the "social" or "fashionable" aspects of philanthropy often devote a good deal of time to what they do, and are very effective at raising money to support important causes.

Some also objected that many donors give quietly and don't want publicity. One man emphasized that he and many others work "to keep our mugs out of the papers," and another said that in his experience, "the big money comes in quietly." One donor argued that the glitzier aspects of philanthropy attract greater publicity, and so appear to be more pervasive than is actually the case. He offered examples of various donors whose more "fashionable" involvements appear in the press, while their other philanthropic efforts go unreported. And another emphasized that neither the "social stuff" nor the other negative aspects of philanthropy, "vitiates the human need to improve the world a little bit. And as a general principle, philanthropy seems to me a good thing. There are faults with those who practice it, but they don't ruin the whole thing. And I don't think most people give money for any of these bad reasons."

The remaining criticism presented to donors was that philanthropy extends the power of the wealthiest over the rest of society. Most disagreed completely, but a number thought there was some truth to the statement in a modified or qualified form.[14] For instance, some thought the comment applies to restricted, but not unrestricted, donations. Some donors addressed the issue in terms of influence or "perks" gained by individual donors, rather than power gained by the wealthy over other groups. One man thus acknowledged that as a large donor to a hospital, he is in a position to help a friend obtain a room or better medical attention. And another agreed that philanthropy "is a means of extending the influence and taste" of the wealthy, but "wouldn't say it extends the power to keep anybody under your thumb. It might promote a more elitist approach to music and art than we would have without it."

Expressing a commonly held view, one donor observed that it is a "fact of life" that wealth brings power, but "it's not philanthropy per se." Similarly, another man argued that it's "a result of the fact that the wealthy tend to have power. It's not causal. It's the tail, not the dog." And one said, "I don't see the rich running society through philanthropy. There are other ways for them to do it." After noting that *influence* was a more appropriate term than *power,* one donor said, "There's probably some truth to that," but added, "The wealthiest are going to have a special—call it what you will—power or influence. And I'd rather have them having it for good, rather than bad."

Some of those who expressed some agreement argued that the influence enjoyed by wealthy donors was not necessarily bad, because the consequences of philanthropy are good. This was the view of a man who replied,

> That is not a fair comment. If the influence of people with money is directed to accomplishing things that have to be accomplished, that are socially important, what's wrong with that? . . . If you've got more money, you dispense more, and you have more influence. But it has to be thoughtful and it has to be done with purpose. . . . And if people have the money to give, it's much more important that they give it than they hold on to it and pass it along in their estates. To me that is a stupid criticism because what are the alternatives? Not giving? Or stupid giving?

Similarly, another responded,

> A lot of the wealth is generated through the private activity, and they have a right to spend some of it. Do individuals who have an undue amount of wealth exercise an undue amount of influence on how it's given to charities? Yes, they do. But I don't think that's bad for society. A great deal of good has been done for society by private philanthropy and it would be terrible if . . . all philanthropy were controlled by the government, or people who profess to know better than other people how to spend their money.

Some donors challenged that the implicit alternative advocated by this criticism was to give more power to government, which would be undesirable. One donor asked, "What are you going to have in its place? What do these people want in the place of philanthropy? They want the government to do it all. It's not going to happen in the fields that I tend to give to. . . . It's not in our American tradition. . . . I don't foresee any kind of change, short of revolution."

Various other objections were offered as well. Some argued that organizations and individuals other than the donor exert influence in philanthropy. One woman pointed to the importance of organizational professionals, noting that "they're not the people giving the money, and they're the people making the decisions." Another donor objected that much of philanthropy is administered by professionals, "who tolerate the rich donors. . . . The donors are important only for their money, not for their ideas." One man suggested that organizations hold the true power and co-opt donors to achieve their goals. Said he, "Maybe an institution reels in a wealthy individual who wants—who thinks—they can pull the levers of power. In a sense, absorbs them and their money for the work and the progress of what the institution is about, and had been about, before they found the donor."

Other donors believed that a variety of checks existed on the power that can be exerted through philanthropy, such as governmental requirements that nonprofits account for their expenditures and actions. One person argued that in democratic societies, if it "gets too out of line, the process imposes limits." Another felt that the comparatively small size of philanthropy, compared with the expenditures of government (and the country in general), limited the degree of influence channeled through philanthropy. Still others contended that philanthropy takes money out of the hands of donors, and objected that the causes supported by philanthropy would not serve to extend power. One person, for instance, said that philanthropy "opens doors," and asked how something like supporting a library would extend the power of the wealthy?

Finally, a number argued that it is social standing or recognition, more than power, that philanthropy brings donors. One man disagreed that philanthropy brings power, but said he could agree that it enhances "*social* power" as seen by the "refined little group" who give to "buy their social acceptance." One woman thought that philanthropy does not increase the power of the wealthy with respect to other members of society, but might give "some members of the upper class power over other members of the upper class . . . maybe knowing more people, or knowing more important people." And one donor dismissed the criticism, by saying: "Baloney! I used to be a leftist. That's all leftist baloney. . . . Philanthropy is a way for somebody to make themselves feel good. They made a big buck, and they finished with that, and they proved themselves. Now they've got to do something else. Prove themselves again."

Donors' responses to all the criticisms reveal their essentially positive view of philanthropy. Their reactions to the last two negative characterizations are of particular interest because they ask donors to address the potentially elitist dimensions of philanthropy. Donors' recognized these and acknowledged that because they command more resources, the wealthy are privileged in philanthropy, as they are in other spheres. Thus one woman said philanthropy is elitist because "those of us who are able to do it in the biggest way, are those of us who are economically at the top of the ladder. But I don't think philanthropy is in and of itself elitist." As this comment illustrates, donors also refuse to essentially characterize philanthropy as an independent tool for maintaining the privileged position of elites. Their reasons range from the idealistic belief that most donors genuinely want to do something of benefit, to the more pragmatic observation that the wealthy will enjoy privilege with or without philanthropy.

Donors do recognize that philanthropy brings returns to philanthropists as well as to recipients. They are well aware that benefits, testimonials, plaques, and namings (e.g., of buildings) variously give donors a chance to show off, enhance their visibility, make connections, and socialize with their peers. They distinguish philanthropy from other uses of money, however, because they characterize it as being of intrinsic value and social benefit. As one donor wryly observed, "There's a lot of social snobbery that is not dignified by giving." Thus, donors do not characterize wealthy nondonors as individuals who miss an opportunity to enhance their own interests, but as people who are cheap and fail to live up to their responsibilities.

Certainly, some would disagree with these donors' claims about the contributions of elite philanthropy. Regardless, it is important to emphasize that donors do defend philanthropy in terms of its societal value. Many were confident that, on its consequences, philanthropy would be judged as positive, and certainly superior to the alternative of exclusive governmental responsibility. Their insistence on the social benefits of philanthropy complements their individualistic position that people should be allowed to determine the uses of their funds. It is both the social and the individualistic rationale that lies at the basis of elite philanthropy and its justification.

CONCLUSION

There is a more general perspective underlying the diversity of philanthropy, which gives unity and meaning to philanthropy as an institution, regardless of its particular sources (such as gender or ethnicity) or direction (such as culture or social services). Donors defend the importance and legitimacy of philanthropy in terms of a pluralistic view of society in which power is dispersed among governmental and private parties. They maintain that because of the limits of government, and the merits of philanthropy, society benefits from their coexistence. The alternative, in their mind, is a system in which government gains an exclusive, and consequently dangerous, degree of power. These convictions represent a set of basic understandings and values concerning how society should be organized, and the place of individuals within society.

The central themes expressed by donors, including distrust of government power and bureaucracy, skepticism about governmental competence, and enthusiasm for private initiative and input through channels outside of government, are not peculiar to the elite. They are concerns and beliefs found more broadly in American society. Survey results reveal greater faith in the effectiveness of voluntary organizations than in government programs on the part of the American public. Fully 72 percent of respondents to a survey conducted by Robert Wuthnow during the late 1980s believed that "private charities are generally more effective than government programs." This same survey also found there was public receptivity to increasing the influence of nonprofit organizations, but that people felt that politicians already have too much influence in society.[15] These findings testify to the widespread support for philanthropy that exists in this country. This favorable attitude toward private initiative and private nonprofit organizations may help to explain the endurance of the charitable tax deduction. Although legislation has periodically been introduced to correct perceived abuses, the law has remained fundamentally encouraging of philanthropic activity.[16]

Thus, in their philanthropy, elites share and respond to widely held attitudes in American society. Taken together, this chapter and earlier ones underscore the fact that the sources of elites' philanthropy are to be found both inside and outside their own group. The basic rationale for philanthropy in general comes from broader values and attitudes in American society. The particular nature, meaning, and organization of philanthropy among wealthy donors, however, is shaped by the culture and organization of the elite. Giving and volunteering among elites, accordingly, may be viewed as an adaptation, in and to a particular social class context, of a more widespread set of cultural norms and activities. Indeed, even within the elite, part of the reason that philanthropy confers prestige is that donors believe they are engaging in more than a mere status ritual of their class, by also doing something of social benefit that enjoys widespread esteem.[17] In this respect, philanthropy may be a mark of status that is particularly appropriate for elites in a society that stresses egalitarian, democratic values. Somewhat cynically, one might say that their philanthropy is conducted in such a way that elites can enjoy the sense that they are making a contribution to society without actually having to interact with members of that society outside of their class.[18]

Donors' comments testify to the high regard in which they view philanthropy. Although they acknowledge the more dubious motives behind some contributions and the importance of appealing to these in fundraising, donors maintain a definition of philanthropy as an essentially positive activity. Thus, donors sometimes distinguished between giving that is and is not "true" philanthropy. One of the times this distinction emerged was during discussions of corporate philanthropy. One donor said that when companies give in order to enhance their public image, "it is not philanthropy, it's public relations." Another explained that out of business considerations, his own company gives as a "goodwill gesture," but this is "not driven by philanthropy." Such comments testify to donors' view that philanthropy among individuals is basically or primarily tied to a genuine desire to do good, which they contrast with the ulterior motives that guide corporations. They also illustrate donors' awareness of the high public esteem in which philanthropy is held, showing how they try to draw on it in order to help their business. Further evidence of this latter point was seen when another donor explained that his company gives in communities where they have a business interest, in the hope that their residents will "think we're great people."

As much as they value philanthropy, donors also believe it has limitations, particularly with respect to dealing with large-scale social concerns. Albeit grudgingly, they often recognized that the very characteristics of government they distrust, such as large size and bureaucratization, made it the only feasible mechanism for addressing certain problems.[19] Some of donors' observations about the limitations of philanthropy are similar to the historical weaknesses of the nonprofit sector identified by research in this area. Moreover, donors' attitudes and convictions illustrate why philanthropy cannot function as a viable alternative to government in a complex society. Although donors feel an obligation to support worthwhile causes (and engage in philanthropy generally), they believe they have the right to choose the causes they wish to support. Their choices reflect their personal interests and concerns, as well as their ideas about the abilities and limits of philanthropy.

Donors exhibit a distinct preference for supporting projects and organizations where they believe that philanthropy, preferably their own donations, can make a difference. This means there is a disincentive to directing philanthropy toward the most pervasive, large-scale social problems.[20] We can thus see why, as Salamon has observed, a "central failing of the voluntary system as a provider of collective goods has been its inability to generate resources on a scale that is both adequate enough and reliable enough to cope with the human service problems of an advanced industrial society."[21]

This does not mean that wealthy individuals never give to causes related to large-scale problems, but rather that their major philanthropic efforts are focused on areas and organizations where they feel knowledgeable, involved, and able to have an impact. In taking this approach, many donors are following the same logic they use in their business decisions, by seeking to invest their money where it can have the "greatest payoff." At the same time, this orientation reflects the way in which philanthropic decisions may be subject to considerations of individual ego and prestige, for donors surely enjoy a greater sense of personal efficacy and public recognition when making gifts with a greater impact.[22] Even donors whose contributions were not large enough to command that level of recognition or impact tried to focus their gifts to avoid a sense that they were just being frittered away. For instance, rather than make twenty-five dollar gifts to many similar organizations, donors would select one institution and make a larger donation. In this way, they could feel that their gift was more important for the existence of at least one particular organization.

Whether consciously or not, we can clearly see that donors define the boundaries of philanthropy (and the responsibilities of government) in a way that essentially legitimates them in following their own personal preferences when making donations. After all, some would surely object that the greater social contribution lies in giving to pressing large-scale problems, even though the donor might have to sacrifice a valued sense of personal efficacy. Philanthropy, in short, allows elites to enjoy the sense that they are making a contribution to society, while defining social benefit on their own terms. Accordingly, support for causes that the individual donor, or the larger elite, value and want to see sustained, is elevated to the stature of doing good.

The findings of this chapter show the importance of distinguishing donors' own outlook from the way that philanthropy's role is frequently depicted in political discourse. These interviews were conducted during the Reagan era, a time of government cutbacks in which the private sector was being asked to take up greater responsibility from government. Yet donors themselves were often critical of government cutbacks, and distinguished between governmental and private responsibilities. As we have seen, they quite consciously stayed away from certain areas, such as large-scale social problems, viewing them as the responsibility of government. Their lack of interest in, if not outright rejection of, the Reagan-era call for the private sector to take over from government reflects their general attitude toward philanthropy. Donors do not feel obligated to assume tasks that they see as governmental responsibilities. Indeed, the very idea that politicians should guide their philanthropic decisions runs directly counter to their very understanding of philanthropy. The fact that donors essentially said no to the Reagan-era proposal further illustrates that philanthropy cannot function as a substitute for government. Donors have their own philanthropic agendas and are not generally interested in redirecting them to take up tasks previously assumed by government.

The fact that wealthy donors feel free to direct their donations to those causes that correspond to their interests and priorities suggests an additional reason that philanthropy cannot function as a substitute for government. An obvious result is that organizations not connected to elite networks and interests or not deemed worthy of support by members of the elite will be at a disadvantage.[23] Thus the very nature of elite philanthropy suggests that it will not address many issues and needs in a balanced way. In this respect, there is a tension between the individualistic sources of philanthropy and its social purposes.

CONCLUSION

THIS BOOK has asked why wealthy donors engage in philanthropy. Philanthropy itself comprises many diverse activities, influences, and people. Our final picture of elite philanthropy must therefore avoid oversimplification without becoming so engulfed in the complexities that we lose sight of general patterns. To understand why the wealthy give, moreover, it is necessary to consider the basic meaning of philanthropy to donors themselves, because the very incentives for philanthropic participation are intimately rooted in the meaning that it holds among the wealthy. Furthermore, philanthropy itself is much more than the concrete act of giving or volunteering; it also includes a whole set of shared meanings and assumptions, beliefs and values. Accordingly, I have considered philanthropy from different vantage points, looking at what unites and differentiates donors and forms of giving, scrutinizing behavior and beliefs, and analyzing the different levels at which philanthropy operates, including the individual and social, symbolic and organizational. We may now integrate and assess the conclusions.

PHILANTHROPY, STATUS, AND ELITE CULTURE

In their basic understanding and defense of philanthropy, wealthy donors share and make reference to broad themes in American society. Individualism, private initiative, suspicion of governmental power and bureaucracy—these are the underlying values and attitudes in terms of which philanthropy takes on meaning as a social institution. The existence of such a framework is important, for it is not obvious or necessary that philanthropy be valued by elites or anyone else. This point is well illustrated by the fact that introducing tax incentives for giving has not automatically resulted in fostering comparable levels of philanthropy in other countries.[1] Elites largely champion philanthropy as a beneficial *social* institution, indicative of the fact that it is deeply connected to certain conceptions of how society should be organized. Thus, I have argued that it is critical to distinguish the particular phenomenon of philanthropy, and its specific institutional manifestations, from the more general issue of altruism or helping behavior. Generosity can take many different forms, and what we must understand are the particular social institutions that exist and are encouraged for channeling generosity, and how these are maintained. To do this requires understanding the ideological and social foundations of philanthropic activities.

The assumptions and attitudes underlying philanthropy—and philanthropy itself—are not unique to the elite. Rather, in the rationales they offer for philanthropy, elites share in broader themes and values in American society. This is often seen as well in their defense of philanthropy. Many of donors' comments resemble general statements about the value of helping and sharing that are not that different from what one hears regularly on television around Christmastime, or in the wake of a disaster.

There is, however, more to elite philanthropy that is very much related to its specific class context. This emerges when we move from the basic rationale for philanthropy to examine how it is conducted, and the meaning, significance, and prestige that the practice takes on within the elite. If the fundraisers and exclusive exhibits and performances were to end, if donors' evaluations of nonprofit organizations were not shaped by elite prestige hierarchies, and if elites were to volunteer in more class heterogeneous settings, elite philanthropy would become a very different activity indeed. Elites take philanthropy and adapt it into an entire way of life that serves as a vehicle for the cultural and social life of their class, overlaying it with additional values and norms. Philanthropy thus comes to function as a mark of class status that is connected to elite identity. In this respect, it resembles other marks of class status, such as aesthetic appreciation, which also bind group members together and differentiate them from others.

Equally important is that philanthropy differs from other marks of class status. Groups typically attempt to monopolize indicators of status for themselves and seek to prevent their appropriation by outsiders.[2] This monopolization strengthens the identification of the status symbol with that individual group. Philanthropic giving and volunteering are not specifically elite activities, either in practice or in terms of symbolic associations. Philanthropy is not associated with the elite in the same fashion as, say, involvement with high culture. The identification between philanthropy and elite status does not stem from the actual or symbolic monopolization of philanthropy as an activity. Rather, its ability to function as a mark of class status is based on the way in which it is conducted, where elites do carve out a separate and exclusive arena for themselves. In elite philanthropy, a set of values and activities are taken from the broader society and given a distinctive meaning within a specific class context. Moreover, the specific kinds of donations made and volunteer work done by elites is deeply influenced by the distinctively class-based adaptation of philanthropy.

The widespread esteem enjoyed by philanthropy makes it a particularly appropriate mark of class status for an elite in a society that stresses democratic, egalitarian values. I have also argued that elite philanthropy shows us something important about the nature and functioning of upper-class culture in the United States. Some have observed that American culture has been dominated by the middle class and that a genuinely upper-class culture has not developed.[3] Indeed, the United States does lack the aristocratic traditions and sharply defined class distinctions found in societies such as England. The case of philanthropy, however, has shown that American elites do fashion a separate cultural world for themselves by drawing on, and reformulating, elements and values from the broader society. Thus, within the context of a middle-class culture lacking a strong aristocratic tradition, elites nonetheless construct distinctive cultures out of elements of the larger society. In doing so, elites both connect themselves to, and differentiate themselves from, the larger society. There are continuities in the nature of philanthropy within the upper class and outside of it, but the way it is conducted and its function as a symbol of class membership is distinctive to the elite. More generally, this indicates that future research is needed not only to establish what is unique in the culture of elite groups, but also to carefully scrutinize cultural practices that appear to cut across class lines, in order to see whether they take on different meanings in different class contexts.

The boundaries surrounding the world of elite philanthropy are, to a large extent, maintained by the simple necessity of having large sums of money in order to participate.[4] Those who cannot afford the cost of a lavish benefit cannot attend, and those who cannot contribute enough will not have access to events arranged exclusively for larger donors. Furthermore, boards of directors select their own members, so that decisions about board composition and the criteria for selecting new members are in the hands of those who currently serve. This is conducive to maintaining the class homogeneity of those boards composed largely of elites. Current board members' social networks are more likely to lead them to know of, and select, other members of their class. Furthermore, to the extent that such factors as ability to contribute or raise money, corporate affiliations, certain kinds of professional expertise, or political connections are considered vital, the very criteria used in board recruitment will clearly favor the selection of members of the elite.[5]

CRITICISMS OF ELITE PHILANTHROPY

Elites are sometimes perceived more as corrupters than practitioners of philanthropy by those outside their class. Volunteers outside the elite and popular stereotypes often depict elite philanthropy as superficial and frivolous. From this perspective, the willingness of the wealthy to become involved does not extend much beyond going to fashionable fundraisers. Such attitudes were expressed, for instance, by volunteers studied by Robert Wuthnow. He found that those who "dirty their hands daily in the trenches" recognized the importance of wealthy patrons to organizations, but were irritated by their "casual and seemingly superficial assistance." For example, one woman spoke of volunteering for a program where the wealthy were willing to serve as trustees, but not to "really get involved."[6]

Such perceptions contrast radically with the way in which wealthy donors themselves experience their philanthropy. For so many of these donors, a deep sense of involvement with particular organizations is the very motivation, and even precondition, for their larger donations. From their perspective, moreover, board membership represents the height of involvement and identification with an organization. As board members, they do not see themselves as detached, but as functioning at the very "core" of an organization, dealing with major decisions and policies. Similarly, the affluent attorneys and business people who donate their professional services to organizations would surely object that they are indeed giving of themselves. Donors are well aware of the social aspects of philanthropy, which some also criticized. Yet those (generally women) who invest considerable time and energy in organizing benefits, would see all their logistical work and planning as "working in the trenches" to produce events that raise so much money for organizations.

The characterizations of volunteers outside the elite and popular stereotypes do, however, correspond to certain truths about elite philanthropy. In particular, they reflect the separate and exclusive nature of elite philanthropy that we have discussed. It is not that the wealthy are unconcerned with the organizations they support, or unwilling to give of their time. Clearly, many were deeply committed to the causes they supported, and maintained their commitments over very long periods. What is true, however, is that the elite do keep their distance, and remain apart, in their philanthropy. In essence, their philanthropy is an extension of, not a departure from, their general existence as elites. Their participation in nonprofit organizations parallels their participation in the business world—they are at the top.

Although there were exceptions, the volunteer work of these wealthy donors typically focused on serving organizational entities rather than directly and personally assisting people. Thus, serving on a hospital board was a typical volunteer activity, but this was not true of working with patients. Affluent volunteers serve in capacities that involve them in issues of policy, planning, and decision making at the highest organizational levels. As board members, for instance, they participate in hiring and firing the institution's director. Fundraising, organizing benefits, and serving on advisory committees, as well as board membership, were also characteristic activities. The people with whom the wealthy deal in such volunteer roles tend to be their social and business peers, and the organization's top professional personnel. In short, many wealthy donors care about the organizations that they support, but in the ways in which they involve themselves and demonstrate their support, they function in a separate and privileged arena—as elites. The boundaries separating the elite from others are not ones that the wealthy are generally any more interested in crossing or blurring in philanthropy than they are elsewhere.

Critics of the nature of the recipients of elite donations also suggest that the wealthy corrupt, rather than practice, philanthropy. The wealthy have been criticized for failing to give more to the poor, and for favoring causes such as cultural and educational organizations.[7] Such criticism assumes that redistribution is a basic aim of philanthropy and criterion by which it should be measured. These are assumptions that others have recently questioned.[8] This study shows that although wealthy donors believe philanthropic gifts should have a public benefit, they do not equate it with redistribution for the poor. Indeed, they view gifts to hospitals, museums, and the broader range of philanthropic institutions as equally legitimate. Some wealthy individuals, such as Carnegie, have even rejected the notion that the role of philanthropy was to provide aid for the destitute.[9] In general, affluent donors often argued that philanthropy was best suited for handling smaller-scale issues than large-scale social problems. In this respect, we have seen that affluent donors define the boundaries of philanthropy (and, by contrast, the responsibilities of government) in a way that validates them in following their own preferences when making donations. Many donors ardently defended the social value of philanthropy. Yet the way in which they interpret philanthropy allows them to enjoy the sense that they are making a contribution to society while defining social benefit on their own terms.

Evidence indicates that whether consciously or not, the above orientation toward support for the poor is not confined to the wealthy, since a comparatively small amount of philanthropy in general is directed to the poor.[10] In supporting museums and universities, members of the elite may well be doing what others also do in their philanthropy—supporting the organizations with which they are involved. It is the consequences (such as giving to the arts rather than to churches) that differ. Whether philanthropy should go to the poor, and whether it is desirable to provide tax deductions if it does not, are questions of value and opinion. In assessing the contributions and the failings of philanthropy in practice, however, it is important to keep in mind what its definition has been in practice, and what it is that donors themselves have believed they are doing. This is equally important to keep in mind with respect to ideas concerning the relative willingness or ability of private philanthropy to pick up funding responsibilities of government. While some may conceptualize private and governmental sources as substitutable, we have clearly seen that donors themselves are generally committed to personal philanthropic agendas, and neither want nor believe they should reorient these in order to take up tasks previously assumed by government.

ELITE DIFFERENTIATION AND PHILANTHROPIC DIFFERENTIATION

Elites construct a separate and relatively insular philanthropic world for themselves. Compared with those who are not members of the elite, the wealthy donors in that world are quite similar. From an intra-elite perspective, however, they are far from a homogeneous or tightly knit group. Although all are affluent, they are differentiated by other distinctions and hierarchies. Major themes of this book have been that elites and philanthropy are both heterogeneous phenomena, and that elite differentiation is associated with variations in philanthropic choices. A consideration of the particular variations that exist revealed a larger pattern. Specifically, internal distinctions and hierarchies within the elite are carried over into the distinctions and hierarchies within philanthropy itself. Moreover, they are distinctions that serve as a source of the donor's identity.

Variations in philanthropic patterns further illustrate that philanthropy responds to influences both inside and outside the elite. For instance, distinctive patterns of giving among Jewish donors reflect Jewish philanthropic traditions as well as the significance of ethnicity as a status barrier within the elite. Similarly, elite women's donations respond to wider societal conceptions of gender roles and women's philanthropic traditions, but are also influenced by the way in which gender functions as an organizing principle within the elite.

This emphasis on elite differentiation is fully consistent with and complements my characterization of philanthropy as an expression of elite culture and identity. I have argued that donor identity is a key factor in shaping philanthropic choices. Donors are not only members of the elite, but also potentially hold multiple group identities and affiliations (in addition to that associated with their class) and participate in subgroup traditions that cut across class lines. A central issue is which of these affiliations donors actually will identify with and express through their philanthropy. It is a choice that influences whether donors will support specific causes affiliated with particular subgroups, as well as the degree of variety present in their major donations. In the social elite, where class identity tends to overwhelm other associations, major giving is far more exclusively focused on the prestigious areas of education and culture. By contrast, the presence and strength of alternative identities is a major factor in other donors' willingness to deviate from the prestige hierarchy of their class, as seen in the major giving of women and Jewish donors.

The significance of particular affiliations within the elite affects the strategic choices of donors. Elite philanthropy functions as an organized social arena, and individuals' donations and volunteering are related to their advancement within that world, such as to valued board positions. If people believe they will face barriers at certain organizations (because of ethnicity, gender, or other reasons), they may be more inclined to make their philanthropic investments elsewhere. Individuals' relationships to particular affiliations also varies according to their position in the elite. The fact that social elite membership overshadowed ethnic and religiously linked patterns of giving suggests that donors' philanthropy is more likely to be expressive of those of their affiliations that have the greater prestige in the elite.

Because of the variations that exist, generalizations made either on the basis of patterns in the elite as a whole, or on the basis of one particular elite subgroup, are likely to convey a distorted picture. This certainly applies to conclusions about philanthropic priorities and the distribution of gifts. Looking at donors in the aggregate, for instance, we would conclude that religious congregations are rarely recipients of major gifts. Yet when we break them down, we find that this does not hold for Protestant donors. Similarly, it would be true to say that culture and education are the near exclusive focus of major giving within the social elite. It would not, however, be true of women or Jews, who also commonly support the social services (chosen by Jewish donors even slightly more than culture). Because the impact of some affiliations or characteristics varies depending on others, we must take care even when generalizing about subgroups. For example, to characterize women's giving on the basis of married women's donations would also be misleading. In short, when offering conclusions about elite philanthropy, it is critical to distinguish among donors, and specify which groups are being discussed.

Differentiating donors into subgroups, moreover, permits us to discover the truly common patterns that cut across groups. Simultaneous consideration of the commonalities and differences enhances our understanding of how philanthropy functions in relation to elite culture and organization. In particular, we have seen that not all subgroups are equal with respect to philanthropy. A prestige hierarchy exists in philanthropy that reflects the prestige hierarchy in the elite. The priorities of the social elite not only are relevant within that group but also serve as a wider reference point. Thus the cultural and educational institutions valued by the social elite enjoy widespread prestige among the broader elite as well. These common values contribute to defining a distinctive and shared culture of philanthropy among the elite.

The concept of "philanthropy" also needs to be disaggregated. In certain respects, it is legitimate to view philanthropy in a unified fashion, for there are underlying political, social, and cultural attitudes that cut across the diversity of giving and volunteering. Once we examine how philanthropy is actually conducted, however, we must go beyond the general concept. I have differentiated philanthropy according to area of activity. The results confirm the usefulness of this approach. Area of activity contributes to defining the meaning, attraction, and prestige of various philanthropic involvements to donors. Moreover, variation exists in the factors that influence giving to different areas. The same holds true for board membership, where social elite membership, for instance, was influential in culture, but not elsewhere. An important area for additional research would be to look further at how giving and volunteering is shaped by organizational developments in different fields.

Some of my findings indicate that area of activity may have a differing importance for various kinds of donations. Donors made individual gifts to the arts, for instance, as part of a general cultural involvement. Yet gifts to education largely reflected commitments to particular colleges and universities. Such findings suggest the usefulness of additional research on the nature and sources of philanthropic involvements with specific kinds of organizations, such as colleges. In general, differentiating philanthropy by area complements, and should not preclude, analysis of the particular recipients of gifts within areas.

CONTINUITY AND CHANGE IN ELITE PHILANTHROPY

Elite philanthropy has evolved and changed, but this change has occurred within the context of a larger continuity. Although the position of particular members of the elite may have weakened, the institution of elite philanthropy itself remains strong. It has proved resilient in the face of considerable change within the elite, the nonprofit world, and New York City. A basic insight of elite theory is that elites and their institutions must change to survive, a process that includes rejuvenation through the assimilation of new people. The findings of this book indicate that this was precisely what occurred during the 1980s in the world of elite philanthropy in New York City.

Former boundaries in elite philanthropy shifted and weakened. Membership in the core status group of the elite remains a valuable asset, but those in the social elite must increasingly share valued board positions with others, by whom they may be outnumbered. Contributing large sums, for example, facilitated access to boards as well, regardless of the donor's affiliation with the social elite. Thus, advantages as well as impediments based on status declined.

Elite philanthropy has, however, remained *elite* philanthropy. It continues to be exclusive with respect to those outside the elite, and its character and role within the elite has endured. There has been a fundamental continuity of values among the participants, even as there has been a shift in their composition or prominence. The newly wealthy and the formerly excluded shared the priorities of previously established elites and valued similar organizations. The philanthropic values of the social elite function as a reference point for the broader elite. This provides an important and basic source of continuity to elite philanthropy. Although the relative dominance of the members of the social elite may have declined in philanthropy, their values have not been rejected, but have been universalized and institutionalized within the larger elite.

In discussing intra-elite boundaries within philanthropy, I have emphasized that while intimately connected, philanthropy and broader elite organization and culture cannot be equated. In particular, the intra-elite boundaries in philanthropy have proved to be more permeable than those within the broader elite. This contrast, I have argued, highlights the tensions in philanthropy's ability to serve as a mark of class status.

Philanthropy has also continued to maintain its basic role as the elite has undergone change. The basis of elite status has increasingly shifted from family and community to organization.[11] In philanthropy, managers chosen on the basis of their corporate position, rather than family ties or social status, have increasingly been joining the ranks of trustees.[12] Yet the use that elites make of philanthropy within their group has endured. Indeed, to the extent that the elite is becoming a more atomized collection of corporate managers,[13] philanthropy's role may become even more important. In an elite whose members are less likely to be drawn from a closely integrated group, philanthropy may assume particular importance in providing a shared culture, identity, and setting for interaction outside of business. Furthermore, because the boundaries in philanthropy are more fluid than those within the elite itself, philanthropy may further facilitate elite integration by providing a common meeting ground for more separate segments of the elite.[14]

Continuity in the nature of philanthropy's function within the elite has also been fostered by the ways in which exclusivity has been maintained under changed organizational circumstances. Even as nonprofits' services are utilized by growing numbers of people, and they move into commercial ventures at odds with more clublike, former ways of operating, elites carve out a separate world for themselves by the way they organize their philanthropy. Through charity benefits, board memberships, private events open only to large donors, and related mechanisms, elites maintain a separate relationship and sense of identification with the nonprofits they value.

Dynamics of continuity and change in elite philanthropy are also shaped by the organizational character of contemporary elite philanthropy itself. Tensions between the financial needs of nonprofit institutions and class-based status concerns are virtually inherent to contemporary elite philanthropy. A central conclusion of this study is that, ultimately, more entrenched members of the elite were willing to open up the doors to "outsiders" in order to preserve the organizations they value. This conclusion need not presuppose any inordinate degree of rationality, omniscience, or coordination among the elite. The concern and behavior of donors, fundraisers, and board members toward the organizations with which they are involved is sufficient. I refer here particularly to the willingness of members of a board to admit new trustees able to make large donations, whom they might otherwise prefer to exclude. We can thus see that board membership does represent more than just a status game to participants, who have feelings of loyalty and responsibility to the organizations they oversee. It further shows that organizations are not merely conduits for philanthropy or intermediaries between individual donors and beneficiaries, but are themselves the focal point of donors' interests and concerns. It would be interesting to further scrutinize the conclusion that I have drawn by examining whether organizations that suffered financially and otherwise during the same period had boards that were unwilling to open their doors and lower former barriers.

In the face of the numerous developments of the 1970s and 1980s, elites and elite philanthropy adapted and endured. Yet while old barriers have weakened, others remain, and new ones can develop. The relative importance of time, money, and status as resources in elite philanthropy shifted during the 1980s, but can shift again. Elite philanthropy does not exist in a vacuum. As the nonprofit world, New York City, and the nature of the elite itself evolve, we must continue to follow the balance between continuity and change in elite philanthropy.

METHODOLOGICAL APPENDIX

THE TWO-STAGE sampling procedure used in this study is described in the Introduction. This Appendix provides additional information to supplement that discussion.[1]

THE ORGANIZATIONAL SAMPLE

The areas of activity from which to select organizations were determined in two stages. First, a set of categories was developed, based on existing classifications of nonprofit organizations.[2] These preliminary categories were deliberately broad and intended to be as inclusive as possible. They were then revised and refined based on reviews of lists of large organizations in New York City.[3]

The primary source used to identify large New York City nonprofit organizations was the New York State tape distributed by the National Center for Charitable Statistics of Independent Sector in Washington, D.C.[4] Since the tape includes nonprofit organizations in many areas of activity, it was particularly suitable for my purposes.[5] The tape did not, however, contain information on universities in New York, so it was supplemented with information from *Voluntary Support of Education.*[6] Where available, other specialized sources were also consulted to verify and, if necessary, supplement the New York State tape.[7] Selection of organizations was made from those with at least $2 million in operating expenditures, and $2 million in total annual private contributions.[8]

As noted, most organizations (75 percent) were willing to provide donor lists. Of the sixteen organizations that refused, one did provide a list of donors, but the baseline contribution size was too low for the purposes of identifying large donors. Two organizations indicated that they do not receive many large gifts from individuals and did not have the data available. The remaining thirteen indicated that they do not publish this information, and they also felt that they could not make it available for the study.

THE DONOR SAMPLE

The interviews with the formal sample of eighty-eight donors were conducted during 1988; the eleven pretests were conducted during 1987. As noted earlier, these eighty-eight donors represent a response rate of

80 percent. Of the twenty-two individuals who declined to be interviewed, thirteen said they had no time or simply did not care to participate, three said they did not wish to discuss philanthropy because it was a private matter, two cited poor health, one cited a recent death in the family, and three cited travel out of the country for extended periods.

NOTES

INTRODUCTION

1. Payton 1989.

2. Legally, these are contributions to private nonprofit institutions eligible to receive tax deductible donations, as defined by Section 501(c)3 of the Internal Revenue Code. A broad category, it includes, among other things, institutions organized for "religious, charitable, scientific, testing for public safety, literary, or educational purposes" (Simon 1987, p. 69; see also Salamon 1992, p. 29).

3. For an extended recent example, see Odendahl 1990; for an early work in this tradition, see Lundberg 1937; for recent efforts to ascertain the redistributional effects of the nonprofit sector, see Clotfelter 1992; for commentators who question or disagree with the assumption that redistribution is a primary aim of the nonprofit sector, see Aaron 1992, pp. 242–243; Cnaan 1993; James 1992, p. 255; Levy 1992, p. 261. As an aside, it may be noted that actual redistributional effects have turned out to be quite difficult, if not impossible, to determine (see Clotfelter 1992; Simon 1987, pp. 84–85).

4. See Bremner 1977; Payton 1989; Simon 1987.

5. Bremner 1977, p. 99.

6. James 1992, p. 255; Jencks 1987, p. 322; Ostrander 1989, p. 221.

7. Schervish and Herman 1988, p. 157.

8. For particular historical examples, see Bremner 1977; DiMaggio 1982; Hall 1982; Jaher 1982; McCarthy 1982; Story 1980; Tomkins (1970) 1989.

9. Bellah et al. 1985.

10. The identification of such activities, institutions, and mechanisms has been a major component of elite research. Prominent examples include prep schools and social clubs (Baltzell 1964; Cookson and Persell 1985; Domhoff 1970, 1974, 1983; Useem 1980). Research on culture reveals that arts participation serves a similar role (DiMaggio 1982; DiMaggio and Useem 1978, 1982). As researchers have recognized, these kinds of activities and organizations can have consequences for other domains, with elite cohesiveness facilitating unity of action in other spheres such as business and politics (Domhoff 1983). For other discussions of various aspects of philanthropic activities (such as charity benefits, board membership) that bear on elite solidarity, see also, e.g., Daniels 1988; Odendahl 1990; Useem 1980.

11. Schervish 1992, p. 332.

12. These themes are not confined to the elite but are found more generally in American society, as Wuthnow's (1991) study of volunteers and Bellah and his associates' (1985) exploration of American individualism demonstrate. They are discussed in greater detail in chapter 6.

13. This is seen in comparative studies of culture (see Montias 1982; Schuster 1985a, 1985b).

14. Similar considerations apply if philanthropy is viewed as a mechanism for the attainment of more self-serving ends, for we are still left asking why indi-

viduals pursue their interests through certain social channels rather than others. Generosity and self-interest undoubtedly exist among elites of all countries, and consideration must be given to the social institutions into which these are channeled.

15. Lundberg 1937; Odendahl 1990.

16. For instance, much giving in the United States goes to religious congregations (Salamon 1992; White 1989), most of whose expenditures go to provide services for congregation members (Biddle 1992; Jencks 1987). Estelle James concludes that "when people make voluntary payments to nonprofit organizations, they generally do so with the object of getting some private benefit in return" (1992, p. 255).

17. For an extensive discussion of prestige as an incentive in fundraising and giving, see Galaskiewicz's study of corporate philanthropy (1985). See also Daniels's discussion in her study of women volunteers (1988). The subject is given further attention in the next chapter.

18. Blau (1964) 1986. In the case of giving among the wealthy, these may be organizations or programs in organizations started by donors themselves.

19. DiMaggio and Useem 1982. This last point is also important because it emphasizes the need to consider the boundaries of organizational exclusivity from the vantage point of donors themselves. Odendahl argues that philanthropy serves the self-interest of wealthy donors, benefiting the rich and middle class to a greater extent than the poor (1990). From the perspective of elites, however, a greater openness of nonprofit institutions with respect to even the middle class may clearly be in tension with their "elite" character. The fact that many nonprofit organizations have become more open in this respect raises important questions about the continued interest of elites in supporting these causes, considered in this book.

20. Phillips 1990.

21. The New York Public Library increased its maximum board size from twenty-five to thirty-five in the mid-1970s, and then to forty-two during the mid-1980s (Dain 1991). Carnegie Hall, the New York City Ballet, and the Metropolitan Opera all enlarged the size of their boards as well. Carnegie Hall went from twenty-eight board members in the early 1970s to forty-two by the early 1980s, and forty-seven by the early 1990s. The New York City Ballet board grew from twenty-six members in the early 1980s to thirty-six by the early 1990s. The Metropolitan Opera reorganized its board into various subcategories, increasing overall board size from forty-four in the early 1970s to seventy-eight by the early 1980s, and eighty-two in the mid-1990s. I have gathered these figures from the following sources: New York City Ballet (performance, programs for January 1982 and June 1992); Carnegie Hall (performance programs for September 1972, October 1982, and May 1992); Metropolitan Opera (performance programs for September 1972, March 1982, and April 1992). Those listed as ex-officio, emeritus, or honorary trustees are not included in these figures. A trend toward larger board size has also been found in other cities (Abzug 1993; Abzug et al. 1992).

22. For instance, the Metropolitan Museum increased its board size by a smaller amount, but created a new body in the early 1980s, called the Chair-

man's Council. Its purpose was to serve as a "new vehicle by which important supporters who wish a closer involvement with the Museum can provide significant help on an annual basis" (Metropolitan Museum of Art, *112th Annual Report of the Trustees,* 1981–1982). The Chairman's Council was to be "of an importance second only to the board of trustees" (p. 4).

23. Carnegie Hall provides a good example. During the mid-1970s, the organization announced its first campaign, to start an Endowment Fund, noting that while it had not previously relied on such drives, they had now become a necessity ("A National Endowment Fund for Carnegie Hall," *Stagebill,* October 1977).

24. Baltzell 1964; Pareto 1935.

25. Smith observes that "what was once a closed corporation now trumpeted ticket availability in newspapers, on radio, and through the mails" (1983, p. 31).

26. Metropolitan Museum of Art, *122nd Annual Report of the Trustees,* 1991–1992 p. 8. Attendance during the 1981–1982 year was 3.5 million (Metropolitan Museum of Art, *112th Annual Report of the Trustees,* p. 4).

27. The two terms have been used interchangeably (Zweigenhaft and Domhoff 1982).

28. Baltzell 1964; Domhoff 1983; Useem 1984.

29. Baltzell 1964; Zweigenhaft and Domhoff 1982.

30. Domhoff 1983, p. 218.

31. Baltzell 1964, 1991.

32. Marcus 1983, pp. 42–43; see also DiMaggio 1982.

33. Domhoff 1983; Baltzell (1953) 1966. Clubs and schools are listed in Domhoff 1983, pp. 44–47. Examples of some of the clubs include the Colony, Knickerbocker, Links, and River. Examples of schools include Emma Willard, Foxcroft, Groton, Lawrenceville, and St. Mark's.

34. This topic is of sufficient breadth and complexity to require separate treatment and will be addressed in chapter 6.

35. Out of seventy-three donors responding, 82.2 percent agreed with that view. One additional person was unsure.

36. In fact, the address at which this woman lived was so uncharacteristic for a wealthy person that I initially feared having contacted the wrong person. This is important to note, because overconsumption was also criticized by some who were obviously living very expensive lifestyles. It was clear that in the eyes of such donors, "ostentation" had to do with a style of using and displaying wealth, rather than with the expensiveness of a lifestyle per se.

37. Ostrander 1984.

38. Weber (1946) 1977, p. 271. The issue of what constitutes "deserved" wealth for these donors will be considered in chapter 5.

39. This subject will be considered at greater length in the following chapter.

40. Of the sixty-eight respondents providing usable answers, 61.8 percent knew one or more individuals of substantial means who make no major contributions, 25 percent did not know anyone like this, and 13.2 percent were unsure (because they were not aware of what other people gave). Of those who know people who make no major contributions, fully 78 percent said that they think less of them for this reason. It should be borne in mind that these re-

sponses represent donors' perceptions of the generosity of acquaintances, which may not correspond to actual behavior. Of interest, however, is donors' willingness to incorporate philanthropic behavior into their judgments about other people. Even the few donors who did not believe that philanthropy is an obligation shared this attitude. Indeed, every one of these five respondents who knew a wealthy person in this category said that this influences their attitude toward that person. Moreover, even those donors who said they do not think less of people who do not contribute substantially, qualified their responses (e.g., one person said her opinion of an acquaintance has not been affected "only because he is remarkable in other ways").

41. On the other hand, another man was baffled about why one couple he knows are such "tightwads," because they come from a "good family" and were "brought up in the Church." Since nothing had gone wrong, he could not understand their failure to contribute more generously.

42. Little difference existed on this issue between inheritors and others. Of the eleven inheritors who knew a wealthy person who does not give much, 90.9 percent said this affected their attitude, as opposed to 72.2 percent of those eighteen who inherited no wealth, and 72.7 percent of those eleven who inherited some money, but less than $1 million.

43. Norms concerning philanthropy were also indicated by the fact that donors even recounted jokes they had heard about nondonors. One man recounted the following "famous story about the man who was approached for a gift": "The man says, 'You ask me for a gift. I have a brother who is very, very sick—hospitalized, and his kids are in trouble. His wife has to go out and work days and nights.' They say, 'Gee, we didn't realize you had this obligation.' The man says, 'I don't mean that. I don't give [to] him. Why should I give [to] you?'"

44. "The community," and which organizations are central to it, are subject to interpretation. For instance, Daniels observes that when affluent women volunteers describe themselves as leaders in "the community," they obscure their city's diversity, and their position at the top of its economic hierarchy (1988, p. 76). Furthermore, even within their own class, donors sometimes portray their own causes as more important for some larger social body (the city, society, etc.), criticizing those who favor other things as ignoring the needs of the general community.

45. Based on responses by forty-six donors who are members of a congregation and twenty-five who are not. $P \leq .05$ (Fisher's test) for the relation between congregation membership and viewing philanthropy as obligatory. While 89.4 percent of congregation members viewed philanthropy as an obligation, 68 percent of nonmembers did so.

46. Wood and Houghland (1990) suggest that churches and synagogues influence philanthropy because at the same time that they impart relevant values they encourage and provide opportunities for the implementation of those values.

47. The difference between Independents and others was significant at the .10 level, and this observations is offered in a speculative and preliminary fashion. Based on seventy-one respondents. The percentages viewing philanthropy

as an obligation were: Republicans (N = 30), 83.3 percent; Democrats (N = 30), 90 percent; Independents who split their vote (N = 11), 63.6 percent. The relationship between philanthropy and general forms of social participation presents an interesting area for further research.

48. Yet some apparently wish to maintain a distance from family causes. One respondent thought it "unseemly to be too involved with something that has the same name that you do," and believed that being too involved would make it appear that "I'm not being very creative." In another study, an attorney with wealthy clients reported seeing "terrible battles" break out when parents expected children with other interests to continue their philanthropy (Ostrower 1987). The subject of carrying on family members' philanthropy is discussed further in the next chapter.

49. Charitable giving increases with age (Auten and Rudney 1987; Jencks 1987; see also Odendahl 1987). Jencks observes that this may reflect either a greater willingness to give as people age, or a change in the population, so that people born more recently have a different attitude about giving. The findings in this study reveal that some donors' interest in and level of giving did grow with age for various reasons. Some felt freer to contribute more money because they felt confident that family members were cared for adequately. For others, retirement coincided with the donor's realizing greater wealth (as from the sale of a business, or taking money out of a partnership), leading to increased giving.

50. For a discussion of women's volunteer work as an "invisible career," see Daniels 1988.

51. See Methodological Appendix.

52. Wolpert and Reiner 1984, p. 202; Wolpert 1989, p. 386.

53. This was particularly true since the nature and organization of elite groups has historically differed in major American cities (Jaher 1982).

54. Therefore, of course, no implications are made about other communities.

55. *Forbes*, "The Forbes Four Hundred." *Forbes*, special issue, October 27, 1986, p. 216.

56. Higley 1992, p. 97. Twenty-three percent of all *Social Register* households were located there in 1988. Furthermore, Manhattan alone, with 3,457 such households, accounted for just under 11 percent of all those listed. Manhattan's Upper East Side contains the highest urban concentration of *Social Register* households in the country (Higley 1992, p. 149).

57. For a detailed discussion of the organizational sampling procedure, see the Methodological Appendix.

58. The forty-eight organizations providing usable lists represent a response rate of 75 percent.

59. It was anticipated that younger donors would be more likely to show up in this way because giving as a percentage of income increases with age (Auten and Rudney 1987, p. 18; Jencks 1987, p. 26).

60. Nine percent of those interviewed declined to identify the amount of their total donations in a way that could be classified in the above categories. For instance, one person said he had given more than $20,000, but it is not known how much over this amount was contributed. Of these, it is known that half

(about 5 percent of all donors) had contributed more than $20,000, and 25 percent had contributed more than $100,000 (in one case, more than $400,000). Another donor would not give the amount for the past year, but has previously given gifts in the millions. The balance (3 percent of the entire sample) did contribute in the thousands, but the totals are not known. My guess (based, e.g., on the size of individual gifts they had made) is that they belong in the $5,000 to $20,000 range, but it is possible that they belong in a higher category.

61. Occupation (and whether the donor worked at all) varied so greatly by gender that specific occupational breakdowns are presented separately for men and women, in chapter 3.

62. For the use of various of these approaches, see Daniels 1988; Odendahl 1990; Ostrander 1984; Schervish and Herman 1988.

63. The basis upon which perceptions of generosity are formed would itself be an interesting topic for future research. For discussion of debates over the use of the "reputational method" in elite studies generally, see Domhoff and Dye 1987; Friedland and Palmer 1984. For an interesting account of how a reputational method was used in a study of corporate philanthropy, along with suggestions for strengthening this method, see Galaskiewicz 1987.

64. See e.g., Domhoff 1970, chapter 2; Ostrander 1984.

65. See Nielsen 1990.

66. Weber 1988, p. 21. Other evidence indicates that large variations exist in terms of the amounts contributed (Auten and Rudney 1987). These comments, therefore, are not meant as a judgment on the generosity of the wealthy, but simply as evidence of a widespread pattern of giving among this group.

67. Indeed, the 82 percent figure mentioned earlier does not even include all New Yorkers from *Forbes* who are donors—only those who gave to the specific organizations in my study. I am confident that many of the other 18 percent are also donors. One indication that this is true is that at least two-thirds of these remaining individuals are affiliated with a family foundation.

68. Domhoff 1983, p. 41.

69. Simmel (1908) 1971, pp. 172–173.

CHAPTER ONE
PHILANTHROPY AND STATUS BOUNDARIES AMONG THE ELITE

1. Baltzell (1953) 1966, pp. 268, 271; 1964 pp. 61, 138; see also Domhoff 1974, 1983, p. 17; Useem 1980, pp. 55–56; See previous chapter.

2. Donors were asked to describe the main reasons they made each gift, and why they had contributed to that organization rather than another in the same field. Since responses to the two questions were highly repetitive and overlapping, and since each question allowed for multiple responses, the answers were analyzed together.

3. The notable exception, to be considered in the next chapter, was gifts made to a Jewish-affiliated fund in the social services. While organizational involvements are absent here, relations with other people do play a role.

4. A health organization's mission can assume a particularly strong personal

meaning because of the donor's relationship with someone suffering from the problem. One man who had long searched without success for a cause to focus on, developed an interest following a family member's experience with a particular illness (through which he became familiar with a health organization and its staff). He found that "having a personal interest makes a great difference. . . . If you fasten on one cause . . . it becomes like a religion." Indeed, because of the prevalence of giving prompted by a family member's experience with an illness, the "other health" category had one of the higher percentages of largest gifts connected to donors' relationships with other people.

5. For the category "board member/volunteer," other data were available for comparison. Some instances were found in which donors had donated where they volunteered, but not given this as a reason. If they had, the percentages for the board membership category would have risen by the following number of points: culture (1.9); churches/temples (7.7); hospitals (9.1); education (10.3); rights/advocacy/policy (11.1); youth services (20). In 56.3 percent of these cases, however, the donor had mentioned another relationship. In the education category, other data also allowed for a comparison between the percentage of largest gifts made to donors' schools (44.8) and the percentage for which the donor cited attending the school as a reason (42.5), and they were quite close.

6. At least one of these factors was present in 95 percent of all gifts. This question was not asked of all donors (including eight who do not attend benefits), but data are available on forty cases.

7. At this level, "small" gifts may involve considerable sums. One donor regarded annual gifts of $1,000 to an organization as a "nominal" donation. Another donor described his $2,500 gifts as among the smaller donations he makes just to satisfy the person requesting the donation.

8. Data on the 165 most recent gifts of $1,000 or less made by sixty-five donors were also consistent with the pattern of giving accompanied by ties, although the frequency of particular kinds of ties varied from those in largest gifts.

9. The allocation of largest gifts to an area varies markedly with board membership in that area. Close to 79 percent of those on culture boards, as compared with 25.5 percent of other donors, made a largest gift to culture. Similarly, 66.7 percent of those on the board of an organization in the animal and environmental area, but only 6.5 percent of others had made a largest gift in that area. It is understandable that those interested enough to serve on boards in a particular field would make a largest gift there, and vice versa. What is notable, however, is that such a high percentage of donors who did not sit on a college or university board made a largest gift to such an institution. Although 88.2 percent of university board members gave a largest gift to a university, so too did 53.7 percent of other donors. Even the area with the next highest percentage, culture, received largest gifts from only 25.5 percent of nonboard members. This is consistent with the fact that gifts to one's college appeared to be a norm among elites, which was widely regarded by donors as an obligation. Furthermore, attending a school provides a strong alternate source of involvement with recipient institutions. Donor attitudes toward giving to colleges and universities are discussed further in chapter 4.

10. See chapter 4.

11. One way his office does this is by learning about donors' interests, in order to invite them to relevant events at the organization.

12. Simmel (1908) 1971, p. 163.

13. Even one unusual donor who said he disapproved of ongoing support, paused and acknowledged that he consistently gives to his schools, because he feels alumni are "logically . . . the only place they can go."

14. For discussions of prestige as a tool of fundraising in other contexts, see Daniels 1988; Galaskiewicz 1985.

15. See, e.g., Allen 1987; Daniels 1988; Galaskiewicz 1985; Lundberg 1968; McCarthy 1982; Odendahl 1990; Ostrander 1984; Ross 1954.

16. Blau (1964) 1986.

17. The idea of exchange is applicable to philanthropy in a further way. Gift giving in general, which involves the obligation to give, receive, and return gifts has been analyzed as a form of social exchange. Because social exchange involves parties in long-term relations of reciprocal debt, it fosters feelings of trust, gratitude, and obligation, thereby generating solidarity among parties to the exchange (see Blau [1964] 1986, p. 94; Mauss [1925] 1967; Schwartz 1967). While this may not occur among the elite donor and beneficiaries who receive philanthropic gifts, it is one way to view the exchange of contributions for one another's causes that occur among donors themselves.

18. On average, respondents attended about two benefits a month (standard deviation of four), although there were wide differences. Thus, while twelve donors attend about two benefits a year, nine attend about four or more per month. Calculations are based on seventy-one cases for any attendance, sixty-nine cases for frequency of attendance, and include those who never attend. One donor got her calendar to show me how many of these she was scheduled to attend. She said, "It's crazy," but added that she goes because "I enjoy the camaraderie."

19. The wealthy have held parties and weddings at the Metropolitan Museum of Art, for example. A *New York* magazine article observed that for many of them, the museum is important not only because of great art, but also because "it's a great place to have a party," and that this is because of the institution's high status (John Taylor, "Party Palace: The High Life at the Gilded Metropolitan Museum," January 9, 1989).

20. The appropriateness of lavish benefits for charity was an issue that was debated among wealthy New Yorkers in the press, with some charging the money should go to the recipient charity, while others argued that the opulence was needed to attract donors (see, e.g., Kathleen Teltsch, "Misgivings on Benefits Split City Social Circle," *New York Times*, May 11, 1986; Ron Rosenbaum, "Society Dissidents," *Manhattan, inc.*, April 1986).

21. Other donors also noted the rather glamorous setting in which elite philanthropic activities occur, but did indicate that they would personally have no difficulty with less luxurious surroundings, such as one who finds benefits "somewhat nauseating" because of the money spent on decorations and related items.

22. It will be recalled that these represent the three largest gifts made by the donor during the twelve months prior to the interview.

23. This observation makes no assumptions concerning the comparative amount of use of these organizations by members of different classes. The point here is simply that they are used and valued by elites, regardless of how much they may be used by others. Similarly, although obviously correlated, it is important to keep the question of areas of giving analytically distinct from the question of intended beneficiaries. Thus, for example, a wealthy donor might contribute to a prestigious alma mater in order to support a scholarship fund.

24. The Ivy League includes Brown, Columbia, Cornell, Dartmouth, Harvard, University of Pennsylvania, Princeton, and Yale. One indication of the selectiveness of the other schools is their high rating on the Astin Index of Selectivity, which ranges from 1 (least selective) to 7 (most selective) (Astin 1971). Ninety-six percent of the twenty-six schools rated (i.e., excluding professional and other unrated schools) received a 5 or higher, and 56.4 percent received a 7.

25. Based on thirty-seven of the donor lists collected. To ensure comparability, eleven of the lists that started at a baseline of more than $1,000 were excluded. Two additional lists began at a level between $1,000 and $1,500 but were retained because the difference was so small and including them did not depress the average and median numbers of gifts for their area.

26. College prestige was measured by use of the Astin Index of Selectivity (see above for description). Among graduates of schools with an index of 5 or less ($N = 13$), 15.4 percent had made a largest gift to their school. The figure rises to 25 percent among graduates of schools with an index of 6 ($N = 16$), and to fully 57.1 percent among graduates of schools with the highest rating of 7 ($N = 42$).

27. Specific subgroups and patterns will be the subject of the following chapters.

28. DiMaggio 1982; Hall 1982; Jaher 1982; Story 1980.

29. Similarly, having a prominent member of the elite take an interest in an institution can help it to rise in prestige.

30. Donors told of organizations asking for permission to publicize their support because it would help them to raise money from others. One donor was told that his "name there would certainly make a great difference with certain types of people."

31. This point is supported by the fact that no statistically significant differences in giving to particular areas (such as culture, education, social services) were found between those of inherited wealth and those of self-made wealth. This indicates that the newly wealthy do indeed share the philanthropic priorities of those with inherited wealth.

32. DiMaggio and Useem 1982.

33. In thinking about the following comments made by donors, remember that these donors are also trustees who have often served on boards for long periods of time, and thus have personal experience of how boards function and change. Furthermore, boards select their own members, so that donors also

speak from personal experience with the process of recruiting people to boards. Similar observations were made by donors who serve on different boards, suggesting that a larger process was taking place that affected numerous institutions.

34. This brings to mind Mannheim's observation that aristocratic groups pretend not to notice such "elementary concerns" as food and money. Although he says this "extreme delicacy" is not found in the first generation, descendants tend to "look away from the 'facts of life' until they no longer live in the world of real things but in a second world of artificial symbols" ([1933] 1971, pp. 311–312).

35. DiMaggio and Useem 1982. See also Bourdieu's distinction between the "naive exhibitionism of 'conspicuous consumption'" and the attitude that "sets the aesthete apart from the common herd by a radical difference which seems to be inscribed in 'persons'" (1984, p. 31).

36. One donor, a self-described member of the "nouveau riche," believes those who come from upper-class families are particularly susceptible to snob appeal. Pointing to one nonprofit board with many well-known, prestigious members, he said, "You know something—at bottom I think it's a snob organization that people are attracted to because it's an old organization that their parents may have given some money to."

37. It is interesting that comments about "buying in" were often made by those affiliated with cultural institutions. Social network data collected during the interviews reveal that this is precisely the area in which there is a higher level of social acquaintanceship among donors. Because donors form more of an interacting group in this area, they may well be more likely to notice and/or resent the appearance of newcomers. It may also be that newcomers are particularly likely to seek admittance to the cultural arena because of the high interaction that occurs among its donors.

38. To reiterate, a donor is classified as a member of the social elite if he or she is listed in the *Social Register*, or is a member of an elite club, or is a graduate of an elite prep school.

39. While detailed discussion is deferred to future chapters, it may be noted that variables for ethnicity and gender were also examined and were not significant.

40. Breaking this analysis down further, to separately examine serving on any board and serving on multiple boards, is instructional as well. Being a member of the social elite was the sole consideration associated with serving on any board. In absolute terms, the social elite were nonetheless outnumbered as board members by other donors, who exceed them in number: 90 percent ($N = 26$) of the social elite were trustees, as compared with 65.4 percent ($N = 34$) of other donors ($p < .05$). Looking solely at those donors who serve on boards, however, only the amount of a donor's contributions is associated with serving on more boards. The results support the conclusion that while members of the social elite remain highly valued as trustees, they must share board positions with other members of the elite to a considerable degree, and may well find themselves outnumbered on any particular board.

41. Logistic regression results, which simultaneously examine the impact of multiple variables, are presented only for the areas of culture, hospitals, and universities—the areas with the greatest numbers of trustees. It should be noted, however, that bivariate analyses, performed for areas where fewer cases of board members were available, also revealed no association between social elite membership and board membership. (The areas were other health and rehabilitation organizations, animal and environmental causes, educational institutions below college level, and social service organizations.) Members of the social elite did initially appear to have an advantage in the single area of rights, advocacy, and policy. Yet once controls were introduced for either business association or total dollars contributed during the past year, the relationship disappeared, indicating that the advantage did not stem from membership in the social elite per se.

42. The situation may also reflect the fact that cultural institutions rely more heavily on private sources of funding than do other nonprofits (Salamon 1992). This may make it more important for cultural nonprofits to retain close ties to the core social group within the elite. It may suggest, as well, that such organizations are less susceptible to influences that would force greater diversification.

43. I compiled these figures by looking trustees up in the *Social Register* volumes for the relevant years.

44. DiMaggio and Useem 1982.

45. Bourdieu (1966) 1969, 1986; for a discussion of this aspect of Bourdieu's work, see DiMaggio 1979.

CHAPTER TWO
RELIGION, ETHNICITY, AND JEWISH PHILANTHROPY

1. See Alba and Moore 1982; Allen and Broyles 1989; Baltzell 1964; Coleman and Rainwater 1978; Domhoff 1972, 1990; Useem 1980, p. 59; Zweigenhaft and Domhoff 1982.

2. The term *ethnicity* is more appropriate here for several reasons. First, it reflects the way many affluent Jews think about their own Jewish affiliation. Second, it reminds us that upper-class exclusion of Jews has been directed at both religious and nonreligious Jews.

3. See Baltzell 1964.

4. Baltzell 1964; Zweigenhaft and Domhoff 1982.

5. Baltzell 1964, p. 138.

6. A sense of identification with a particular religious or ethnic community in relation to philanthropy was raised in far greater detail by Jewish donors than others interviewed for the study.

7. See Baltzell 1964; Coleman and Rainwater 1978.

8. For instance, it would be important to include donors from each religion who are actively involved with various causes associated with their religion.

9. Among Jewish donors, 62.7 percent identified with a particular denomination, as follows: Reformed (59.4 percent), Conservative (34.4 percent), and Orthodox (6.3 percent). This information is missing for one Jewish respondent. Most Protestants were Episcopalian (52.2 percent) or Presbyterian (26 percent),

with the remainder divided among various denominations. Of the four with no religious affiliation, one each grew up in a Protestant, Jewish, and Catholic household. The fourth person's family had no religious affiliation.

10. It should be noted that this is not the result of response bias, or a greater willingness of Jews to participate in the study. While the religion of all twenty-two people who declined to be interviewed is not known, it is known that eight are Jewish. Thus, even under the most conservative (and unlikely) assumption that these were the only Jewish nonrespondents, the sample would still have been 55 percent Jewish had all agreed to participate.

11. Sirota and Alper 1988, p. 31.

12. Tabulations on high-income donors were made available upon request, and the generous assistance of Bill Alper of Sirota, Alper and Pfau (who conducted the survey) for providing this information is gratefully acknowledged.

13. This interpretation is strengthened by the fact that the Sirota and Alper study used a different method for sampling donors (random digit dialing) than my study, which sampled from donor lists. Furthermore, groups of affluent donors identified in other ways also contained an overrepresentation of Jews and underrepresentation of Catholics relative to their presence in the general population (Boris 1987; Odendahl 1987). Ethnographic material also indicates that wealthy Jews and non-Jews perceive Jews as being particularly large donors (Odendahl 1987, pp. 227–228).

14. Baltzell 1964; Birmingham 1987, p. 299.

15. Interestingly, while Protestants exhibited the most directly "religious" pattern by giving to churches, they were less likely to feel their donations had been influenced by their religious beliefs. Only 47.6 percent of Protestants ($N = 21$) believed this was the case, as compared with 66.7 percent of Catholics ($N = 9$) and 64.3 percent of Jews ($N = 42$). Four donors had no religious affiliation, three said they did not know, and data are missing for the balance.

16. While best categorized in the social services, it should be noted that funds are also channeled to other areas. Moreover, it should be emphasized that while the organization's affiliation is Jewish, the services funded are not confined to Jews. Being Jewish was also associated with making largest gifts to health and rehabilitation organizations. These gifts, however, were not religiously linked in the same sense of going to organizations with a religious affiliation.

17. Four of the seven gifts to churches went to a church the donor currently belongs to and attends. Of the others, one went to the church the donor belonged to as a child and attended school, and another was made by a widowed donor to his wife's church. The remaining gift was made to a donor's local church, although he said that he virtually never attends.

18. While there are comparable organizations with a Protestant and Catholic affiliation, these were not the recipients of any largest donations. This indicates that we cannot explain the divergent pattern of Jewish giving in terms of the simple presence of such an organization.

19. One study observes that for Jews in the corporate elite, philanthropy and fundraising are the "primary means of demonstrating commitment to being Jewish" (Zweigenhaft and Domhoff 1982, p. 99).

20. These descriptions of distinctive fundraising techniques further highlight the fact that Jewish philanthropy exists as a distinctive organizational and cultural philanthropic world. Donors volunteered this information to explain how this world operates.

21. As this comment indicates, it is important to keep in mind that often donors were not merely offering abstract reflections, but discussing shifts they had witnessed during the course of their philanthropic careers.

22. Moreover, while donors believed that barriers had weakened, they did not necessarily feel the obstacles had disappeared. One donor who thinks that boards have become much more open to Jews also said that he serves on one board that is trying to reduce its number of Jewish trustees, and on another that contains "pockets of anti-Jewish feeling." Another donor was angry at an institution because he suspects that its board either excludes or permits only a token presence of Jews.

23. Chapter 1 described philanthropy as a field in which individuals compete to position themselves, drawing on the resources at their disposal. If Jewish donors believe that they will be unable to advance (e.g., to gain board memberships) in the world of prestigious cultural institutions and the like, it will make more sense for them to "invest" elsewhere.

24. In this respect, there is a parallel between philanthropy and political behavior among affluent Jews, which has also been explained in terms of the influence of internal community values as well as the relationship between Jews and non-Jewish members of the elite, and concerns about anti-Semitism (Domhoff 1990, p. 245).

25. Milton Goldin, "Does Jewish Philanthropy Have a Future?" *Midstream*, November 1983, p. 23.

26. $P < .01$. This includes gifts to any organization with a Jewish affiliation, regardless of its area of activity. Based on twenty-eight Jews who do not serve on a cultural or university board and twenty Jews who do. Data are missing for four cases.

27. Baltzell 1964.

28. This point holds even when we focus on donors of inherited wealth (which members of the social elite are more likely to be). Among those who reported inheriting $1 million or more, fully 90.9 percent of Protestants as compared with 25 percent of Jews were in the social elite.

29. Baltzell 1964, p. 63; see also Zweigenhaft and Domhoff 1982, who argue that class identification assumes primary importance for Jews in the corporate elite who have been assimilated into the social elite.

30. By contrast, 40.5 percent of Jews outside the social elite had made such a gift. Among Jewish donors, $p \leq .05$ for the relationship between making a largest gift to the Jewish-affiliated fund and social elite membership. Furthermore, while being Jewish continues to be associated with making a largest gift to a health and rehabilitation organization outside the social elite ($p \leq .05$), the relationship disappears in the social elite.

31. Thus, for instance, seven out of nine Jews in the social elite had made a donation to the Jewish-affiliated fund—but not one of their largest gifts (one did not give, and it is not known whether the final person did so). Similarly,

Zweigenhaft and Domhoff conclude that class identification assumes primary importance among Jews in the corporate elite who have been assimilated, but note that this does not mean that Jewish identification disappears (1982, p. 110).

32. While 18.8 percent of Protestants in the social elite made a largest gift to a church, 66.7 percent of others did so. The relationship between social elite membership and largest giving to a church, however, was not quite significant at the .05 level ($p = .053$). The difference between Protestants and other donors in giving to churches was statistically significant outside, but not inside the social elite. Given the very small number of Protestants outside the social elite (six), these findings must be treated as preliminary, but they warrant further research.

33. Earlier a similar observation was made with respect to the effects of access to cultural and university boards. It would be of considerable interest to try to disentangle the effects of incorporation into the elite and integration into non-religious nonprofits on major giving to Jewish causes. The number of cases and high correlation among variables does not permit me to do so here, but the subject provides an area for future research. It is worth noting, however, that outside the social elite, fewer Jews on university/cultural boards gave to Jewish-affiliated causes than did other Jews. In the social elite, all but one Jew sat on such boards, and, as we have seen, virtually no one gave to any Jewish-affiliated cause. The overall findings lead me to suspect that serving on nonreligiously affiliated cultural/university boards and social elite membership are essentially indicators of varying degrees of overall assimilation by Jews into the general elite.

34. Within the social elite, $p \le .01$ for the relationship between being Jewish and making a largest gift to rights/advocacy/policy. Outside the social elite, 10.8 percent of Jews ($N = 37$) and 7.1 percent of non-Jews ($N = 14$) had made a largest gift in this area. Interestingly, three of the four rights/advocacy/policy gifts made by Jews outside the social elite, but none made by Jews in the social elite, went to an organization with a Jewish affiliation.

35. This was true of all three (out of four) organizations that could be classified in this fashion (the donor to the fourth organization described himself as "basically liberal"). Given the small number of cases, any conclusions must be preliminary, awaiting analysis using a larger sample.

36. Allen and Broyles 1989; Domhoff 1972, 1990; Lenski (1966) 1984, p. 84.

37. Among non-Jewish members of the social elite, 15 percent were Democrats and 5 percent were Independents. Class apparently does not replace ethnicity as the "independent variable" in political party affiliation in the social elite.

38. As noted earlier, political behavior among affluent Jews has been seen as reflecting internal Jewish community values, concerns about anti-Semitism, and residual wariness toward gentile members of the elite who so long excluded Jews from their institutions (Domhoff 1990, p. 245).

39. It should be emphasized that the ethnic barriers discussed in this chapter were not absolute. Jews did not begin serving on major boards in New York City in the 1980s or even the 1970s. In a study covering the years 1895 to 1970, Dain found that while the board of the New York Public Library remained overwhelmingly Protestant, it also appointed its first Jewish and Catholic members

by 1905, for political reasons (1991, p. 222). Similarly, Birmingham notes that "despite the anti-Semitic cast of the Met," Jacob Schiff, who was Jewish, was invited to join the Opera's board in the early 1900s. He declined, but recommended Otto Kahn, who was also Jewish, and who went on to play a major role in the development of the Metropolitan Opera (1967, p. 305).

40. Dain 1991. The newspaper was the *Village Voice*, which is quoted by Dain (p. 234).

41. That is, with respect to the worth of particular nonprofit institutions.

42. Marcus 1983.

43. Baltzell 1964, 1991.

44. Indeed, Baltzell suggests that changes in patterns of giving are "often excellent indexes of change within the elite and the upper-class structures" (1964, p. 61). He notes that at one time, Russian and German Jews had separate charitable organizations. As the Russians were accepted into the ranks of the German Jewish upper class, however, they were also assimilated into the charitable organizations of the Germans, and eventually the charities of the two groups merged (Baltzell 1964, pp. 61–62).

45. In making these gifts, donors give huge sums to a federated fund, virtually never a recipient of major giving. In doing so, they are donating large sums without knowing the specific, ultimate use to which it will be put, a situation that affluent donors generally regard with considerable wariness.

46. This is not, however, true of all recipient organizations. Indeed, donors often had independent relationships with some of the institutions. Nonetheless, the point is that they were willing to give to the federated fund as a whole, rather than make the decision on their own regarding the allocation to individual agencies.

47. Higley 1992.

48. While 30.4 percent of Jews served on a cultural board, and 39.1 percent served on a cultural or university board, only 19.2 percent were members of the social elite. These figures exclude those Jewish donors missing data on social elite membership. Among all Jewish donors (including those missing data on social elite membership), 34 percent sat on a cultural board and 42 percent sat on a cultural or university board. This, of course, does not include the additional numbers who serve on nonreligiously affiliated causes of other kinds.

49. Weber (1946) 1977, p. 192. Interestingly, some members of the social elite expressed the opinion that while philanthropy would not make the newly wealthy socially acceptable, it might serve to "launder" them so that their children would be.

50. These considerations are further supported by findings from current research I am conducting on nonprofit boards of directors.

CHAPTER THREE
GENDER, MARRIAGE, AND PHILANTHROPY

1. See Collins 1988; Daniels 1988; Domhoff 1970; Hacker 1975; McCarthy 1990; Odendahl 1990; Ostrander 1984; Tickamyer 1981.

2. Dye 1990; Moore 1988.

3. Daniels 1988; McCarthy 1990.

4. McCarthy 1990, p. 1.

5. See Collins 1988; Daniels 1988; McCarthy 1982, 1990; Odendahl 1990; Ostrander 1984; Tickamyer 1981.

6. Thus, most of the men worked and also were involved with the business world. A business involvement was not confined to those in business specifically, but also characterized many attorneys. Fully six of the eleven lawyers were associated with the large law firms whose presence in New York leads Hoffman to characterize the city as the "hub of corporate law" (1982, p. 35). The careers of three of the remaining five attorneys also involved a business focus. The business involvement of the remaining two are unknown. For a discussion of the close links between major law firms and the corporate and financial institutions that are their clients, see Burch 1981; Hoffman 1982.

7. One professional woman, who had a connection to a small business, was the sole woman with a career connection to a business.

8. Half of unmarried women (and 60 percent of unmarried men) made a largest gift to an organization where they served as a trustee. Only three of the sixteen married women had inherited wealth ($1 million or more). When they are excluded, we still find 38.5 percent of married women sitting on the board of an organization to whom they made a largest gift. In the sample as a whole, 44.8 percent of the women and 19.6 percent of the men in the study were not married.

9. In a sole case, a donor said that all three of her largest gifts (which she considered as joint) basically reflected her husband's interests and connections. Even in this case, the donor said that she makes other contributions on her own, without consulting her husband.

10. The correlation between the number of hours per month volunteered by donor and spouse was .38 ($p < .05$). Data on the hours volunteered by the donor's spouse were available for only 61 percent of married donors, so this finding is a preliminary one. The subject of volunteering among members of a couple would be a fruitful area for future research.

11. The fact that women are generally more dependent on a spouse for funds apparently does not make them more likely than men to think of giving as a joint activity. Thus, 65.1 percent of married men and 68.8 percent of married women viewed all or most of their philanthropy as done jointly with a spouse. Furthermore, over half of each group said all of their contributions were made jointly. By contrast, male members of the social elite stood out from others because of the high percentage (54.6 percent) who said they make none, or almost none, of their gifts jointly. Only 33.3 percent of women in the social elite, 6.9 percent of other men, and 14.3 percent of other women said this was the case. The possibility that the difference stemmed from the higher percentage of inheritors in the social elite was examined, on the theory that such people might view their giving as more of a tradition of their distinct families, but this proved not to be the case.

12. Bear in mind that we are dealing here with a sample of donors. The extent to which women more generally feel free to allocate funds to causes of their choosing awaits a random sample of wealthy women.

13. These differences persist when we consider only donors in the social elite,

where no men and 30 percent of women had made a largest gift to the social services. Thus, even as members of a group that exhibits greater conformity to the elite pattern of major giving to culture and education, women continue to pursue a distinctive pattern in the social services.

14. Women were no more likely to be Jewish than were men, and a logistic regression analysis confirmed the independent relation of gender (chi-square = 5.6, $p \leq .05$) and being Jewish (chi-square = 6.2, $p \leq .01$) to having made a largest gift to the social services (1 = yes).

15. McCarthy 1990.

16. $p < .10$.

17. Among women, 27.6 percent had less than a college education, 37.9 percent had a college degree, and another 34.5 percent had an advanced degree. By contrast, only 3.5 percent of men had less than a college education, 29.3 percent of men had their highest degree from college, and 67.2 percent had obtained an advanced degree.

18. Remember, it is the percentage of gifts received from women being discussed here, not the percentage of all women making donations. A far higher percentage of women made gifts to cultural organizations, for instance, although culture received fewer of its total gifts from women.

19. Women's support for animal and environmental causes would also be consistent with a historical pattern identified by Domhoff, whereby affluent women participate in social movements designed to "take some of the roughest edges off a profit-oriented business system" (1970, p. 35).

20. The subject of support by elites (both individuals and companies) for environmental causes would also provide a useful area in which to explore other issues, such as the relationship between economic class interests and charitable contributions, and between political and ideological outlooks and philanthropy.

21. Couples were highly concentrated in culture, with 68.8 percent having made a gift to a cultural organization. By contrast, the next highest percentage is the 11.1 percent of couples found as donors to hospitals, a considerably lower figure. Interestingly, female donors to these organizations were also concentrated in culture (58 percent), but this was not true of men (33.9 percent of whom appeared as a donor to culture).

22. It is likely that there are many additional factors encouraging joint giving in culture as well, which would be useful for future research to investigate.

23. $p \leq .01$. The percentage of married women making a largest cultural gift also exceeded the percentage for married men (34.8). The effect of gender here, however, is indirect, reflecting the correlation between being a married woman and being in a nonlegal profession. Four of the five married women professionals were in cultural occupations. That the minority of women who worked were more likely to be in such professions than were men, typically found in business or law, itself reflects gender divisions. Differences between married and unmarried women, by contrast, persist even with controls for occupation.

24. This was not the case for men. A lower percentage of married men than unmarried men had actually made a largest gift to culture, but the relationship was not significant.

25. The findings are also consistent with the idea that married women attend to status or the more "refined things," while men generate resources (see Collins 1988; Daniels 1988; Hacker 1975; Veblen [1899] 1953). My own view emphasizes the greater likelihood of the woman to express her identity as a member of a couple through philanthropy.

26. 58.3 percent of unmarried women, as compared with 37.5 percent of married women, made a largest gift to the social services. Although culture is the more typical choice among married women (75 percent), the difference in the frequency of support for the social services between married and unmarried women was not statistically significant.

27. These results are based on 142 matched women/couple sets and 410 matched men/couple sets. The lower number of women/couple matches is partly due to the greater difficulty of matching women and couples, since the wife's first name is often omitted in listing a couple (e.g., "Mr. and Mrs. John Smith"), whereas her first name is often used when she gives alone (e.g., "Mrs. Mary Smith").

28. The standard deviation was 40 for women and 42 for men. There was considerable variation in the hours spent volunteering, and the median was 17.5 for women and 10 for men. Based on data for seventy-six cases.

29. The standard deviation was 43.7 for men and 40.7 for women; the median was 20 for men and 18.8 for women.

30. As seen in the multiple regression analysis presented in chapter 1, gender was not a significant predictor of the overall numbers of boards on which donors serve. The bivariate relationship between gender and number of boards was also not significant. Men were, however, more likely than women to serve on very large numbers of boards. Fully 36 percent of men sat on four or more boards, as compared with 13.8 percent of women ($p < .05$). Men's advantage here is due primarily to their greater likelihood of having a business connection.

31. The subject of gender and board membership in various areas of activity will be taken up in a later section with another set of data. The interview data permit multivariate analyses of the determinants of serving on culture and hospital boards, including gender, which was not significant. In bivariate analyses, the sole area in which gender was related to serving on a board ($p \le .05$), was university/college-level education, where a higher percentage of men (26.3) than women (6.9) served. Those with a business connection were more likely to serve on such boards, and the impact of gender apparently results from men's greater likelihood of having such a connection. A more conclusive interpretation awaits a larger sample that includes women in business. Women were also less likely (3.5 percent) than men (19.3 percent) to serve on the boards of a rights/advocacy/policy organization ($p < .10$), a relationship that diminished when business connections or having made a largest gift to the field was taken into account. Taken together, these results highlight the usefulness of further research into how women's absence from the business world affects their presence in distinct areas of philanthropy.

32. See Collins 1988; Daniels 1988; Odendahl 1990; Ostrander 1984.

33. Ostrander (1984) argues that volunteering offers women class-related returns that could not be matched by paid work. Daniels (1988, p. 37) observes

that the women she studied speak less of maintaining their class through volunteering than those studied by Ostrander. The women I spoke with are more similar to those in Daniels's study in this regard.

34. See chapter 1.

35. Some businesses specifically encourage volunteer work (Ross 1954; Useem 1984), and some businessmen in this study worked in such organizations, but that was not associated with volunteering more hours or serving on boards. My own interpretation is that this indicates the multiplicity of factors available to encourage members of the elite to serve on boards, rather than the unimportance of the organizational factor.

36. The rationale for volunteering becomes more similar among men and women once the former are retired, for retired men are also looking for involvements they feel are useful and fulfilling outside the world of paid work.

37. Although beyond the scope of this study, an area for further investigation concerns potential differences in what men and women do as board members. For instance, female trustees in this study appeared to be more active in organizing benefits than were men, while men appeared more frequently involved in issues of organizational finances. For discussions of elite women on boards, see Covelli 1989; Daniels 1988.

38. One exception was a woman who did discuss her experiences in gender terms, describing difficulties she had faced as a female trustee. These had been at organizations outside of New York City, suggesting the usefulness of comparing differences in the assimilation of women onto nonprofit boards in various cities. A rare comment concerning shifts in women's presence on boards was made by a man who observed that he had been on one board when it admitted a woman, requiring a revision in their use of the male pronoun in the by-laws.

39. Despite the relatively insular nature of elite philanthropy, recipient organizations are often highly visible outside the elite and need to maintain relationships with other groups, such as government, for whom issues of diversity may be of concern.

40. Information on board membership was gathered for twenty-one organizations. In most cases, it was collected from the *Directory of Directors in the City of New York* (1971–1972 edition), and the *Directory of Directors in the City of New York and Tri-State Area* (1982 and 1992 editions). For the remaining cases, it was collected from other sources for the same years as follows: Metropolitan Museum of Art (Annual Reports for the years 1971–1972, 1981–1982, 1991–1992); Carnegie Hall (performance programs for September 1972, October 1982, May 1992); Lincoln Center for the Performing Arts (performance programs for 1972 [Metropolitan Opera, June Festival program], October 1982, April 1992); Metropolitan Opera (performance programs for September 1972, March 1982, April 1992). The percentage of women on fifteen boards increased as follows (percentages are for 1972, 1982, and 1992): Carnegie Hall (10.7, 19.0, 19.1); Lincoln Center (9.0, 14.7, 18.9); Metropolitan Museum (21.0, 27.8, 38.8); Metropolitan Opera (20.0, 28.9, 37.8); Barnard College (48.0, 53.8, 54.5); Columbia University (0.0, 12.5, 14.3); New York University (10.8, 5.7, 22.7); Union Theological Seminary (15.4, 24.2, 24.0); Hospital for Joint Diseases (8.8, 13.9, 15.6);

Memorial Sloan-Kettering Cancer Center (10.0, 19.5, 20.3); New York University Medical Center (12.5, 17.2, 20.6); Presbyterian Hospital (9.5, 12.2, 20.0); Roosevelt Hospital (1972)/St. Luke's-Roosevelt Hospital Center (1982, 1992) (5.4, 22.2, 27.5); Citizen's Budget Commission (0, 4, 6); YMCA of Greater New York (0, 6.9, 8). The boards of five organizations examined remained essentially the same (or, in one case, dropped slightly), as follows: New York Philharmonic (28.6, 35.7, 30.2); Museum of Modern Art (28.9, 36.8, 31.6); Community Service Society (31.3, 37.5, 30); The Conference Board (0, 3.4, 3.4); American Museum of Natural History (17.9, 14.3, 15.1). One board, the YWCA of the City of New York, was all female at each time period. In some cases, trustees' gender was explicitly identified by a "Mrs." or "Miss" preceding the name, but usually the determination was made based on the person's name. Where a determination could not be made, the case was excluded from the analysis. In all but five cases (four organizations at five times) the percentage of all trustees whose gender was unknown was less than 3 percent. For the cases where it exceeded 3 percent, the following gives a range, where the first percentage figure assumes all unknown cases were male and the second assumes all were female: Columbia University, 1972 (0–4 percent); The Conference Board, 1982 (3–6); Presbyterian Hospital, 1992 (19.4–22.6); Union Theological Seminary, 1972, 1982 (24.2–27.2, 24–32). As we can see, recategorization of the gender of the donors in these cases would not affect the findings. While these figures clearly show that many major New York nonprofits were increasing the presence of women on their boards, additional research on greater numbers of large New York boards would be useful to establish precisely the scope of the trend.

41. There is considerable overlap between these organizations and those from which the donor list data were collected. With the exception of the rights, advocacy, and policy category, the criteria for inclusion were identical. Board and donor information were not both available in some cases, resulting in some variation in the organizations included. The board data do contain an additional category (rights, advocacy, and policy) not included in the procedure for sampling donors. The idea of including it there was considered but not adopted for various reasons, including the fact that some institutions received gifts from organizational rather than individual sources, that the heterogeneity of other organizations made it difficult to regard them as constituting a distinct area of activity, and the difficulty of obtaining donor information from others.

42. Of the 11,281 gifts of $1,000 or more, 39.4 percent were made by men, 24.7 percent were made by women, and 35.9 percent were made by combinations of individuals, primarily couples (see Table 3.2). The percentage of women drops to 15.1 percent when we move to gifts of $100,000 or more, a figure that is twice as high (32.1 percent) for men. The bulk of these gifts (46.7 percent) were made by couples, with the small balance coming from other combinations of individuals.

43. Since women from the corporate world are likely to connect their board membership to their business skills, as is true of men, it will also be interesting to see whether we find such women assuming different roles and tasks as board members than has traditionally been the case.

CHAPTER FOUR
EDUCATION, CULTURE, AND THE INSTITUTIONALIZATION OF
PHILANTHROPIC VALUES

1. The emphasis on higher education is apparent if one looks at total contributions as well as largest gifts. Whereas 92 percent of donors had made some contribution to a university or college during the previous year, only 65.3 percent had given to another kind of educational institution. And 25 percent of all donors had given more than $25,000 to a college or university, but less than 7 percent had given this much to other educational causes. Based on seventy-five cases for giving to colleges/universities and seventy-two cases for other education.

2. In 57.1 percent of cases, the gift went to the donor's alma mater, and in 23.8 percent, it went to a school attended by a family member (in all but one case a spouse or child).

3. These last comments accord well with Hansmann's view that giving to higher education "serves at least in part as a system of voluntary repayments under an implicit loan system," whereby private schools charge rates below cost in exchange for an implicit commitment that students will "repay" the school after graduation (Hansmann 1987, p. 36). Much alumni giving, however, goes beyond settling a precise debt, as illustrated by respondents who clearly gave more than the cost of repaying their "loan"—in some cases contributing millions of dollars.

4. Some donors (11.8 percent) did make major contributions to colleges or universities they or a family member had not attended. In one case, however, a family member did have a professional relationship with the school, and in another the donor's business had a relationship. Interestingly, three of these ten gifts involved Jewish donors supporting an educational institution with a Jewish affiliation. Other gifts involved specific projects, in most cases relating to a friend of the donor. In two unusual cases, the donors had simply become quite personally involved and supportive of a school that they did not attend.

5. College was the important cutoff, with virtually no difference in the percentage of those making largest gifts to education among those with college degrees (74.1 percent) and those with more advanced degrees (72.9 percent). Of the four gifts to education made by noncollege graduates, two made gifts to their childrens' schools.

6. Entered as the independent variables in a logistic regression, donors' educational level and having children were each independently and significantly related to making a largest gift to education (chi-square = 1.52, $p < .05$ for each). Based on eighty-five cases.

7. Fully 56.3 percent of donors had a postcollege degree, another 32.2 percent held a college degree, and the remaining 11.5 percent had less than a college education. Seventy-five of those interviewed had children.

8. (For the Astin Index of Selectivity, see Astin 1971.) Although selectivity and prestige are not identical, they are related, and selectivity is a good indicator of prestige for the schools attended by these respondents. Of the forty-four cases in which donors attended a college or university rated 7, 61.4 percent were in

the Ivy League, and all but one of the remaining institutions were highly competitive colleges. Furthermore, analyses were performed to compare graduates of Ivy League schools with graduates of other institutions with the same rating, and their behavior was found to be the same. The suitability of the Index is further illustrated by the women's colleges that received a rating of 7. Of the nine cases where donors attended a women's school, seven were in the group of colleges (such as Smith, Vassar, and Wellesley) known to be favored by upper-class women (see Domhoff 1970, p. 37), testifying to their prestige within their class. Most of the seventy-four college graduates (69.5 percent) attended a school rated 7, 23 percent attended schools with a rating of 6, 13.5 percent graduated from a school rated 5, and the remaining 4 percent attended schools rated 4 or 3. One donor attended a university outside the United States that is not ranked and is thus excluded from the current analysis.

9. Indeed, an unusual donor who graduated from a less selective school but gives substantially to his alma mater, spontaneously referred to his school's relative lack of prestige when explaining his donations. Although "it's not a fancy Ivy League school," he explained, he had "had a fantastic experience."

10. See chapter 1.

11. As one study concludes, although admission to a prestigious college is of extreme importance to prep school students, "the days when preps could automatically expect to go to an Ivy League or other highly selective college are over" (Cookson and Persell 1985, p. 188). On the declining percentage of students at highly selective schools drawn from private prep schools, see also Baltzell (1991), who argues more generally that these universities have been transformed from "class institutions" to "elitist meritocracies."

12. This example is meant to illustrate one donor's awareness of changes at his school. It should not be taken to mean that donors—whether in the social elite or not—are never angry or never lower their contributions if a child or other relative is refused admission.

13. During one year, for instance, branches of the University of California, Louisiana State University, Penn State University, University of Kentucky, and several other state schools were among the recipients of the largest contributions made to education (American Association of Fund-Raising Counsel 1985).

14. $p \leq .05$.

15. Most graduates of private schools (69.8 percent), but no public college graduates, had attended an institution rated 7 (most selective). By contrast, most public college graduates (81.8 percent) attended institutions rated 5 or below, while only 6.4 percent of the private institutions were in this lowest category.

16. When analysis is confined to the far larger group of donors who attended private schools (sixty-three), there continue to be differences in levels of giving according to institutional ranking. Furthermore, both characteristics were entered as independent variables in a logistic regression, with having made a largest gift to one's alma mater as the dependent variable. School selectivity (0 = below 7, 1 = 7) remained significant (chi-square = 4.1, $p < .05$), but public/private status did not (chi-square = 1.1). Based on seventy-one cases of college graduates.

17. Only eleven donors had attended a public college as compared with sixty-three who attended a private school. The small number of state university alumni may reflect the study's East Coast/New York geographical focus. Domhoff reports that graduates of private schools outside of New England (he cites examples from California and Texas) "most frequently attend a prominent state university in their area" (1983, p. 27).

18. A review of the Astin Index revealed that there are comparatively few public colleges with a rank of 7, but some do exist, and the comparison would be an interesting one.

19. Thus, 36.8 percent of donors had contributed more than $10,000 to cultural causes during the past year, and 32.4 percent had contributed more than $25,000. The comparable percentages for colleges/universities were 41.4 percent and 26.7 percent. Hospitals also received large total contributions from a high percentage of people (25 percent of donors had contributed more than $25,000), but they did not attract the same widespread support as culture and higher education. Fully 25 percent of donors had contributed no money to a hospital during the previous year, while fewer than 9 percent each had given no donations to culture or to colleges/universities. Based on seventy-five cases for universities and colleges, sixty-eight cases for culture. It should be noted that $25,000 represents a cutoff point; in many cases the total sums contributed to the area far exceeded that amount.

20. The median number of gifts received was 461 in education (the mean was 451) and 362 in culture (the mean was 600.6). The other five areas were hospitals, other health organizations, animal and environmental causes, social services, and youth organizations (not elsewhere classifiable). After culture and education, the figures drops to a median of 210, and a mean of 305.7 in the area of hospitals.

21. Overall, nine significant relationships were found between the various areas, of which seven were negative. Six of these negative relationships involved culture, and ranged in size from a low of −.17 (phi coefficient) in the case of animal and environmental causes to a high of −.26 in the case of the social services ($p \leq .001$ for all six relationships). The seventh, smaller, negative relationship was between hospitals and animal and environmental causes (phi = .07, $p <$ .05). The two positive relationships involved social services and youth organizations (phi = .14, $p \leq .001$), and social services and health and rehabilitation (phi = .08, $p \leq .01$). The former, larger relationship reflected the fact that organizations in the youth category shared donors with social service organizations that focus on youth. When these social service organizations were reclassified in the youth category, the phi coefficient dropped to .06 ($p \leq .10$). This illustrates how a particular class of beneficiary, as well as an area of activity, can become a focus of elite philanthropy. It also is consistent with my general impression (based on compiling the list of New York's largest nonprofits and the interviews), that in terms of beneficiaries, the young tend to be among the more favored groups.

22. See chapter 1.

23. She noted that the opening night at one cultural organization had been transformed into a social event to such an extent that she had ceased to attend.

24. Seven donors actually worked in a cultural occupation (e.g., as a writer or an artist), and an eighth was in the closely related field of teaching. Seven of these people had made one of their largest gifts to a cultural organization.

25. It would be equal to one if every person were socially acquainted with every other person.

26. See chapter 1.

27. The figure then drops to 19.8 percent for donors who served on college or university boards.

28. On clubs, see Domhoff 1974; Useem 1980, p. 56; on cultural resources and elite interaction, see DiMaggio 1987; DiMaggio and Mohr 1985; DiMaggio and Useem 1978, 1982.

29. Baltzell 1964, 1991. On the exclusivity of the Protestant Establishment, see the former, and on the shift to a more atomized elite, see especially the latter.

30. Zweigenhaft and Domhoff 1982.

31. By contrast, the absence of a focus on policy organizations by the social elite suggests that their major philanthropy is shaped more by their status interests than by class interests in shaping broader policy agendas. I do not question the well-documented involvement of members of the social elite with influential policy organizations, but I do suspect that much of this involvement flows from their position within the business community rather than from their personal philanthropic efforts. In this respect, their involvement here may be more a reflection of the position within the corporate hierarchy than within the social elite.

32. See chapter 1.

33. Ibid.

34. Looking at donors who inherited no wealth at all, we find that 70.3 percent gave a largest gift to education, and 40.5 percent gave one to culture. The comparable percentages for those inheriting $1 million or more are 76.2 percent for education and 45 percent for culture. (Among those who inherited some wealth, but less than $1 million, the percentages are 62.5 and 41.7. Although the education figure is a bit lower for this group, it is still the most frequent choice.)

35. Based on reports of social acquaintanceship by Jewish members of the social elite, the density of ties was .09 between them and other Jews, and .08 between them and non-Jews outside the social elite. Based on reports of social acquaintanceship by non-Jewish members of the social elite, the density of ties was .01 between them and Jews outside the social elite, and .02 between them and non-Jews outside the social elite. Within the social elite as a whole, the density of ties was .12 (three times that for donors as a whole). The density of ties between Jewish and non-Jewish members of the social elite was .11 based on the former and .09 based on the latter (indicating that Jews identified non-Jews as social acquaintances somewhat more frequently than the reverse). So virtually all social acquaintances identified by non-Jews in the social elite were also in the social elite, but this was not the case for their Jewish counterparts.

36. White 1989, p. 67.

37. Indeed, one donor suggested the analogy when she spoke of her initial

introduction to philanthropic involvements through childhood participation in the church. Said she, "You were reared in the church, and if there was a church supper, you contributed in your own little way." Another donor went so far as to characterize art as his religion.

38. Caplow 1984.

CHAPTER FIVE
ATTITUDES TOWARD INHERITANCE AND PHILANTHROPIC BEQUESTS

1. Mills 1956, p. 12. For a historical discussion of tensions concerning inheritance in the American context, and the mechanisms developed to allow intergenerational transfers of wealth, see Hall 1988.

2. Two additional donors (2.6 percent) gave some other answer. Based on responses by seventy-seven donors. It is important to keep the relative nature of the comparison in mind. Donors who plan to give less by bequest may still be contributing considerable sums, just as those giving more by bequest may give large amounts during life.

3. Such comments are of particular interest because philanthropic bequests have been characterized as one of the surest routes for the perpetuation of control over wealth (see Ostrower 1989 for a review). For a discussion of donor control and foundations, see Simon 1978.

4. $p = .013$. Based on eight donors with no children and sixty-nine donors with children.

5. As noted, some of those leaving more by bequest did have children and thus had other reasons. One woman explained that her financial situation necessitates that she operate from income rather than assets, thereby restricting funds available for lifetime giving. Another hopes to make a substantial gift by bequest, but feels that "we can't give that away before, because we have to be sure there's enough to see both of us through whatever may come."

6. Of the remaining donors, 21 percent had no bequests, and another 19.7 percent were unsure of their plans.

7. It should be noted that giving by bequest is not the only vehicle for making donations after the donor's lifetime. For instance, some had started private foundations that will continue after the donor dies.

8. Only 9.5 percent felt that government should tax most of an estate, 9.5 percent felt the estate should be equally split, 6.3 percent did not know, and the remaining respondent said only that if you give to charity, the government does not tax the money, which he believes is appropriate. The question was asked of sixty-three respondents. It should be emphasized that "most" includes anything over 50 percent of the estate. Indeed, a number of donors said they did not oppose estate taxes per se, but rates perceived as too high. One donor, for instance, could "live with" the government taking 40 percent. By contrast, four people believed there should be no estate taxes. These figures are presented to give a rough overview of donors' attitudes, which qualitative materials are used to explore. In light of the uniformity among donors, it would be of interest to use more finely graded categories in future research.

9. To get an overview of their attitudes, I asked donors whether they thought that inheritance has either negative or positive economic consequences. Only 33.3 percent believed inheritance has positive economic consequences, 13.6 percent believed it was negative, 16.7 percent felt it had mixed consequences, 24.2 percent said it depends (e.g., on who inherits the wealth), 6.1 percent felt it was not positive or negative, and 6.1 percent said they did not know. Based on sixty-six donors.

10. When donors were asked which of various views about inheritance came closest to their own, 18.6 percent said the wish to leave as much as possible to children, 25.7 percent felt children should not be left too much wealth, 24.3 percent said that it depends on the child, 12.9 percent said their position was mixed, 12.9 percent said they were unsure, and 5.7 percent provided some other answer. These responses are also indicative of reservations about leaving great wealth to children. But remember that we are examining attitudes and dealing with amounts in relative terms. For instance, those who believe children ought to get only a "basic" amount, or some help starting out, may still be leaving their children sums that far exceed what most people inherit. The issue here, however, concerns attitudes toward giving wealth to children in relation to the overall disposition of the donor's estate.

11. For a discussion of concerns that children will dissipate the family fortune and mechanisms used to guard the life of the fortune from those who inherit among dynastic families, see Marcus with Hall 1992. For the argument that philanthropy itself, notably private foundations, has served a dynastic function for families of great wealth, see Marcus with Hall 1992; see also Odendahl 1990. On the subject of foundations and dynasty more generally, see Simon 1978.

12. As might be expected, those who had inherited larger sums were less likely to say that inheritance has negative consequences. No inheritors, but 19.6 percent of others held that view ($p \le .05$). At the same time, they were not disposed to characterize inheritance as positive. Thus, 31.6 percent said it had positive consequences, 31.6 percent said it had mixed consequences, and 21 percent said it depends on the recipients. The rest were split among those who felt it had neither consequences, did not know, or gave some other response.

13. Comments such as these were made even where donors did not feel their own incentive had suffered. This suggests that such views may reflect collective attitudes about inheritance as much as personal observations about the actual fate of those who inherit wealth.

14. Weber (1922) 1963, pp. 106–107.

15. Bellah et al. 1985, p. 198.

16. Some donors distinguished between the freedom one has to use inherited wealth as opposed to earned wealth. One person said that someone who earns money is "much more free to do whatever he or she wants," but "money inherited should stay in the family." Another said she would have "no business" leaving all her money to charity, because it was her husband's money and he expected it to go to their children. One donor felt that "if it came from someone else, you kind of owe it to that person to think about what they would have liked you to do with it." These comments also indicate that for some donors, inheri-

tors' wealth is not viewed as being theirs in the same way as wealth that is earned. This discussion provides further illustration of how money assumes meanings for these donors that go beyond the economic.

17. Interviews left the impression that living on inherited wealth without working is less of an issue for women than for men (although it was for some). Women seemed more willing to simply say they were fortunate to have this money available. Still, women's comments do indicate that it was also important to them to have independent achievements, and they often pointed to their volunteer activities as examples (see chapter 3).

18. Donors were asked to consider all the money they have to bequeath as 100 percent and to indicate what portion of it they plan to leave for philanthropic purposes.

19. The comparison should not, however, detract from the fact that the percentages indicate that philanthropy is also a significant option for donors with children.

20. As might be expected, there was a correlation between having a negative attitude toward inheritance and believing that children should not inherit too much (phi = .61). Although it might be anticipated that attitudes about inheritance would be associated with having children, this was not the case, suggesting that these attitudes and having children have distinct relationships with estate planning.

21. Collapses of variables (asset level, marital status) into dichotomous categories were based on exploratory analyses. A likely explanation for the effect of asset level is that donors with great wealth can give higher percentages for philanthropic purposes while still leaving very large sums to children. The reason that married donors donate a higher percentage of their wealth to philanthropy, however, is less clear and would be of interest for future research to explore.

22. The same analysis was conducted using donor views on leaving children too much wealth instead of viewing inheritance as having negative consequences. Although the relationship to leaving wealth to philanthropy was also positive, the view of inheritance as having negative consequences appeared to be the stronger determinant.

23. Remember that we are dealing here exclusively with people who have been philanthropically active during their lifetime. A study of bequests made by other wealthy individuals might reveal a different balance of influences.

24. Weber (1922) 1963, pp. 106–107.

CHAPTER SIX
GOVERNMENT AND PHILANTHROPY: ALTERNATIVES OR COMPLEMENTS?

1. Only 4.1 percent were favorable to this proposal, and 5.5 percent placed themselves somewhere in the middle. Based on seventy-three cases. An additional two donors were unsure, two said it would depend on the particular area, and another thought it was a good idea but would work out badly in practice.

2. Donors' belief that philanthropy provides services that would not be maintained by government accords well with Weisbrod's (1975, 1988) analysis

of the nonprofit sector as a mechanism for providing goods for those who remain undersatisfied with levels of governmental provision (which respond to majority demands).

3. For each area, beliefs about what should happen to government spending were as follows:

Donor Beliefs about Government Spending by Area (in Percentages)

Area	Increase	Reduce	Continue	Don't Know	Other
Health Care	68.1	6.8	11.4	9.1	4.5
Arts	55.5	8.9	15.6	17.8	2.2
Higher Education	59.1	2.3	11.4	22.7	4.5
Social Services	65.9	6.8	9.1	13.6	4.5
Animals/Environment	68.2	0.0	9.1	20.5	2.3

Time only permitted these questions to be asked of half the respondents, and percentages are based on forty-four cases (forty-five for the arts). It is hoped that these issues will be examined in greater detail in future research on a larger sample.

4. By area, the percentage of donors who said government should administer funds directly, channel them through nonprofits, or who chose another response are as follows:

Donor Attitudes toward Administration of Government Funds (in Percentages)

Area	No. of Donors	Admin. Directly	Use NPOs	Do Both	Depends	Either
Health Care	28	10.7	39.3	14.3	21.4	14.3
Arts	23	0.0	52.2	13.0	21.7	13.0
Higher Education	24	4.2	45.8	16.7	25.0	8.3
Social Services	28	10.7	42.9	14.3	21.4	10.7
Animals/Environment	29	10.3	41.4	13.8	20.7	13.8

My conclusion concerning donors' openness to seeing some government role is based on combining the "Do Both," "Depends," and "Either" categories. Clearly, however, donors are not as prepared to give unqualified support to governmental administration as they are to administration by nonprofits. Note that these figures include only those donors who thought government spending should be increased in an area.

5. With respect to centralization allowing for better coordination, fully 76.4 percent disagreed, only 6.9 percent agreed, 11.1 percent did not know, and 5.6 percent gave some other response (such as one who favored anything that minimized government's role but declined to respond to the individual item). Based on seventy-two cases. With respect to government distributing funds in a fairer way, 79.7 percent disagreed, only 1.4 percent agreed, 14.5 percent did not know, and 4.3 percent gave another response. Based on sixty-nine cases.

6. Thus, 83.1 percent agreed that an enhanced governmental role would re-

duce variety, 2.8 percent disagreed, 9.9 percent did not know, and 4.2 percent simply said they opposed putting matters in the hands of government and declined to address the individual item. Based on seventy-one cases. Similarly, 79.2 percent of donors agreed that government funds would be used less efficiently, only 9.7 percent disagreed, 8.3 percent did not know, and 2.8 percent gave another answer. Based on seventy-two cases.

7. Donors' antigovernment attitudes are consistent with the negative view of civil servants among American business elites observed in other contexts, and the social distance between members of the two groups (Domhoff 1983; Useem 1984). Domhoff and Useem connect this to the divergent class backgrounds of members of the two groups, observing that in Europe, members of both more frequently share a similar (upper) class background. This may be a contributing factor in the attitudes observed here, but attention must be given as well to the more general antigovernmental ideology in this country. Indeed, this may contribute to upper-class members avoiding government careers in the first place. Also, antigovernmental sentiments were found both among those who were and those who were not from wealthy backgrounds, and even among those who were involved in government service.

8. As this quote suggests, antipathy toward large bureaucratic structures exhibited in donors' criticisms of government also influences their decisions about philanthropic beneficiaries. Donors expressed wariness about nonprofits they believe spend too much on overhead. Excessively large size, complexity, and bureaucracy were also cited as reasons for not giving to certain organizations.

9. Bremner 1977, pp. 89–90.

10. Only one person (1.2 percent) felt there was any truth to this at all. By contrast, 91.6 percent disagreed with the statement and 7.2 percent gave some other answer. Based on eighty-three respondents.

11. Of the eighty-one responding, 53.1 percent disagreed, 34.5 percent expressed some agreement, and 12.3 percent gave another answer (generally that they did not know).

12. Of the seventy-nine responding, 62 percent expressed some agreement, 26.6 percent disagreed, and 11.4 percent gave another answer (primarily that they did not know).

13. A related, extended discussion of prestige and philanthropy may be found in chapter 1.

14. Of the eighty-two responding, 57.3 percent disagreed, 39 percent expressed at least some agreement, and 3.6 percent gave some other answer. Members of the social upper class were more likely to agree with this criticism (60.7 percent) than were other donors (33.3 percent, $p \le .05$).

15. Wuthnow 1991, pp. 230–231. Those who believed nonprofits should have a greater influence in society outnumbered those who believed their influence should be reduced by a ratio of three to one. Seven in ten people thought politicians have too much influence, but only one in ten thought they have too little influence. Similarly, another survey found that nonprofit organizations enjoy greater public confidence than several other institutions, including Congress (an Independent Sector survey conducted by the Gallup Organization cited by Wuthnow 1991, p. 230). On the preference of Americans for voluntary

associations over politics, and the negative connotations of government and politics to middle-class Americans, see also Bellah et al. 1985.

16. Increasing governmental regulation of private foundations in 1969, for instance, was justified on the grounds that funds were being used for other than philanthropic purposes and not on the basis that philanthropy per se ought to be curtailed (Ostrower 1989, pp. 288–289).

17. At the same time, the widespread esteem for philanthropy can also be used by elites when seeking to legitimate the benefits they derive from philanthropy.

18. One interesting exception is that many donors enjoy the contact with artists that sometimes results from their philanthropy. The opportunity to mingle with prominent performers (e.g., at benefits), is sometimes used as a "perk" to encourage donations.

19. The ambivalent recognition of the need for bureaucratic structures, and the tension between the desire for government to achieve certain goals and fear of government expansion are also more general themes in American society (see Wuthnow 1991, pp. 264–265).

20. To the extent that donors do focus on such problems, one would expect to see them do so in ways that allow them to feel they can have an impact. For example, one would expect to see philanthropic gifts going more readily to fund research or provide seed money for a pilot project than for direct support for victims of a disease.

21. Salamon 1987, p. 111. For the related observation that the Great Depression "shattered the myth" that philanthropy could care for the poor in bad times, leading to the acknowledgment that government involvement was necessary, see Bremner 1977, p. 97.

22. While beyond the scope of this discussion, the ways in which organizations structure fundraising appeals so as to make donors feel that their gifts will have an impact would be an interesting area for future research.

23. This outcome reflects the problem of philanthropic particularism, identified by Salamon (1987) as one of the historical weaknesses of the voluntary system.

CONCLUSION

1. This is seen in comparative studies of culture (see Montias 1982; Schuster 1985a, 1985b).

2. DiMaggio and Useem 1982; Goffman 1951.

3. Bellah et al. 1985.

4. My impression is that members of the elite generally do not think or worry about philanthropy's exclusivity with respect to those outside the elite. This is not due to indifference, for their comments show that they are quite conscious of this exclusivity and its importance as an incentive for philanthropy. Rather, it more likely reflects the absence of their sensing any significant challenges to this exclusivity. The point of reference for these donors are the fellow members of their class. The challenges to exclusivity that do arouse attention and concern are those that pertain to boundaries between different groups within the elite.

5. This is not to imply, however, that there are no countervailing pressures on boards. It would be of interest, for example, to investigate whether and how such factors as the changing demographic character of cities, government funding, political pressures, issues of public legitimacy, and calls for greater diversity currently influence board composition. Historically, such factors have led boards to recruit members they might otherwise not have chosen. Dain reports that a largely Protestant board of the New York Public Library appointed its first Jewish and Catholic members by 1905 for political reasons, and that more diverse ethnic representation on library boards was achieved in cities "where political considerations figured in appointments" (1991, pp. 222–223).

6. Wuthnow 1991, pp. 234–236 (quotes are from p. 236).

7. Odendahl 1990; see also Lundberg 1937, pp. 345–346; Ostrander 1989.

8. See Aaron 1992, pp. 242–243; James 1992, p. 255.

9. Bremner 1977, p. 99.

10. See James 1992, p. 255; Jencks 1987, p. 322; Ostrander 1989, p. 221.

11. Baltzell (1953) 1966, pp. 268, 271; 1964 pp. 61, 138; see also Domhoff 1974, 1983, p. 17; Useem 1980, pp. 55–56.

12. DiMaggio and Anheier 1990; Jaher 1982, p. 272; Useem 1984.

13. Baltzell 1964, 1991.

14. This appears to have occurred, for instance, among Jews and Christians (see Zweigenhaft and Domhoff 1982).

METHODOLOGICAL APPENDIX

1. An extremely detailed account of the methodology, which includes step-by-step discussion of the procedural issues encountered and how these were handled, may be found in Ostrower 1991.

2. Sources consulted were: American Association of Fund-Raising Counsel 1985; Bureau of the Census 1982; Commission on Private Philanthropy and Public Needs 1975; Disney et al. 1984; Hodgkinson and Weitzman 1984, 1986; Morgan et al. 1979; documentation for the New York State tape distributed by the National Center for Charitable Statistics of Independent Sector in Washington, D.C.; Salamon and Abramson 1982; Yankelovich et al. 1986. A very detailed taxonomy, the National Taxonomy of Exempt Entities, was subsequently released by the National Center for Charitable Statistics in 1987. The classifications used in the study are consistent with that taxonomy.

3. For instance, after reviewing the lists, two categories ("animal and environmental causes" and "youth, not elsewhere classifiable") were added to include organizations that did not fit into the initial scheme.

4. The tape is compiled from registration forms filed by nonprofit organizations. Data were for 1983.

5. By contrast, other sources are specialized by type of organization (e.g., libraries, museums). Another advantage was that organizations could be readily identified by size, whereas printed sources would have required sifting through alphabetical lists of hundreds of institutions to find the largest ones. Extracting institutions in New York from other sources would also have posed considerable difficulties.

6. *Voluntary Support of Education* 1984–1985.

7. Other sources consulted include: *American Hospital Association Guide to the Health Care Field*, *American Library Directory*, *Theatre Profiles*, and the *Museum Program Survey* tape (undertaken by the National Center for Educational Statistics at the request of the National Institute of Museum Services). In some cases, I obtained current financial information directly from organizations to make a final determination about eligibility. In total, five organizations were selected solely on the basis of sources other than the New York State tape or *Voluntary Support of Education*.

8. Large organizations were selected to facilitate the goal of identifying greater numbers of larger donors. The figure for total private contributions had to be used because gifts from individuals, corporations, foundations, and bequests could not be distinguished. Two million dollars seemed to be a reasonable figure that would obtain organizations with large individual donors while allowing for the giving by those other sources.

BIBLIOGRAPHY

Aaron, Henry J. 1992. "Commentary." In Charles T. Clotfelter, ed., *Who Benefits from the Nonprofit Sector?* Chicago: University of Chicago Press.

Abzug, Rikki. 1993. "Comparing Trusteeships across Cities: Some Predictions and Some Surprises." Paper prepared for the Fifth Annual International Conference of the Society for the Advancement of Socio-Economics, New York.

Abzug, Rikki, Paul J. DiMaggio, Bradford H. Gray, Chul Hee Kang, and Michael Useem. 1992. "Changes in the Structure and Composition of Non-Profit Boards of Trustees: Cases from Boston and Cleveland, 1925–1985." Program on Non-Profit Organizations, Yale University. Working Paper 173.

Alba, Richard D., and Gwen Moore. 1982. "Ethnicity in the American Elite." *American Sociological Review* 47:373–383.

Allen, Michael P. 1987. *The Founding Fortunes: A New Anatomy of the Super-Rich Families in America.* New York: Truman Talley Books.

Allen, Michael P., and Philip Broyles. 1989. "Class Hegemony and Political Finance: Presidential Campaign Contributions of Wealthy Capitalist Families." *American Sociological Review* 54:275–287.

American Association of Fund-Raising Counsel. 1985. *Giving USA.* New York: American Association of Fund-Raising Counsel.

American Hospital Association Guide to the Health Care Field. 1984 ed. Chicago: American Hospital Association.

American Library Directory. 1985. Edited by Jacques Cattell Press. New York: R. R. Bowker.

Astin, Alexander W. 1971. *Predicting Academic Performance in College: Selectivity Data for 2300 American Colleges.* New York: The Free Press.

Auten, Gerald, and Gabriel Rudney. 1987. "The Variability of the Charitable Giving of the Wealthy." Program on Non-Profit Organizations, Yale University. Working Paper 126.

Baltzell, E. Digby. 1991. *The Protestant Establishment Revisited.* Chapters 3, 5, and 6. Edited by Howard G. Schneiderman. New Brunswick, N.J.: Transaction.

———. (1953) 1966. "'*Who's Who in America*' and '*The Social Register*': Elite and Upper Class Indexes in Metropolitan America." In Reinhard Bendix and Seymour M. Lipset, eds., *Class, Status and Power: Social Stratification in Comparative Perspective.* 2d ed. New York: The Free Press.

———. 1964. *The Protestant Establishment.* New York: Vintage Books.

Bellah, Robert, Richard Madsen, William Sullivan, Ann Swidler, and Steven Tipton. 1985. *Habits of the Heart: Individualism and Commitment in American Life.* New York: Harper & Row.

Biddle, Jeff E. 1992. "Religious Organizations." In Charles T. Clotfelter, ed., *Who Benefits from the Nonprofit Sector?* Chicago: University of Chicago Press.

Birmingham, Stephen. 1987. *America's Secret Aristocracy.* Boston: Little, Brown.

Birmingham, Stephen. 1967. *"Our Crowd": The Great Jewish Families of New York*. New York: Harper & Row.

Blau, Peter M. (1964) 1986. *Exchange and Power in Social Life*. New Brunswick, N.J.: Transaction.

Boris, Elizabeth T. 1987. "Creation and Growth: A Survey of Private Foundations." In Teresa Odendahl, ed., *America's Wealthiest and the Future of Foundations*. New York: The Foundation Center.

Bourdieu, Pierre. 1986. "The Production of Belief: Contribution to an Economy of Symbolic Goods." In Richard Nice, James Curran, Nicholas Garnham, Paddy Scannell, Philip Schlesinger, and Colin Sparks, eds., *Media, Culture and Society: A Critical Reader*. Beverly Hills, Calif.: Sage.

――――. 1984. *Distinction*. Cambridge: Harvard University Press.

――――. (1966) 1969. "Intellectual Field and Creative Project." *Social Science Information* 8(2):89–119.

Bremner, Robert H. 1977. "Private Philanthropy and Public Needs: Historical Perspective." In *Research Papers* sponsored by The Commission on Private Philanthropy and Public Needs, 1:89–114. Washington, D.C.: Department of the Treasury.

Burch, Philip H., Jr. 1981. *Elites in American History: The Federalist Years to the Civil War*. New York: Holmes & Meier.

Bureau of the Census. 1982. *Census of Service Industries: Geographic Area Series*. Washington, D.C.: Department of Commerce.

Caplow, Theodore. 1984. "Christmas Gift Giving in Middletown." *American Journal of Sociology* 89:1306–1323.

Clotfelter, Charles T., ed., 1992. *Who Benefits from the Nonprofit Sector?* Chicago: University of Chicago Press.

Cnaan, Ram A. 1993. Review of *Who Benefits from the Nonprofit Sector?* edited by Charles T. Clotfelter. *Nonprofit and Voluntary Sector Quarterly* 22:184–188.

Coleman, Richard P., and Lee Rainwater with Kent McClelland. 1978. *Social Standing in America*. New York: Basic Books.

Collins, Randall. 1988. "Women and Men in the Class Structure." *Journal of Family Issues* 9:27–50.

Commission on Private Philanthropy and Public Needs. 1975. *Giving in America*. Washington, D.C.: Department of the Treasury.

Cookson, Peter W., Jr., and Caroline Hodges Persell. 1985. *Preparing for Power: America's Elite Boarding Schools*. New York: Basic Books.

Covelli, Lucille. 1989. "Dominant Class Culture and Legitimation: Female Volunteer Directors." In Robert D. Herman and Jon Van Til, eds., *Nonprofit Boards of Directors*. New Brunswick, N.J.: Transaction.

Dain, Phyllis. 1991. "Public Library Governance and a Changing New York City." *Libraries and Culture* 26:219–250.

Daniels, Arlene K. 1988. *Invisible Careers: Women Civic Leaders from the Volunteer World*. Chicago: University of Chicago Press.

DiMaggio, Paul. 1987. "Classification in Art." *American Sociological Review* 52:440–455.

――――. 1982. "Cultural Entrepreneurship in Nineteenth-Century Boston, I:

The Creation of an Organizational Base for High Culture in America." *Media, Culture and Society* 4:33–50.

———. 1979. "Review Essay: On Pierre Bourdieu." *American Journal of Sociology* 84:1460–1474.

DiMaggio, Paul J., and Helmut K. Anheier. 1990. "The Sociology of Nonprofit Organizations and Sectors." In W. Richard Scott and Judith Blake, eds., *Annual Review of Sociology*, vol. 16. Palo Alto, Calif.: Annual Reviews.

DiMaggio, Paul, and John Mohr. 1985. "Cultural Capital, Educational Attainment and Marital Selection." *American Journal of Sociology* 90:1231–61.

DiMaggio, Paul, and Michael Useem. 1982. "The Arts in Class Reproduction." In Michael W. Apple, ed., *Cultural and Economic Reproduction in Education*. London: Routledge & Kegan Paul.

———. 1978. "Cultural Democracy in a Period of Cultural Expansion: The Social Composition of Arts Audiences in the United States." *Social Problems* 25:179–197.

Disney, Diane, Madeleine Kimmich, and James Musselwhite. 1984. *Partners in Public Service: Government and the Nonprofit Sector in Rhode Island*. Washington, D.C.: Urban Institute Press.

Domhoff, G. William. 1990. *The Power Elite and the State*. Hawthorne, N.Y.: Aldine de Gruyter.

———. 1983. *Who Rules America Now? A View for the Eighties*. Englewood Cliffs, N.J.: Prentice-Hall.

———. 1974. *The Bohemian Grove and Other Retreats*. New York: Harper & Row.

———. 1972. *Fat Cats and Democrats*. Englewood Cliffs, N.J.: Prentice-Hall.

———. 1970. *The Higher Circles: The Governing Class in America*. New York: Vintage Books.

Domhoff, G. William, and Thomas R. Dye. 1987. Introduction. In G. William Domhoff and Thomas R. Dye, eds., *Power Elites and Organizations*. Newbury Park, Calif.: Sage.

Dye, Thomas R. 1990. *Who's Running America? The Bush Era*. Englewood Cliffs, N.J.: Prentice-Hall.

Friedland, Roger, and Donald Palmer. 1984. "Park Place and Main Street: Business and the Urban Power Structure." *Annual Review of Sociology* 10:393–416.

Galaskiewicz, Joseph. 1987. "The Study of a Business Elite and Corporate Philanthropy in a United States Metropolitan Area." In G. Moyser and M. Wagstaffe, eds., *Research Methods for Elite Studies*. London: Allen & Unwin.

———. 1985. *Social Organization of an Urban Grants Economy*. Orlando, Fla.: Academic Press.

Goffman, Erving. 1951. "Symbols of Class Status." *British Journal of Sociology* 2:298–312.

Hacker, Helen Mayer. 1975. "Class and Race Differences in Gender Roles." In Lucile Duberman, ed., *Gender and Sex in Society*. New York: Praeger.

Hall, Peter Dobkin. 1988. "A Historical Overview of Family Firms in the United States." *Family Business Review* 1:51–68.

———. 1982. *The Organization of American Culture, 1700–1900: Private*

Institutions, Elites, and the Origins of American Nationality. New York: New York University Press.

Hansmann, Henry. 1987. "Economic Theories of Nonprofit Organizations." In Walter W. Powell, ed., *The Nonprofit Sector: A Research Handbook.* New Haven: Yale University Press.

Higley, Stephen Richard. 1992. "The Geography of the 'Social Register.'" Ph.D. diss., University of Illinois at Urbana-Champaign. Distributed by UMI Dissertation Services, Ann Arbor, Mich.

Hodgkinson, Virginia A., and Murray S. Weitzman. 1986 and 1984. *Dimensions of the Independent Sector: A Statistical Profile.* Washington, D.C.: Independent Sector.

Hoffman, Paul. 1982. *Lions of the Eighties: The Inside Story of the Powerhouse Law Firm.* Garden City, N.Y.: Doubleday.

Jaher, Frederic Cople. 1982. *The Urban Establishment: Upper Strata in Boston, New York, Charleston, Chicago, and Los Angeles.* Urbana: University of Illinois Press.

James, Estelle. 1992. "Commentary." In Charles T. Clotfelter, ed., *Who Benefits from the Nonprofit Sector?* Chicago: University of Chicago Press.

Jencks, Christopher. 1987. "Who Gives to What?" In Walter W. Powell, ed., *The Nonprofit Sector: A Research Handbook.* New Haven: Yale University Press.

Lenski, Gerhard. (1966) 1984. *Power and Privilege: A Theory of Social Stratification.* Chapel Hill: University of North Carolina Press.

Levy, Frank. 1992. "Commentary." In Charles T. Clotfelter, ed., *Who Benefits from the Nonprofit Sector?* Chicago: University of Chicago Press.

Lundberg, Ferdinand. 1968. *The Rich and the Super-Rich.* New York: Bantam Books.

————. 1937. *America's 60 Families.* New York: Vanguard Press.

Mannheim, Karl. (1933) 1971. "The Democratization of Culture." In Kurt Wolff, ed., *From Karl Mannheim.* New York: Oxford University Press.

Marcus, George. 1983. "Elite Communities and Institutional Orders." In George Marcus, ed., *Elites: Ethnographic Issues.* Albuquerque, N.M.: University of New Mexico Press.

Marcus, George E., with Peter Dobkin Hall. 1992. *Lives in Trust: The Fortunes of Dynastic Families in Late Twentieth-Century America.* Boulder, Colo.: Westview Press.

Mauss, Marcel. (1925) 1967. *The Gift.* New York: Norton.

McCarthy, Kathleen D. 1990. "Parallel Power Structures: Women and the Voluntary Sphere." In Kathleen D. McCarthy, ed., *Lady Bountiful Revisited: Women, Philanthropy, and Power.* New Brunswick, N.J.: Rutgers University Press.

————. 1982. *Noblesse Oblige: Charity and Cultural Philanthropy in Chicago, 1849–1929.* Chicago: University of Chicago Press.

Mills, C. Wright. 1956. *The Power Elite.* New York: Oxford University Press.

Montias, J. Michael. 1982. "Public Support for the Performing Arts in Western Europe and the United States: History and Analysis." Program on Non-Profit Organizations, Yale University. Working Paper 45.

Moore, Gwen. 1988. "Women in Elite Positions: Insiders or Outsiders?" *Sociological Forum* 3:566–585.

Morgan, James, Richard Dye, and Judith Hybels. 1979. *Results from Two National Surveys of Philanthropic Activity.* Ann Arbor: Institute for Social Research, University of Michigan.

Nielsen, Waldemar A. 1990. "Self-Interest Is Not the Whole Story of Philanthropy." *Chronicle of Philanthropy.* May 1, 1990, pp. 35–36.

Odendahl, Teresa. 1990. *Charity Begins at Home: Generosity and Self-Interest Among the Philanthropic Elite.* New York: Basic Books.

———. 1987. "Wealthy Donors and Their Charitable Attitudes." In Teresa Odendahl, ed., *America's Wealthy and the Future of Foundations.* New York: The Foundation Center.

Ostrander, Susan. 1989. "The Problem of Poverty and Why Philanthropy Neglects It." In Virginia A. Hodgkinson, Richard W. Lyman and Associates, eds., *The Future of the Nonprofit Sector.* San Francisco: Jossey-Bass.

———. 1984. *Women of the Upper Class.* Philadelphia: Temple University Press.

Ostrower, Francie. 1991. "Why the Wealthy Give: A Study of Elite Philanthropy in New York City." Ph.D. diss., Yale University. Distributed by UMI Dissertation Services, Ann Arbor, Mich.

———. 1989. "Donor Control and Perpetual Trusts: Does Anything Last Forever?" In Richard Magat, ed., *Philanthropic Giving: Studies in Varieties and Goals.* New York: Oxford University Press.

———. 1987. "The Role of Advisors to the Wealthy." In Teresa Odendahl, ed., *America's Wealthy and the Future of Foundations.* New York: The Foundation Center.

Pareto, Vilfredo. 1935. *Mind and Society*, vol. 3. New York: Harcourt, Brace.

Payton, Robert L. 1989. "Philanthropic Values." In Richard Magat, ed., *Philanthropic Giving: Studies in Varieties and Goals.* New York: Oxford University Press.

Phillips, Kevin. 1990. *The Politics of Rich and Poor: Wealth and the American Electorate in the Reagan Aftermath.* New York: HarperPerennial.

Ross, Aileen. 1954. "Philanthropic Activity and the Business Career." *Social Forces* 32:274–280.

Salamon, Lester M. 1992. *America's Nonprofit Sector: A Primer.* New York: The Foundation Center.

———. 1987. "Partners in Public Service: The Scope and Theory of Government-Nonprofit Relations." In Walter W. Powell, ed., *The Nonprofit Sector: A Research Handbook.* New Haven: Yale University Press.

Salamon, Lester, and Alan Abramson. 1982. *The Federal Budget and the Nonprofit Sector.* Washington, D.C.: Urban Institute Press.

Schervish, Paul G. 1992. "Adoption and Altruism: Those with Whom I Want to Share a Dream." *Nonprofit and Voluntary Sector Quarterly* 21:327–350.

Schervish, Paul G., and Andrew Herman. 1988. *The Study on Wealth and Philanthropy Final Report.* Social Welfare Research Institute, Boston College.

Schuster, J. Mark Davidson. 1985a. "Tax Incentives as Arts Policy in Western Europe." Program on Non-Profit Organizations, Yale University. Working Paper 90.

Schuster, J. Mark Davidson. 1985b. *Supporting the Arts: An International Comparative Study.* Washington, D.C.: Policy and Planning Division, National Endowment for the Arts.

Schwartz, Barry. 1967. "Social Psychology of the Gift." *American Journal of Sociology* 73:1–11.

Simmel, Georg. (1908) 1971. "The Poor." In D. N. Levine, ed., *On Individuality and Social Forms.* Chicago: University of Chicago Press.

Simon, John G. 1987. "The Tax Treatment of Nonprofit Organizations: A Review of Federal and State Tax Policies." In Walter W. Powell, ed., *The Nonprofit Sector: A Research Handbook.* New Haven: Yale University Press.

———. 1978. "Charity and Dynasty Under the Federal Tax System." Program on Non-Profit Organizations, Yale University. Working Paper 5.

Sirota and Alper Associates. 1988. *New York City Volunteers and Gives.* Prepared for Daring Goals for a Caring Society.

Smith, Patrick J. 1983. *A Year at the Met.* New York: Alfred A. Knopf.

Story, Ronald. 1980. *The Forging of an Aristocracy: Harvard and the Boston Upper Class, 1800–1885.* Middletown, Conn.: Wesleyan University Press.

Theatre Profiles. 1984. Volume 6. New York: Theatre Communications Group.

Tickamyer, Ann R. 1981. "Wealth and Power: A Comparison of Men and Women in the Property Elite." *Social Forces* 60:463–481.

Tomkins, Calvin. (1970) 1989. *Merchants and Masterpieces: The Story of the Metropolitan Museum of Art.* New York: Henry Holt.

Useem, Michael. 1984. *The Inner Circle: Large Corporations and the Rise of Business Political Activity in the U.S. and U.K.* New York: Oxford University Press.

———. 1980. "Corporations and the Corporate Elite." In Alex Inkeles, Neil J. Smelser, and Ralph Turner, eds., *Annual Review of Sociology*, vol. 6. Palo Alto, Calif.: Annual Reviews.

Veblen, Thorstein. (1899) 1953. *The Theory of the Leisure Class.* New York: Mentor.

Voluntary Support of Education 1984–1985. 1985. 30th Anniversary Survey Report. New York: Council for Financial Aid to Education.

Weber, Max. (1946) 1977. "Class, Status, Party" and "The Social Psychology of the World Religions." In H. H. Gerth and C. Wright Mills, eds., *From Max Weber: Essays in Sociology.* New York: Oxford University Press.

———. (1922) 1963. *The Sociology of Religion.* Boston: Beacon.

Weber, Michael E. 1988. "Individual Income Tax Returns for 1987: Selected Characteristics from the Taxpayer Usage Study." *Statistics of Income Bulletin* (Department of the Treasury, Internal Revenue Service) 8:3–21.

Weisbrod, Burton A. 1988. *The Nonprofit Economy.* Cambridge: Harvard University Press.

———. 1975. "Toward a Theory of the Voluntary Non-Profit Sector in a Three-Sector Economy." In Edmund S. Phelps, ed., *Altruism, Morality, and Economic Theory.* New York: Russell Sage Foundation.

White, Arthur H. 1989. "Patterns of Giving." In Richard Magat, ed., *Philanthropic Giving: Studies in Varieties and Goals.* New York: Oxford University Press.

Wolpert, Julian. 1989. "Key Indicators of Generosity in Communities." In Virginia A. Hodgkinson, Richard W. Lyman and Associates, eds., *The Future of the Nonprofit Sector*. San Francisco: Jossey-Bass.

Wolpert, Julian, and Thomas Reiner. 1984. "The Philanthropy Marketplace." *Economic Geography* 60:197–209.

Wood, James R., and James G. Houghland, Jr. 1990. "The Role of Religion in Philanthropy." In Jon Van Til and Associates, eds., *Critical Issues in American Philanthropy*. San Francisco: Jossey-Bass.

Wuthnow, Robert. 1991. *Acts of Compassion: Caring for Others and Helping Ourselves*. Princeton: Princeton University Press.

Yankelovich, Skelly, and White Inc. 1986. *The Charitable Behavior of Americans*. Washington, D.C.: Independent Sector.

Zweigenhaft, Richard L., and G. William Domhoff. 1982. *Jews in the Protestant Establishment*. New York: Praeger.

INDEX

age and giving, 18, 149n.49. *See also* retirement: and philanthropic involvement

altruism: philanthropy distinguished from, 8–9, 25, 132

alumni giving: among graduates of public vs. private institutions, 91–92; as a norm among donors, 87–89, 151n.9; prestige of school, as influence on, 90–92, 165n.8, 166n.9

animal and environmental philanthropy: gender and, 74–76, 161n.19

artists: donors' enjoyment of contact with, 174n.18

arts organizations. *See* cultural philanthropy

Astin Index of Selectivity, 90, 153n.26, 165n.8

Baltzell, E. Digby, 12, 62, 65, 96

Bellah, Robert, 6, 170n.15

benefits. *See* charity benefits

bequests, philanthropic, 100–112; attitudes toward estate taxation and, 101, 103–105; attitudes toward inheritance and, 100–101, 105–112, 170nn.9 and 10; childlessness as influence on, 102–103, 108–110; determinants of, as percentage of donors' estate, 108–110, 171n.20; vs. lifetime giving, 101–103, 169n.5

Blau, Peter M., 37

boards of directors: business involvement and participation on, among men, 79–80, 162n.30, 163n.35; "buying" onto, discussed by donors, 43–45, 95, 154n.37; class homogeneity of, 48, 84, 134; corporate managers' increasing presence on, 140; determinants of membership on, 45–47, 154n.40; external influences on changes in, 67, 81, 84–85, 163n.39, 175n.5; gender and membership on, 46, 78–85, 162nn.30 and 31, 163nn.37 and 40; giving and membership on, 29, 32, 151n.9; growth in size of, 10, 146n.21; Jewish donors and membership on, 59–62; prestige of, 37–39, 68, 95, 141; social ties and, 33–34, 38; status competition and, 42–45; weakening in barriers to mem-

bership on, 26, 42–47, 59–60, 67–68, 81–85

boundaries: gender, 69–70, 81–85; Jewish donors and ethnic, 50, 59–62, 64–68, 158n.39; newly wealthy and, 43–45, 48–49, 64, 67–68, 85, 95, 97, 159n.49; philanthropy and the definition and maintenance of elite culture and, 3, 6, 28, 36, 47, 140; in philanthropy and the elite, compared, 67–68, 140; status competition and, 42–45; weakening of, in philanthropy, 45, 48–49, 59–62, 64–68, 81–85, 140–141. *See also* cohesion of elites; exclusivity of elites

Bourdieu, Pierre, 48

Bremner, Robert H., 122

bureaucracy, suspicion toward: in government, 8, 117–119, 128–129; in philanthropy, 173n.8

business involvement: as determinant of board membership, 45–46, 162n.30; gender and, 69–70, 75, 83–85, 160n.6, 162n.31; and men's volunteering and board membership, 79–81, 162n.30, 163n.35; as path to elite philanthropy, 17–18

capitalism: as context for attitudes toward inheritance, 101, 111–112; philanthropy discussed in terms similar to, by donors, 118

Carnegie Hall, 47, 81, 146n.21, 147n.23, 163n.40

Catholics: religiously affiliated giving pattern among, 53–56; in sample, 51–53

change in philanthropy. *See* continuity and change in philanthropy

charity: compared with philanthropy, 4–5

charity benefits, 31, 37–38, 124, 152nn.18 and 20

churches. *See* religious congregations

closure in elite philanthropy, 33–35, 38. *See also* exclusivity of elites

club membership, 12, 96

cohesion of elites: cultural activities and, 94–95; philanthropy as facilitating, 6, 36, 94, 101, 133–134, 140, 152n.17. *See also* boundaries; exclusivity of elites

About the Author

FRANCIE OSTROWER is Associate Professor of Sociology at Harvard University. She has written on arts participation and contributed articles on philanthropy to various books.